PRINCE OF THE GHETTO

PRINCE OF THE GHETTO

Maurice Samuel

published by MERIDIAN BOOKS, INC. *New York*
and THE JEWISH PUBLICATION SOCIETY
OF AMERICA *Philadelphia*

MAURICE SAMUEL

*Born in Rumania in 1895 and educated in England,
Maurice Samuel came to the United States in 1914.
After a term of service in the United States Army
during the First World War, he acted as an interpreter at the Peace Conference, and still later he
was with the Reparations Commission in Berlin and
Vienna. After ten years in Palestine (1929-39)
he returned to the United States.
Mr. Samuel is the author of a number of books,
among them* THE WORLD OF SHOLOM ALEICHEM,
LEVEL SUNLIGHT, HARVEST IN THE DESERT, THE GREAT
HATRED, THE GENTLEMAN AND THE JEW, CERTAIN PEOPLE
OF THE BOOK, THE PROFESSOR AND THE FOSSIL, *and a
novel on the Borgias,* THE WEB OF LUCIFER. *He has
also translated numerous works, including Yiddish
writings by Sholem Asch and I. J. Singer.*

M

First published by Meridian Books, Inc., and The Jewish
Publication Society of America, October 1959
First printing September 1959

❀ v ❀

Contents

❀

CONTENTS

PRINCE OF THE GHETTO

CHAPTER I

I Meet a Dead Man

❀

THE man who has been alienated from his people and its ways during a number of formative years should enjoy a certain advantage when he has made his return: he should be able to see them from without and from within. He should be able to combine the appreciation of a stranger with the love of a kinsman, and, being of two worlds, he should—granted certain gifts—be well placed to act as interpreter between them.

There is, of course, a corresponding disadvantage: he will never, in his position, become the unquestioning carrier of the tradition of his people. No matter how deeply he becomes implicated again in the folkways, he can never be the thing that he is explaining. His relationship to it will not be tacit, primal, and indivisible. He is touched with duality. His advantage is the advantage of an imperfection.

I had to all intents and purposes forgotten, by the time I was a young man, whatever I had picked up in early childhood of the languages of my people; I had to sit down to learn them again. I had for years been indifferent to the destiny of the Jews and willingly ignorant of their peculiar creations. When, for reasons that are not relevant here, I felt again the irresistible tug of the relationship, the recall was incomplete. I was of the Western world and would never wholly relinquish it; English was my language, and so remains in a sense that will never be true of Yiddish and Hebrew. Moreover, I was already uncentered, with a certain cosmopolitanism which has its charm and uses, but which excludes me from the tacit inmost circle of Jewishness.

I long ago recognized the defect and decided to exploit the opportunity. If it is impossible for me to be a genuine insider because I have known what it is to be an outsider, I will at least put my reborn interest and affection at the service of permanent outsiders. If I cannot be a creator of Jewish values, I will try to be the interpreter of some of them.

These personal remarks are by way of apology and credentials. I know dozens of men with a deeper understanding of the subjects I deal with in this and other books on Jewish themes. But most of them write in Yiddish and in Hebrew. And what is more to the point, even when they write in English, and do it well, they never came to Jewishness with the relish and curiosity and astonishment of a half-stranger. They did not "choose" to become Jews again. They have no notion what it feels like to have been ignorant of Jewish things. But I have, and that is a major part of my equipment.

Of the man whom I call here "Prince of the Ghetto" I had heard in my boyhood as one hears of a Hindu fabulist or an Arab philosopher: someone distant, exotic, and vaguely tempting, of whom one says: "I must really find out something about him some day." When, at the age of twenty, I began to read Yiddish hesitantly, still handicapped by a complete ignorance of Hebrew (the handicap will be explained later), I came across a few beautiful

4

stories of his. But Isaac Loeb (Yitzchok Leibush) Peretz remained a name to me until in 1919 I first met Polish Jewry; it was then that I became aware, through his effect on an entire people, of the massive reality of his spirit.

He had been dead four years and in a sense was not yet buried; for his death had occurred in Warsaw in the first year of the first World War, and though a hundred thousand Jews had attended his funeral, the loss had not sunk in. It was a time of wild changes—a prelude to the wilder changes of the second World War. A few months after Peretz's death, in 1915, the Germans overran Poland and, mad as it sounds today, behaved better toward the Jews than the Russians had done. Three years later the Germans withdrew after their defeat in the west. An independent Poland was established, and signalized its re-entry into the family of free nations by a series of pogroms against the Jews. In those years the leisure and security that are necessary for a proper mourning were wanting; and so, in spite of the hundred thousand at the funeral, it was as though the urn had not yet left the chapel. You heard on every hand, as one actually hears in a chapel: "Why, I was speaking with him only the other day."

It made me feel as if I could have met him in person had I only arrived in Warsaw a day or two earlier; and at moments I even had the impression that I had not quite missed him. He was always, so to speak, round the corner. It was still possible for someone to make a slip of the tongue and admonish me: "Well, now you are here, you must of course call on Yal Peretz." And this queer effect of immanence left a permanent imprint on my mind, so that if I live long enough I may yet be saying: "Yes, I met Peretz in Warsaw in 1919."

There were other reasons than the suspended obsequies to account for the vividness of his presence. Peretz, who

5

appears in this book primarily as the writer, was one of those national phenomena which are unintelligible apart from their people's history. The word was his implement; his conscious task was the intellectual improvement of his people. He was obsessed by the spiritual and physical destiny of Polish Jewry as Mazzini was by the spiritual and physical destiny of Italy. He was in the highest and the humblest sense a teacher—he wrote editorial exhortations on modern education and he conducted classes in elementary science for workingmen and workingwomen; he fought superstition and clericalism; he preached a Jewish national awakening; and he excoriated the jingoisms of Jews and non-Jews alike. And he had finally established such an intellectual dominance over Polish Jewry that years had to pass after his death before he could be spoken of in the past tense.

The literary life of Jewish Poland revolved about him. The present generation of Yiddish writers—Sholem Asch and I. J. Singer (but recently dead, before his time) and Menahem Boraisha and I. Opatoshu (I mention only a few)—drew inspiration from him in their early years, and not at a distance but in personal contact. No one with a touch of genuine talent, no one capable of adding to Jewish values, was a stranger to Peretz. And so when one came into Warsaw thirty years ago, a whole world was his coterie. He was everywhere. And everywhere he was discussed not simply as the artist, but as the man and Jew.

And yet, as will be seen, there was a kind of misunderstanding about him at the time; and Peretz himself shared it. Such a man as I have briefly described above could not be called "Prince of the Ghetto." Teacher, perhaps, or leader—but not prince. But the truth is that thirty years ago the mortal Peretz still overshadowed the immortal Peretz; his conscious programmatic work obscured his

6

true character. His great creations, the folk tales and the Chassidic tales—which make up most of the substance of my study—were regarded as almost incidental to his educational purpose. It was a hopelessly false perspective.

Actually his public activity was not more important than the activities of a score of his contemporaries. There was no lack of exhorters, modernizers, and teachers; with or without him Polish Jewry thirty and forty years ago would have been much as it was. What Peretz did was to distill in his Chassidic and folk tales the spirit of east-European Jewry. He, who on the surface was apparently a modern "public worker," was secretly a legendary prince, entrusted with the timeless treasures of his people, the accumulated inheritance of many generations. Incognito during his lifetime, even to himself, he was to become the eternal representative of Polish Jewry by the grace of God.

It may be that this was already in the air when I "met" Peretz; and it is also possible that I owe something of my first impressions to my own state of sensitivity in those days. I had come to Poland as a secretary on an American Pogrom Investigation Commission. I was making my first contact with east-European Jewry and with the howling wilderness of hatred that surrounded it. I was drawn powerfully toward these communities which, in a miraculous way, had retained the Jewish ethos in the midst of unspeakable moral discouragement; I was drawn toward the teachers who sustained and were sustained by them. If Peretz stood out among them it may well have been because the prince in him, unrecognized as such, gave an extraordinary touch to the commoner.

It is possible again that the years between have colored the memories which filter through them. I may be persuading myself that I remember more vividly than I do. And on the other hand the intervening horror, the destruc-

7

tion of Polish Jewry, may in fact bring to the surface recollections that in a normal way would remain buried forever. However that be, it is a highly personal experience with me. Chiefly I recall from that time in Poland an extraordinary Jewish aliveness and a fantastic blossoming of hope—the spirit of Yal Peretz. They and he—the three and a quarter million Jews of Poland and Yal Peretz—believed that a better time was coming! They believed that the follies of mankind were transient, its fundamental goodness and wisdom permanent. Therefore it behooved them to prepare for the permanent, to slough off their own follies and errors, and to enter the bright new world as the equals of its noblest artificers.

There is a little sketch of Peretz's in which the hero (probably himself) confesses to a dreadful sin: he is a writer, but his source of livelihood, his only one, is a young pupil, the son of a pious and superstitious Jew. The father wants his son to have the rudiments of a modern education, but he warns the teacher: "On no account must you teach him that the earth goes round the sun, or out you go!" And the teacher, who has a sick mother to support, consents to the dishonesty. What a crime against the child! What a crime against the Jewish people, which had to modernize itself in order to be worthy of partnership with the Polish people in the happy new world!

The Polish Jews who were the objects of Peretz's passionate and scrupulous concern have been wiped out by the modern world. Of the three and a quarter million, three million were done to death—gassed, machine-gunned, bombed, burned or buried alive. It did not matter at all whether they believed in the astronomy of Maimonides, derived from Ptolemy, or in Copernicus's; whether they were superstitious or scientific, antisocial reactionaries or social idealists. And nothing they could have done could

8

have averted their fate! A whirlwind of human evil, altogether beyond their control and not to be evaded by any stratagem, came upon them. And if human wisdom and goodness do ultimately triumph, there will be no Polish Jewry to take part in the universal rejoicing. Perhaps it is this reflection that throws back upon my contact of thirty years ago a quivering, sensitive light.

It was Peretz's hope that the Polish Jewry of tomorrow (that is, our today) would combine the strongest and most wholesome Jewish values with the highest achievements of the present. He was, in his stories, something of the *maggid,* or traditional preacher; he was also the modern student of sociology. He loved and understood, with a depth which few have approached, the queer, futile kabbalistic dreamers in the ancient, out-of-the-way Talmudic academies; and he hated and despised the empty, shifty, and shiftless lives of the economically unproductive middle-class Jews. He did not look to Palestine as the solution of the Jewish problem. He wanted it solved on the spot. And he never knew that his political views and programs and formulas were only his personal self, whereas his love of the tradition was the essence of his princely, representative being.

That was one source of division in him. There were others. He wanted a great and creative Polish Jewry in the midst of a great and creative Polish nation. And yet he understood only too clearly the implacable character of the anti-Semitism that gripped the Polish people; he knew only too well that whatever the faults and failings of the Jewish people (and who was better acquainted with them than he?), they are irrelevant to the fluctuations of the anti-Semitic pestilence. He was on solid ground when he sought to improve his people simply because he loved it; not so when he exhorted it to "merit" partnership in the

9

modern world, for he more than once admitted that in an anti-Semitic world (and why only in that kind of world?) merit and reward are not related ideas. He by-passed the difficulty by assuming that sooner or later anti-Semitism would disappear. The horrible thought did not occur to him that Polish Jewry would disappear first.

There was still another division in him. His desire to conserve the traditional moral values of the Jewish teachers was founded in a partial distrust of the modern world and modern methods. He could not see how mankind could be made moral by means of a-moral scientific adjustments; he understood the value of statistics, but he could not accept them as the exclusive instruments of man's salvation. The peculiarly modern belief that the perfect society will be produced by an intelligent balance of mutually antagonistic moral imperfections, egotism competing with egotism, outraged him. It had been the nemesis of capitalism; it would be the nemesis of any other system conceived in the same spirit. For him there was hope only in one combination: the humility, self-effacement, and love preached by the old teachers, and the social-economic principles formulated by the new. But while his mind accepted the second, his heart—and his princely destiny—accepted the first. And so, while he dealt, all his life, with programs and theories, with action, organizations, meetings, classes, he fulfilled himself and his people in the folk stories.

This intellectual-moral division had its cultural counterpart in him. That which he desired for Polish Jewry—modernization, Europeanization—he achieved for himself: part of him became the complete European. That part of him chafed at the loving bonds which held him to his own world. On the one hand he was, like Sholom Aleichem, a Jewish folk figure; on the other hand, and un-

like Sholom Aleichem, he was the subtle, many-sided
European intellectual. But the European in him was frustrated in two ways: Europe never knew him, and to his
own people he is—as the European—of no importance.

Now I, the returned stranger, must explain the work of
this complex figure to other strangers. As in the case of
Sholom Aleichem, I must do it in a roundabout way. It is
useless to present the reader with a body of translations
and say: "There you have the man. Judge him for yourself." The most characteristic of Peretz cannot be translated outright. Honest attempts have been made—again as
in the case of Sholom Aleichem—and they may be read
for what they are worth. These men must be interpreted.
One must talk about them, and around them, and around
their people and its problems; one must retell their stories,
one must hint and allude, interpolate, digress, find anal-
ogies; their work must be introduced as it were incidentally
and by way of illustration, even though it is actually the
purpose, and constitutes the bulk, of the enterprise.

There is always much talk about "mutual understanding" between Jews and non-Jews; there is seldom any
reference to the intellectual effort that it calls for. Good
will is not enough; by itself it is nothing more than benevolent indifference, a treacherous thing in a crisis. Decent human relations are established and maintained by
work, and the reader is advised from the outset that he
will be called on to put a certain amount of work into
the reading of this book. It may turn out to be pleasant
work, but it will be work just the same.

And now a brief reference to the method I have employed. I begin with a series of folk tales, a few translated,
most of them retold. These constitute a substantial and—I
hope—attractive introduction to the "princely" aspect of
Peretz. I then turn aside to Peretz the rebel, the modernist,

the anti-traditionalist, the self-contradictory Peretz. I return then to Peretz the lover of Chassidism, that strange democratic religious rebirth in Jewish life over two centuries ago. Thus the inessential publicistic Peretz—who cannot be ignored and who is for that matter fascinating in his own right—is properly flanked on both sides, and to some extent engulfed, and diminished to his right proportions, by Peretz the Prince. I close with some explanatory chapters on the nature of Yiddish, its peculiar, intransmissible characteristics, and the light it sheds on a section of Jewish history.

CHAPTER II

"Devotion unto Death"

❀

T HE first of Peretz's folk tales offered is neither the first
he wrote nor the best-known; it is, however, the one best
fitted to induct us into his essential style.

He calls it *Messiras Nefesh,* which is translated here as
"Devotion unto Death." The Hebrew phrase, which has
been taken over bodily into Yiddish, means, literally, "the
handing over of the soul," to a cause, a person, or God.
Connected with the word *messirah* (which can also mean
"handing over" to the state authorities; that is, denunciation to the police) is *massorah,* or tradition, the handing
over of the faith from generation to generation. On the
surface the story deals with a young girl's uncalculating
devotion to her beloved, the handing over of her soul to
death for his salvation. On a deeper and more important
level it is an illustration of uncalculating devotion to the
highest value in Jewish tradition—Torah. Torah, which
in its restricted sense means the Pentateuch, the first five
books of the Bible, in its wider sense means all Jewish religion, all law, all knowledge, all wisdom as the mani-
festation of God. It is the key-word to the traditional Jewish outlook.

"Devotion unto Death" is a fairy tale for grown-ups, in
which the truths taught are of the spirit. People who be-

lieve that spiritual truths can be conveyed only by "realistic" novels will not be interested in Peretz's folk tales. This one is filled with impossibilities. Its locale, for instance, is a palace in the sacred city of Safed, with windows looking out on the sapphire-blue Sea of Galilee. The Sea of Galilee is unfortunately twenty miles from Safed, with many hills and vales between. Peretz discovered this years after he wrote the story, and apologized for the error. He need not have done so. The story calls for a special setting, in which the sanctity of Safed, the city of the medieval kabbalists, must be combined with the beauty of the Sea of Galilee. Even so did Shakespeare, needing a seacoast for Bohemia, move one a few hundred miles.

The time of the story is indeterminable, and in fact impossible. It tells of a Jewish merchant prince and scholar in Safed, and of a Yeshivah or Talmudical college in Jerusalem, and of a flourishing Jewish community in Palestine, all existing side by side with the great Talmudical academies of Babylonia. There never was such a combination of circumstances in Jewish history. This did not bother Peretz, and it should not bother the reader any more than should the talking snakes, the blossoming staff, and the other fairy-tale incidents.

I said that the truths in the story are of the spirit; its accuracies, too, are on another plane than the physical; they are psychological, and are addressed to grown-ups, not children. They deal with human weakness, with the sources of misbehavior, with the possibility of moral resurrection—all of them matters of deeper moment than geography and history. The miracle of the spiritual rebirth in the story is far greater than the miracle of the physical resurrection of the bride who gave up her life for her young husband.

Chiya, Chananya, and Miriam are the chief protagonists. Chiya we meet as a marvelous young man, compounded of all gifts and virtues, who is imported from Babylon by a scholarly merchant prince of Safed to become the husband of his youngest daughter. So beautiful was Chiya in his youth that strangers passing him on the street would stop short and utter a prayer of thanksgiving; and so modest was he that he concealed from everyone the fact that he was of the seed royal, descended from King David, and therefore one of those in line for ancestorship of the Messiah.

Miriam, Chiya's daughter and only child, inherited from him his beauty and piety, with an additional (if seemingly superfluous) portion of both from her mother, Sarah, who died young. They used to say of Miriam: "Chiya's daughter is as radiant as the sun," and "On Chiya's daughter lie the grace and charm of Queen Esther."

Of Chananya, the husband-to-be of Miriam, I shall tell shortly.

When Chiya was brought as a bridegroom from Babylon to the Holy Land, he lived with his wife in the palace of his father-in-law and devoted himself to study, prayer, and good deeds. This was the palace that stood in Safed and had its windows over the Sea of Galilee: a noble place, surrounded by a great garden in which flourished all manner of trees and shrubs, fruit-bearing and flowering, ornamental and medicinal, a joy to the eye, a comfort and a healing to the body. Wide, sand-strewn paths ran through the garden, and little summer-houses stood on the shores of lakes on which floated the rarest and whitest of swans. It was an earthly paradise, no less. For Chiya's father-in-law was a merchant of immense wealth, a dealer in precious stones, a man as wise as he was fortunate, a true

15

merchant prince and not one of your noisy charlatans, making a big show and always on the verge of bankruptcy, such as the world is full of nowadays.

In the course of time the father-in-law died, and all his possessions descended to Chiya, who was compelled to leave the exclusive pursuit of wisdom and practice of pious deeds and to take over the family business, which entailed long journeys to all four corners of the earth. That he did this successfully, and even bettered his father-in-law's record, is only natural, for it is quite inconceivable—at least in a story of this kind—that a young man steeped in the wisdom of the sages is not more than a match for the shrewdest man of affairs who cannot, God help him, read a page of the Talmud. In short, Chiya became one of the mightiest merchants of his generation.

But you must not imagine for a moment that all this activity led, in Chiya, to a neglect of his sacred studies or of good deeds. By no means. On his travels Chiya took the Word of God with him. When he crossed the desert he had an attendant lead the camel, while he kept his eyes fastened on the sacred book which he held in his hand. And when he traveled by sea—in his own ship, of course —he shut himself up in his cabin and studied the lore, both the revealed and the unrevealed. He was also attentive to secular learning, and from various wise old sheikhs whom he encountered on his journeys he picked up a knowledge of medicine, of the languages of birds and beasts, and even of astrology.

As for his charitable deeds, there was simply no end to them. It goes without saying that one tenth of his earnings he automatically set aside for the poor. That, however, was only a beginning. His hand was open to every needy person; and for the ransom of captives he kept a special account. Being, moreover, by reason of his trade, an inti-

mate of princes and viziers, whose high regard he won by
his honesty, his wisdom, and his handsomeness of person,
he was in a position to render great service to his people.
Here he intervened to obtain the abrogation of an evil decree, there to obtain the release of a Jew unjustly imprisoned or wrongly condemned to death; and many were
the souls he rescued from something worse than death,
namely apostasy under duress.

That was the way Reb Chiya of Safed conducted his
business. Let all merchants who read this story take a lesson from him.

During his long absences from home his pious wife,
Sarah, maintained the sort of household that befitted her
husband's reputation. Reb Chiya's trust in her was complete; he knew that any man who came to the house hungry would go away sated; that the wandering scholar
would receive encouragement, and the wandering collector for good causes a handsome contribution. The
house was always full of the needy and the learned, of
homeless mendicants, of rabbis and of heads of academies.
No emissary of Palestinian Jewry left the country to visit
the Jews of the exile without first making a halt at Reb
Chiya's lordly home; and none returned from abroad, his
mission completed, without calling there again. And in the
matter nearest Reb Chiya's heart, the upbringing of the
lovely Miriam, Sarah was perfection itself. Of the beggars
and saints and emissaries whom she entertained and sent
on their way strengthened, she asked but one return: that
they place their hands on Miriam's head and bless her.
And these blessings, coming from the heart, mounted
straight to the throne of grace, so that Miriam grew in
beauty and godliness and became a byword in the land.

All of which was too good to last, even in a fairy tale.
Suddenly, in the midst of one of his journeys, Reb Chiya

received word that his saintly wife had been struck down by sickness; and he hastened home, over seas and deserts and mountains, through storm and heat, arriving just in time to take a last farewell of his wife. The dying mother's thoughts were concerned chiefly with her little Miriam. Reb Chiya promised that he would be both father and mother to the orphan girl; there would be no stepmother to threaten the growth of the tender plant. In return the dying Sarah promised that in her new abode in the true or upper world she would never forget those whom she had left behind; she would exert herself with the heavenly powers to the end that they might send her daughter a fitting husband. Moreover, should Reb Chiya, remaining a widower in the false or lower world, ever find himself in perplexity in regard to the child, she, the mother, would do her best to communicate with him in a dream. This agreement made, the godly Sarah drew her feet up in the bed, turned to the wall, and rendered up her spotless soul to her Maker.

There he was, poor Reb Chiya, a widower in the prime of life. No thought of remarriage ever entered his head. Indeed, such worldliness as he had till then permitted himself—and, as we know, he had always turned it to pious account—became unbearable to him. No sooner was the month of mourning over than he proceeded to sell his business, disposing of diamonds and rubies and pearls as fast as he could, and at a loss, so eager was he to be freed from worldly burdens. This done, he transformed his palace into a Talmudic academy—but such an academy as you have never heard of before.

He sought out among the Jews of Safed and the vicinity the most promising youngsters, the most gifted students, irrespective of their means. To those who were poor he became father as well as teacher; he lodged them two and three in a splendid room, he clothed them like the sons of the rich, and nourished them accordingly. He anticipated and met all their needs, down to the matter of pocket-money, so that the poorest student might permit himself an occasional innocent pleasure and not be ashamed in the company of his wealthier companions.

He went further, this extraordinary Reb Chiya. When a poor student had reached the traditional age of marriage, which as we know is eighteen, Reb Chiya sent out messengers in search of a suitable bride; nor did he forget that a learned son-in-law is entitled to a few years of keep in the house of his father-in-law, so that the transition from bachelorhood to the married state may not be attended by an abandonment of the habit of study. Likewise Reb Chiya provided the lucky student with a marriage portion, and paid at least one half of the wedding costs; he himself, and none other, conducted the bridegroom to the bridal canopy. Could anyone ask for more—or even expect one half?

Now, if this was the loving care that Reb Chiya bestowed upon the marriage of his students, what was his concern for his own child, his only one, the lovely and gracious Miriam? For her he dreamed of a pearl of price, a paragon among youths, a delight to humankind and a satisfaction to the Lord.

And being himself a Babylonian, having in his day been recommended to his father-in-law by the Prince of the Babylonian Academy, he now addressed himself to the incumbent in Babylon, and wrote to him, in the flowery and allusive phraseology proper to such a subject and to such correspondents, the following letter:

"With the help of Him whose name is sweet (meaning God), I have planted a beautiful garden (meaning the Academy), with many fruit-bearing trees (meaning the students). And as soon as the fruit becomes ripe (meaning the student is ready for marriage), I seek out a worthy taker (meaning a father-in-law), so that the benediction over the fruit may be pronounced (meaning the wedding ceremony). And in the day when I will find a citron without blemish (meaning a perfect young man), it will be the turn of my beloved daughter, Miriam."

So, in the elegant style of a scholar, full of hints and metaphors and quotations, and not with the crass forthrightness of an ignorant man, wrote the Teacher of Safed to the Prince of the Babylonian Academy; and the latter, in pure astonishment, wrote back: "What? Is it possible that your own Academy lacks scholars of distinction?"

Whereupon Reb Chiya replied with a longer letter of exposition, and herewith we reach the deeper purpose of the story of Miriam and her beloved; and the interpreter steps in for a moment to interrupt the narrative. The reader must not imagine that what Reb Chiya wrote to the Prince of the Babylonian Academy, reproduced below, was new to the latter; nor is it conceivable that Reb Chiya was a sententious bore. The letter of Reb Chiya is for the benefit of the reader; and Peretz begins here that moral probing, that search into the mysterious origin of sin, which is the ultimate purpose of most of his folk tales. And let us note that the observations of Reb Chiya, though they are deeply analytical, are such as the simplest person can understand *if he desires*. It is a folk tale for the folk, not for philosophers, literary connoisseurs, and fancy æsthetes. This is what Reb Chiya wrote:

"The Torah, or Word of God, is like a living stream; but not all streams have their springs in paradise—that is, not all men study the Torah in that pure devotion and disinterestedness of spirit which alone is acceptable to Him. One man studies diligently only to indulge his lust for success and conquest; his one desire is to surpass his fellow students and to triumph over them. A second studies for reputation; he would bask in the glory of the Torah; he does not desire to honor the Torah, he desires that the Torah shall honor him. A third brings to his studies a different kind of lust and self-indulgence. He loves mental gymnastics! His desire is not for God's wisdom, but for his own. *His* little tricks, *his* discoveries and interpretations and ingenuities, *his* juggling of texts, fill him to overflowing with delight and pride. And in order that he may display his cleverness he is prepared to pervert and distort the plain meaning of the Torah, to the confusion of the simple. And some there are whose natures are more gross; for them, despite the explicit warning of the sages, the Torah is a spade to dig the dirt with. Their dreams go no higher than a successful marriage, a wealthy father-in-law, fat meals and rich raiment, and, in the fullness of time, a handsome inheritance. And though it be true, as the wise have told us, that a deed may be begun with low intent and finish up nobly—that is, a man may begin to study with a base end in view and finally come to love wisdom for its own sake—still the soul retains some taint of the original sin, a flavor of evil, an imperfection."

In short, what Reb Chiya wanted for his Miriam was a citron of purest quality, fair to look upon and perfect within. No small problem, for more than one man has a noble exterior and is corrupt of heart. Of the unproved man it is written in the Talmud: "Honor him—and keep an eye on him."

To all of which the Prince of the Babylonian Academy answered with a pithy quotation from the Mishnah: "If one says, 'I *sought* and I found,' believe him." Which means that if a man found something without seeking for it, it has no value, and whatever is obtained without effort is worth the effort it cost.

CHAPTER III

"Devotion unto Death"
(*continued*)

❀

R EB CHIYA of Safed had a theory about the human
voice. He was wont to say:

"One would imagine that the eyes reveal the true character of a man. For, look you: the soul sits imprisoned in
the body, and the Lord of the world, in the greatness of
His mercy, has built two windows in the wall of the prison.
These are the eyes, through which the soul may look out
on the world and be recognized by the world. Unfortunately, the windows have curtains—the eyes have eyelids;
and a man whose soul is impure, feeling himself scruti-
nized, lets down the curtains and conceals the soul. You
think it is modesty, but it is really cunning.

"Now, the voice is another matter. Man has been likened
to an earthen pot which can receive the waters of the Torah without losing a drop—that is, if the pot is whole and
uncracked. But how are we to know if the pot has not a
tiny flaw, invisible to the eye, but capable of letting out the
contents? Ah—as to that, there is a simple test. You have
but to tap the pot with your finger. If it rings back full and
true, all is well; there is your perfect pot. And if not—man,
alas, has been likened to a broken potsherd.

"So a man who is not whole may have a voice that is
high or one that is low; he may have a wheezy voice, a

cracked voice, a tremulous voice; but he will never have a full and true voice."

It was a habit with Reb Chiya, when he was not teaching, to sit in his study, which overlooked a part of the garden, and to occupy himself with the unrevealed Torah. At a certain hour of the day the students were free to walk about the garden paths, enjoying the odors of the shrubs, or tasting the fruits after they had made the proper benediction. Walking in pairs or in groups, they would repeat the lesson of the day, or discuss some knotty problem of the Talmud, or indulge in the innocent talk of friends. Then their voices would come up to Reb Chiya's ears. He would take off his spectacles and lay them on the volume before him, and he would listen intently. Not, God forbid, to overhear what they were saying; he had not the desire to do that, nor, from where he sat, could he have distinguished the words. Only the sound of the voices reached him. And never did Reb Chiya hear one that pleased him completely.

This often plunged him into deep sadness; and on one occasion he even began to complain:

"Lord of the world," he sighed, "the birds in the garden have but the common soul of wild nature, and they sing Thy praises; my students have each his individual soul, and they study Thy Torah. . . . Why is the voice of the birds so pure and whole, whereas the voices of my students—"

No, Reb Chiya did not end the sentence. He was not going to denounce his students before the heavenly court. But the sadness in his heart remained; and the search for the perfect bridegroom for Miriam made no progress.

As for Miriam, the orphan, her soul still slept, and she knew nothing of the care that weighed on her father's heart. One day he asked her whether she sometimes visited her mother's grave.

"Indeed I do, Father," she answered, and kissed his hand.

"And do you ever pray there?"

"I pray for your health, Father."

Reb Chiya stroked his daughter's cheek. "My health, God be thanked, is all it should be. There is something else you must pray for at your mother's grave."

"And what is that, Father?"

"Implore her to remember her promise, and to do in heaven whatever she can to bring about what I have in mind for you."

And Miriam answered him simply and without questioning: "I will, Father."

The voice of Reb Chiya's dreams and prayers came at last; and its possessor was the youth Chananya, the predestined husband of Miriam the beautiful. But what a frightful contrast between the voice and the person! And what a contrast between the recommendations that Reb Chiya had brought with him to his Sarah and the history of the youth Chananya. Chananya enters the story wildly. Dressed in beggar's sackcloth, which he refuses to change for decent clothes, carrying a peeled almond branch, which he cannot lay by, but must keep at his side day and night, he comes to Reb Chiya's Academy begging to be admitted as a student. But his qualifications are such as would not admit him to an elementary school. Not a page of Talmud can he read; not even a phrase of the Mishnah. He can barely make his way through the Hebrew prayers—but he does not know the meaning of a single word, for he speaks and understands only the vernacular. And yet he implores the privilege of sitting in on Reb Chiya's lessons. "Perhaps I will remember," he weeps.

"Sick!" thinks Reb Chiya. "Once he knew, and now he has forgotten." But the voice! It is *the* voice.

"My son," says Reb Chiya, "why do you not look at me? Are you hiding your soul from me?"

"Yes, Rabbi," the youth answers. "It is a sinful soul. I have much to be ashamed of."

"Our sages say that no man gives himself an evil name," responds Reb Chiya. "I command you to lift up your eyes."

The youth obeys, and Reb Chiya starts back in terror.

"My son," he says, "there is a curse in your eyes. Who has put it there?"

"The head of the Talmudic Academy of Jerusalem," answers Chananya. "And he it was who sent me to you to confess my sins."

CHANANYA'S STORY

Chananya's mother was a rich widow of Jerusalem, a dealer in spices; and she had two children, Chananya and Esther, Esther being the older by a year or two.

The mother's soul was wrapped up in her son, to the neglect of her daughter; for not only was he the *kaddish*, the male descendant who would say the Sanctification prayer for her after her death, but he was an *ilui*, a child prodigy. The head of the Jerusalem Academy had said as much, after examining him; was even prepared to admit him as a student despite his youthfulness. But the doting mother would not part from her son, and she had him study at home, engaging successive private teachers, each more advanced than the last. And that was Chananya's undoing.

The last of these private teachers, the one who ruined Chananya, was one of those false scholars who are drawn to the Torah not by love of wisdom but by the lust to

25

shine; and he instilled into Chananya his own evil spirit. He taught him the subtle dialectic of negation, the art of disproving and destroying; and he planted in the boy's heart the bitter herbs of pride and triumph. And Chananya soon learned the trick; for indeed this kind of sophistry is only a trick, and not the wisdom of the Torah which was given to us at Sinai. But neither the mother nor the neighbors understood this; and when Chananya declared to his mother that he had completed his studies, that he no longer needed a teacher, the foolish woman saw the gates of heaven opening for her.

Thenceforth Chananya trod the false path alone. Whenever he could he would engage in disputes with students of the Academy or with men of learning, and by the juggling of sacred verses, by ingenious quotations out of context, by intellectual trickery, he would put them all to shame and make them appear to be ignoramuses. This came to the ears of the head of the Academy, who thought: "Youthful follies! He will grow out of them and become a true scholar." And he sent word to the mother to rebuke her son. But the mother, of course, did nothing of the sort; she kissed her son instead and bought him costly presents.

So encouraged, Chananya went further afield. Lacking disputants, he would force himself upon reluctant strangers; he interrupted the studies of young men in the synagogue; he heckled preachers; he barely waited till a speaker had finished, but would spring forthwith on to the pulpit and tear the contents of the sermon to shreds, proving that the preacher was unlettered, or an idiot, or both; and by the swiftness of his tongue and the venom of his manner he so bewildered all those against whom he directed his fury that they became as it were witless and were put to shame.

A second time the head of the Academy sent word to

Chananya's mother: "Punish him again! And this time more severely." And a second time the infatuated woman rewarded her son with kisses and gifts. This being at last told the head of the Yeshivah, he had Chananya brought before him and addressed him thus:

"Hear me, Chananya! All this cleverness of yours serves only to destroy and negate. Our Torah consists of two halves; the one affirms, the other forbids; one half says: 'Thou shalt,' the other half says; 'Thou shalt not.' *Your* cleverness is all negation; therefore you have but one half of the Torah, and representing it as the whole, you preach a lie. And here is the proof: say something of your own that is not a negation."

Chananya was silent, having no answer. His power lay in contradiction and destruction. He said:

"Such things I did not learn from my teacher."

The head of the Academy answered: "Chananya, know that your teacher is dead, and his soul burns in hell. The Torah he learned and taught has no power to save him. And he will continue to burn in hell until you, Chananya, uproot from your heart the evil he planted there. Take pity, Chananya, on your own soul and on the soul of your teacher; repent, return, and study the Torah in the spirit of God."

From the Academy Chananya ran to the cemetery to find out whether his teacher was really dead, for he had had no word of it. Yes, the man had been buried only the day before, and already the freshly dug grave was thickly covered with ugly and poisonous weeds. And Chananya, understanding what this meant, resolved in his heart to repent.

But the way of the penitent is not easy, as we shall shortly see.

There lived in Jerusalem in those days a retired butcher.

a man of infamous character and evil repute, who had become rich by selling tainted and un-kosher meat and who
by his meanness and closefistedness and general impiety
had hounded his wife to an untimely grave. So miserly was
the man that he owned not his money, but his money
owned him; and this was true in all respects save one,
namely his only child, his daughter Hannah. And everything that he denied himself, food and clothes and comfort,
he was eager to bestow prodigally upon her; above all he
was eager to obtain for her a husband of distinction, a
young scholar and pietist whom all the world would envy
him; and for this he was ready, in his strange way, to ex-
pend great sums of money.

But how could this be done? The man's reputation was
such that not all the wealth in the world could offset the
horror of having him as a father-in-law. He sent marriage
brokers through the length and breadth of the land, but
his name had gone before him. He even hired two poor
scholars to travel through the Jewish communities of the
exile, seeking a son-in-law for him; and for two years these
unhappy emissaries, who undertook the mission only under the pressure of great want, did their best, but to no
avail. For though they spoke of the virtues of the bride and
the wealth of the father they were—being honest men—
most eloquently silent on his character; and not even their
praises of the bride-to-be, all of which she merited, could
undo the effect of their significant reticence on the subject
of her father.

Returning empty-handed from their search throughout
the world, the two scholars paused in great perplexity before the walls of Jerusalem, dreading to enter, dreading the
thought of facing their employer. So sitting, they were ac-
costed by a strange, wild youth clad in sackcloth and leaning on a staff which was the peeled branch of an almond

tree. A conversation followed, in which the youth unfolded a wondrous story. For years he had been living in the wilderness, his food the wild grasses, his raiment sackcloth, his sole companion the almond branch; save that every night an old man with brilliant eyes and long, snow-white beard appeared to him and taught him: Talmud and commentary, law and legend, ritual and judgment—everything, in fact, that is comprised in the wisdom of the Torah. The old man taught him by heart, without books, as in the ancient days before all this wisdom had been written down; and taught him perfectly. And only the night before, the old man had taken farewell of him, saying: "Tomorrow you will enter Jerusalem, and there you will find your predestined bride."

A sign from heaven! Overjoyed, the two scholars conducted the young man to the ex-butcher and said: "Look not upon his exterior. Do not be frightened off by his sackcloth garment and his wild staff. This youth has studied in the wilderness, and Elijah the Prophet was his teacher. He is your daughter's destined one."

Without waiting, without questioning, the ex-butcher closed the bargain, and two weeks later he arranged a magnificent wedding; and since it was all for his beloved daughter, he forgot his niggardliness and sent out invitations to every notable and every scholar in Jerusalem. They accepted, not for his sake, but for the daughter's, and for the sake of the sainted mother who, they believed, was responsible for this wonderful match.

Among others came the head of the Yeshivah of Jerusalem, his students, and Chananya, now a penitent. And while the bride was being prepared among the women, the bridegroom, now becomingly clad (the ex-butcher had taken away his sackcloth and staff, to sell them to the ragman after the wedding), delivered his wedding sermon, according to the custom, among the men. And what a sermon it was (recounted Chananya to Reb Chiya)! Gold and silver and pearls and precious stones! Myrrh and frankincense! Ancient wisdom from young lips, eloquence and learning, a river of enchantment! And Chananya listened, indeed, like one enchanted, with never a thought of contradiction, never a touch of envy. On the contrary, he rejoiced with all his heart, thinking: "This will be my friend; he and I will study together in the years to come." And such a love awoke in his heart toward the young stranger, that when the sermon was ended he ran forward to embrace him—and then the evil thing happened.

As he was running forward he heard one of the Yeshivah students say: "The bridegroom is a greater scholar than Chananya," and another answered: "Chananya is a clod by comparison." It was as if a serpent had stung him; no, not *a* serpent, but *the* serpent, that Ancient One, the Spirit of Evil. Something laid hold of Chananya's heart, as if with icy tongs; he stopped dead in his tracks and rose on his tiptoes. He opened his lips, and from them poured a torrent, not of eloquence, but of poisonous and treacherous sophistry: pitch and sulphur and brimstone, lies, evasions, distortions, negations, deceptions. Chananya knew that he was committing a monstrous crime, desecrating the Torah of Elijah the Prophet, the true Torah. He was seized with horror—but he could not stop. Without his will, against his will, the ghastly stream poured on, covering the bridegroom's sermon with such ridicule that the bridegroom fainted away.

The wedding chamber changed suddenly into a madhouse. The ex-butcher sprang to his feet, screaming: "I've been swindled! I've been swindled!" And he ran among the guests, driving them into the street, yelling: "I won't have this wedding feast wasted! Bring in the wretched little carpenter from next door. He shall marry my daughter! And as for you," he howled at the bridegroom, who had just recovered consciousness, "go put on your sackcloth and take your staff!" And he tore off his back the clothes he had given him.

Outside, in the street, the head of the Yeshivah of Jerusalem encountered Chananya, stopped him, and said: "Chananya! Desolation sits on your tongue! Forget all you have ever learned!" In that instant something cracked in Chananya's head; his brain became as empty as a birdless cage; the learning of the years had taken flight.

"Only one ray of hope remained for me," continued Chananya mournfully as he walked side by side under the night sky with Reb Chiya, disemburdening himself. "It so happened that the marriage I had ruined was not a predestined one. The true and predestined husband of the ex-butcher's daughter was, in fact, the little carpenter next door, who was—the head of the Yeshivah told us in confidence—one of the Thirty-six Secret Saints. And the predestined bride of Elijah's pupil was my own sister, Esther. But the curse had been laid on me, and the road of my redemption was to be a long and bitter one. I was bidden to put on the sackcloth of my brother-in-law, to take up his staff, and to wander out into the wilderness. The staff, which you see me holding now, I was to guard as the apple of my eye. I was to walk with it by day and keep it at my head by night. The head of the Yeshivah promised to pray for me, and on the day when his prayer would be answered and I would be cleansed and restored, the dead almond staff would blossom.

"So I went out of my mother's house, an exile and a wanderer, and found myself in a wilderness where my food was wild grass, and my drink the water of stagnant pools. But I did not hunger for bread or thirst for water. I hungered and thirsted after the living word, which I had for-feited. The wild beasts of the wilderness avoided me, and it was as if I heard a voice cry out: 'Touch him not! This man belongs—' but nothing more. To whom or what I belonged was not said.

"Not one word of the sages, not a fragment of the Torah, had remained in my head. I could not even repeat the simplest prayer by heart. One day I took up a handful of sand and poured it on my head; then, standing on one foot, I cried out toward heaven: 'Torah! Torah!' I kept crying out hour after hour until the sun had set; then I fell down and slept. And in my sleep the head of the Jerusalem Yeshivah appeared to me in his graveclothes, for he was already dead. And he said to me:

" 'Arise, Chananya, for the time of your redemption has come. Elijah the Prophet has interceded for you. Arise and go to Safed, to the good man Reb Chiya, and confess to him; and implore him to let you enter his Yeshivah. He will not refuse you. And when, in a few months, you will have reached the age of eighteen, he will find you your predestined bride and will pray for you. And know that the prayers of Reb Chiya avail mightily in the court of heaven. And on the eighth day after the wedding you will awaken, and the staff by your head will have put forth blossoms; and you will remember all the Torah you ever knew, but cleansed of its destructive spirit—it will be a pure and affirmative Torah that you will remember. All this will come to pass, but whether you will live long after that, I cannot foresee.'

"With these words the head of the Jerusalem Yeshivah vanished from my dreams. I woke in the morning and set out for Safed; and here I am according to the instructions I received."

CHAPTER IV

"Devotion unto Death"
(concluded)

❀

Could this be he, Reb Chiya asked himself in great perplexity. Could this be the bridegroom whom the sainted mother in heaven had by her intercessions won for her Miriam? An empty soul, a stranger to the Torah—even though it had been promised him that the Torah would come back to him. But when? And yet, despite that emptiness, there was the voice! The harp and the violins of King David!

But however all this might be, there was no question of turning Chananya away. Only it was proper to warn him of what he faced.

"My son," said Reb Chiya gently, "I for my part am ready to grant your request."

"Rabbi, Rabbi," cried Chananya, "let me sit in your class, somewhere at the back, somewhere in a dark corner. I will not open my lips. I will only listen to what you tell the students."

"I, for my part," repeated Reb Chiya, slowly, "am ready. But what of them? My students—they are young. And, alas, we know only too well of the scholar's contempt for the ignorant man. You will be laughed at, you will suffer."

Chananya caught him up joyously. "Yes indeed! Let me suffer. Is it not part of my penance?"

"Yes," granted Reb Chiya, "and yet the matter is not so simple. You will be doing penance, but they will be committing sin; is it not written that he who puts another to shame in public has forfeited his portion of paradise?"

"Is it indeed so written?" asked Chananya, who before his fall would have known the verse as well as Reb Chiya. "But how is it, Rabbi, if my forgiveness is prepared in advance of the transgression, and I take their jests and gibes in a spirit of love? And as for me, have I not already forfeited my portion in paradise by the shame I put in public on my brother-in-law? Henceforth, then, I shall be studying the Torah without hope of reward; and even if the memory of what I once knew returns to me, I shall cling to it for its own sake, and not for the sake of recompense in the hereafter."

The words of Chananya fell like balm on the soul of Reb Chiya. He consented; and the next day Chananya, clad in sackcloth, staff in hand, took a place on the farthest bench in the classroom.

While Reb Chiya lectured he threw an occasional glance at Chananya, who sat with closed eyes and attentive ears, reddening with joy whenever a sacred word seemed to sound familiar, paling with anguish when the words went over his head. Discussions arose between teacher and students, knotty problems were raised, quick and subtle phrases were thrown back and forth; Chananya alone sat dumb. And more than once a student would stare in his direction with mockery and resentment in his eyes; and Reb Chiya saw it, but made no comment and uttered no rebuke. For he saw also that Chananya looked back at the student with radiant and loving eyes, as if a great favor had been bestowed on him.

So the days passed; during classes Chananya sat in his corner; between classes he sat alone in a little booth in the garden, repeating what he could remember of the day's lessons, and praying desperately to have his knowledge restored. And bit by bit there came to him, not indeed the learning he had forfeited, but a feeling of approach and expectation; as if he were wandering in the desert, parched with thirst, and heard, nearer and nearer at hand, but still invisible, a fountain of fresh waters. This degree of progress, such as it was, he reported to Reb Chiya.

Now, it chanced that one evening Reb Chiya went out into a lonely place in the garden to pray for Chananya, and as he approached with soft tread the booth that Chananya frequented, he suddenly perceived two snakes twined round adjacent oleander trees. They were leaning over to each other, hood to hood, and were engaged in such intimate converse that they remained unaware of Reb Chiya's presence.

Reb Chiya, as we know, was an adept in the languages of birds and beasts; he was, moreover, well acquainted with all the inhabitants of his garden, the creeping things, the running, and the flying. He perceived at once that the snake to the right was a familiar of the place, while the snake to the left was a stranger, a denizen of remote deserts, of the deadly species named Achnai. He heard the home snake ask the visitor what he was doing in Reb Chiya's garden.

"I have come here to sting someone."

"Then you may as well go home again," answered the other. "I have been a resident here many years, and when I first came here I was as fiery and wicked a snake as you could wish to meet. I never let pass a chance to sting one of the students. And today I am as harmless as a dove. I have given up stinging. Do you know why? Every student I stung ran at once to Reb Chiya; and he, having learned in the course of his journeys all the secrets of the healing art from the wisest sheikhs, forthwith applied the proper herbs, and my work was undone. Seeing in time that all my efforts were wasted, I simply gave up. Turn round, then, and go home."

"Foolishness!" answered the stranger snake, and went on learnedly: "The remedies of Reb Chiya are effective only when a snake does its stinging as you do, by virtue of its snake nature, and because of the enmity between man and snake which was decreed of old for the sin of Adam. Such remedies mean nothing to me at this moment. I have come here on a special mission, delegated by the Angel of Death, to carry out sentence against a sinner."

"How can that be?" asked the home snake. "Who among the learned and pious students of Reb Chiya has forfeited his life?"

"The youth Chananya!" answered the stranger snake. "He who sits apart from all the other students. He once put to shame a scholar, a pupil of Elijah the Prophet. And that on the very day of the man's wedding, in the presence of the assembled guests. Therefore the head of the Jerusalem Yeshivah cursed him with the curse of forgetfulness and bade him go into exile and to wander about the earth in sackcloth, a staff of almond in his hand. On the day when the staff will blossom, he will remember his Torah."

"That is, never," commented the home snake.

"Not so," went on the other. "The sentence was discussed at great length in the court of heaven. Some were for the regular sentence—that is, forfeiture of paradise—but the Genius of the Torah would not have it, and a compromise was reached. The youth Chananya was to marry a pious Jewish daughter, and on the eighth day after the wedding he was to die. One half of his sin was to be forgiven him for the sake of the good deed of marriage, the other half for the sake of his death. And because the young woman contributing to the redemption of Chananya was to be left a widow so early, she was to receive an extraordinary recompense: from her was to be born a mighty saint and scholar, the light of his generation and the comfort of the world."

Their converse ended, the snakes uncoiled from the trees and slid away toward the water. Reb Chiya remained where he was, a stunned man.

For there was no doubting the veracity of what he had heard, and he found himself in a frightful dilemma and before a frightful trial. If he did nothing to further Chananya's marriage—with whomsoever it might be—he would be defying Providence; but if he took a hand in it, he would be helping to condemn some pious Jewish daughter to early widowhood: eight days after the wedding!

He looked up into the heavens; they were clouded and unresponsive. But his heart began to beat violently, and a voice within him said:

"Chiya, thou shalt sacrifice thy daughter. Would Father Abraham, who offered his son Isaac to the sacrificial knife, have hesitated in thy place?"

With that the clouds unrolled from the sky, a million stars sprang up, and Reb Chiya addressed his thoughts to his sainted wife, imploring her to visit him according to her promise.

Not long after, toward the end of a fast-day, Reb Chiya fell asleep, and Sarah his wife came to him in a dream. Her face shone with the love and grace of her last moments on earth, and he heard her say clearly, as she placed her hand on his right shoulder: "Fear not, Chiya. The future of our daughter is bright with the brightness of the sun. Have faith in her."

Reb Chiya would have questioned his wife, but she withdrew from his dream and he felt himself being awakened.

It was his daughter Miriam, who stood over him, her hand on his right shoulder.

"Father, forgive me," said Miriam. "The sun has long since set, the moon and stars are out. It is time for you to eat."

"By my life," answered Reb Chiya, "I will not taste food or drink water until you have answered my questions."

He saw the color flow over his daughter's face and he went on:

"My daughter, it is the way of life that a young girl should reveal certain thoughts only to her mother. But you are an orphan, and I must be your mother as well as your father. Therefore you must show me what is in your heart, keeping nothing back."

Miriam covered her face and whispered: "Ask, Father."

"My daughter, the years are passing and I am no longer young. My beard is as white as the snows of Hermon. How will it be on the day when I am called before the court of heaven? In whose hands will I leave you?"

"Father, do not speak of it. I shall always obey you."

"My daughter, is it your desire to be more righteous than Rebecca?"

Miriam smiled. "By no means."

"When Eliezer, the servant of Abraham, came to propose the marriage with Isaac, he was met with the words: 'We will call the damsel and enquire at her mouth.' That is to say, she was not shamefaced, but answered: 'Yes.' "

"Ask, Father, and I will answer you."

"Tell me, Miriam, whom among my students would you choose as a husband?"

"Chananya," answered Miriam, so softly that only a father's heart could have caught the word.

Astounded by the answer, Reb Chiya asked: "Why does he please you, daughter? Have you ever spoken with him?"

"God forbid! Besides—he would never have answered me."

"What then is it? Tell me, daughter," and seeing that she found it hard to speak, he added: "I command it, Miriam, by the law of honor and obedience to a father."

Then she told him that Chananya had pleased her from the beginning; first his voice, which flowed over her heart like a sweet, sacramental oil; second his strength.

"His strength?" asked Reb Chiya.

"Does it not show strength, Father, if a youth goes about in sackcloth among his well-clad fellow students and feels neither shame nor fear?"

"What else?"

"The goodness of his heart, which shines from his eyes whenever he looks up. And his sadness. . . ."

"My child, he is a penitent. A heavy sin lies on his soul."

"God *must* forgive him," cried Miriam. "Sometimes I have passed by his booth and heard his prayers. Can it be that such prayers will not be accepted?"

"Is it only pity you feel for him?"

"In the beginning it was only pity. I used to think that if I were you, I would pray for him day and night. Then another thought came to me: had I been born a man, and his brother, I would surely lay down my life for him. Then suddenly—Father, you have commanded me to tell everything—the blood rushed to my heart, and I said to myself that the utmost sacrifice can come only from a wife. And once, Father, when you and your pupils had gone sailing on the lake—it was the holiday of the Thirty-third Day of the Omer—and I was left alone in the house, I wandered into the garden and fell asleep and had a dream. I saw a white dove being hunted through the skies by a black bird of prey, and a pity stronger than I could bear awoke in me, and I began to scream, to frighten off the bird of prey. It disappeared, then returned, and this happened several times. At last the white dove descended to me and asked: 'Why do you cry out?' I answered: 'Do you not see the bird of prey? It wants to kill you.' Thereupon the dove answered mournfully: 'No, it does not *want* to kill me. It *must* kill me. And it *will* kill me unless someone offers up his life for me. And that no one will do.' 'I will do it,' I cried out; 'I swear it.' Then the dove asked me: 'And you will not regret the oath?' 'Never,' I answered. With that the dove flew away, and I awoke and knew the meaning of the dream. I knew that the dove was Chananya, and that only a wife could show devotion unto death."

For a while Reb Chiya was silent; then he asked, sadly:

"How is it, my daughter, if the decree has gone out that his years shall be few? He is to beget a son who will be a mighty saint and scholar, but he himself will die young."

"Whatever years have been decreed him, they shall be happy ones."

"And how is it if his life is reckoned not in years, but in days?"

"Days, then, but they shall be good days."

"And you will remain a widow?"

"A widow, but blessed of God."

Then Reb Chiya, in a last trial, told Miriam the details of the heavenly decree against Chananya, and of the serpent Achnai, which was to sting him on the eighth day after his marriage—that is, immediately after the ceremony of the Seven Nuptial Benedictions. But, far from being terrified, Miriam showed only joy. Her eyes became irradiated as with a light of prophecy, and she said: "I believe and trust that the decree against him will be nullified. How that will happen I cannot tell; but I shall offer my life up for his."

Then Reb Chiya understood that all this came from

40

God, and he resolved there and then to proceed with the marriage. Nevertheless, in the perplexity of his heart he dispatched that night two identical letters to the heads of the academies of Jerusalem and of Babylon: "Tomorrow," he wrote, "we shall celebrate the betrothal of my daughter, Miriam, God grant her long life. There are moments when I feel that I am setting a crown upon her brows; and there are moments when I feel that I am leading my little one, my one lamb, to the slaughter. I will not oppose the will of God. The wedding is set for a month from this day. Meanwhile I wait for word from you—counsel and comfort; and I beg you to pray for me, and for my daughter Miriam, and for the penitent, Chananya."

The next day the students of the Academy and the inhabitants of Safed were amazed to hear that the youth Chananya and the maiden Miriam, daughter of Sarah and Chiya, were betrothed. An incredible thing! And the days passed, and no word came back to Reb Chiya from Jerusalem or Babylon. The morning of the wedding arrived, and Reb Chiya remained faithful to his word.

An incredible wedding it was, too: a bridegroom in sackcloth, with an almond staff in his hand, and a bride in an old workday dress, for Miriam had resolved that her wedding clothes should be no finer than her husband's; but far stranger than all this, a bridegroom unable to deliver a wedding sermon, even of the simplest kind, so that the bride's father had to speak for him. Yet when the time came for the bride to be unveiled, her face shone and her eyes were pools of faith.

And a week later the ceremony of the Seven Nuptial Benedictions was celebrated in the garden of the Academy; the bride sat like a beggarwoman at a rich feast, and the bridegroom like a wordless clod among Rabbis and scholars, who held forth to each other on the wisdom of the

41

Torah. But whether he himself was holding forth or whether he was listening to others, Reb Chiya was ill at ease; his eyes kept wandering to the shrubs and flower-beds, and now and again he caught a glimpse of the serpent Achnai gliding in and out, and sometimes slipping unperceived among the guests.

In the evening, after the last of the Seven Nuptial Benedictions, Reb Chiya drew his daughter aside and in an unnatural voice said:

"My daughter, tomorrow is the judgment day. Be of strong heart."

"I am strong," answered Miriam, "I am blessed of God. I will redeem my husband from death."

The next morning when Reb Chiya came to visit the young couple, Miriam was already dressed, but Chananya was still abed, and with closed eyes he asked his father-in-law's forgiveness, saying that some slight indisposition kept him from rising. But Reb Chiya's eyes were fixed on the almond staff, which stood by Chananya's head, and Reb. Chiya could scarcely believe what he saw; for the surface of the staff was slowly turning green, and veins began to swell upon it, and among the veins tiny blossoms appeared. Reb Chiya drew nearer, to inspect the miracle more closely; but, glancing at Chananya, he saw a change come over the young man's face, which was taking on color. And Chananya opened his eyes, and they were clear and tranquil, unshadowed by malediction. Reb Chiya, startled, looked round for his daughter, but she had vanished. A moment later Reb Chiya forgot his daughter, forgot the serpent Achnai and the miracle of the almond staff. For Chananya had launched upon a discourse, and from his lips flowed the endless and unfathomable wisdom of the Torah, the revealed and the unrevealed alike. Before Reb Chiya's inward eye a marvelous garden rose, a paradise in which blossomed the tree of life and the tree of knowledge of good and evil and countless other wondrous trees. Wide upon the landscape shone the light of the original seven days, pouring out gold on branches and leaves and blossoms; a multitude of birds played among the trees, and there was a universal singing and burgeoning and unfolding of life. . . . Chananya spoke, and it seemed to Reb Chiya that the soul of the world was speaking. The bliss which filled Reb Chiya was something not to be conveyed in words, and as for the secrets of the Torah which Chananya revealed in that discourse, behold, are they not written in the Book of the Righteous, which is the Book of Chananya, that same book which Reb Chiya issued in later years, bound in gold? And since these things are not to be described, let us leave the two mighty spirits of the Torah, the expounder and the listener, and turn our attention to the beautiful and pious Miriam.

She, witnessing the miracle of the almond staff and seeing her father absorbed in it, had snatched up the sackcloth raiment of her husband and fled from the room. Quietly she ran through the palace and, pausing in a little outer vestibule, threw off her own clothes and put on those of her husband. "Lord of the world," she whispered, "forgive me that I transgress against Thy law, which forbids a woman to wear the habit of a man. But Thou knowest that a life is at stake, and danger of death overrides the law." Therewith, still unseen, she stole into the garden and seated herself at the foot of an oleander tree.

And while she prayed with all her soul that God might accept the sacrifice of her life, she looked about her for Achnai, and when she saw him gliding toward her she covered her face with her hands, so that her outer appearance was like that of Chananya. Between her fingers she watched the serpent drawing nearer and nearer; and he

43

came on slowly, at his leisure, knowing that the victim was prepared for him and would not flee. And seeing Chananya (as he thought) sitting motionless, with covered face, he said to himself: "His heart is filled with foreboding! He is praying, or perhaps confessing." Therewith he drew still nearer and uncovered his fangs, so that Miriam saw them, and saw the spotted skin, and heard the rustle of the coils on the ground. Then she closed her fingers and, having prayed: "Lord of the world, accept my sacrifice," she uttered the confession with lips that did not tremble, and when she had ended she felt the bite of the fangs.

With that she fell to the ground, crying: "Lord of the world, forgive me for the mighty saint and scholar I was to have borne, and who now dies with me! Let Chananya live in his place!" Then the death pangs came on her, and with anguish the soul tore its way out of the young body.

But is not God the God of true judgment?

As the soul of Miriam ascended to heaven, the saints came forth from paradise to meet it, thinking it to be the soul of Chananya, which was then being expected. And she was led before the court of heaven, according to the ritual. The examination began:

"Soul, wert thou honest in thy dealings on earth, in thy buying and selling?"

"On earth I had no dealings; I neither bought nor sold."

"Wert thou diligent in the study of the Torah?"

"Lord of the world," answered the soul of Miriam, smiling, "when didst Thou command the daughters of Israel to be diligent in the study of the Torah?"

Consternation in heaven!

"Who art thou? Who art thou?"

"Miriam, daughter of Sarah and Chiya, wife of Chananya!"

44

Consternation, tumult, and confusion! It is discovered that the woman has offered up her life for her husband, and Achnai, the messenger of death, has been tricked! A thousand voices cry:

"Back to earth, soul, back into your body, before someone finds it and moves it."

"Not I!" answers Miriam. She knows her rights! To suffer twice the pangs of death is beyond all mortal obligation. No, she will not return to her body unless—unless this first death of hers be credited to Chananya's account, and he be permitted to live.

As with a single voice the members of the heavenly court cry out: "Agreed! Agreed!" No time for delay!

On the instant the soul of Miriam re-entered her body, and she rose from the ground completely healed, so that not even a mark remained where the serpent had stung her. Filled with joy, she ran to her husband and father, and barely had she finished telling them what had befallen her when messengers arrived from Jerusalem and from Babylon with the long-delayed answers of the heads of the academies to the letters of Reb Chiya; and both answers consisted of one and the same word:

"Mazel-tov! Felicitations!"

45

CHAPTER V

The Secret Places

❀

O F MAN'S first disobedience, of the dark corners of
the human heart, of the small beginnings of great trans-
gressions—of these and of similar things Yitzchok Leibush
Peretz sang at length in his folk tales. He was endlessly
fascinated by the origin of evil, by the human power of
self-deception which covers the first departure from the
right path, and by the subtle disguises which the Enemy of
Mankind assumes. Sometimes he treated the subject som-
berly; sometimes his tone was light; somber or playful, he
was always serious. The moral nature of man was the
fundamental substance of his meditations.

It began in his boyhood. At the age of fourteen, a
Talmud student in his native Polish townlet of Zamoshch,
he already knew the torments of doubt and self-question-
ing. He tells us in his unfinished autobiography: "I went
about distracted, a wanderer in the upper worlds, steeped
in gloom, my thoughts and dreams occupied with the
cosmic tragedy." *The Guide to the Perplexed* of Maimonides was his first handbook to the eternal riddles.
"What is the purpose of man?" he asked himself. "Whence
come sorrow and suffering, and what end do they serve? Is
there such a thing as free will?"

Among his mature works there is a humorous sketch of

two youths who, on a hot summer's day, steal away from cheder, or Hebrew school, to bathe in the river; but while undressing on the bank they become so absorbed in philosophic discussion that they forget entirely what purpose brought them to this place. Much of Peretz's work is autobiographical; in the actual biography he himself frankly furnishes the key to a great variety of pieces—this particular sketch, "Back to School, You Rascals!" among others. It is himself and a friend he is describing. There they sit, the two boys, their stockings halfway off, the cool water lapping at their feet, the sun blazing overhead, completely abstracted from the world about them.

"Do you know, Berel," says one of them, "I just can't understand what the great Rabbi Tam is driving at. According to him the Almighty doesn't want to humiliate man by offering him paradise for nothing, as if it were a piece of charity. The point is, says Rabbi Tam, that man ought to *earn* paradise without losing his self-respect. But what sort of humiliation is he talking about? When God gives me something, am I taking it from a stranger? Am I taking it from a human being, who is left with less? Does it cost the Almighty anything?"

"That's right enough," says the other, "and still, when you come to think of it, you're on a higher level if you don't get something for nothing, even from the Almighty —if you've earned it, if it's honest payment."

"But haven't the sages told us: 'Do not serve God as a slave does his master, in the hope of payment'?"

"That's quite a different matter."

The two young foreheads are wrinkled in thought, hands gesticulate, fringes of ritual garments fly right and left.

"All right, let it be payment. But what about punishment? What's punishment for?"

47

"But don't you see, it's for the same purpose—that man may be better, may repent if he has sinned?"

"That's all very well for life in *this* world. But what's the sense of punishment in the *next* world."

"You've got the answer right there, in Rabbi Tam. Punishment in the next world is for the purification of the soul, to remove the blotches that have gathered on it in this world."

"Well and good; but on the other hand . . ."

Sunk in debate, the two boys neither see nor hear the long, lean, perspiring woman who is running toward them, flourishing a broomstick, and crying: "Rascals! Heathens! What is this? Playing truant? Bathing in the middle of the day?"

"On the other hand, isn't the soul rather to be pitied? Sure, it has sinned; but doesn't Rashi himself quote a passage from the Talmud: 'No man commits a sin unless a lunatic spirit has entered into him.' You've got to be crazy to commit a sin. That is, if you do it deliberately, and not by mistake."

"Yes, but suppose the Evil Spirit is mighty?"

"That proves my point! The poor sinner's been forced into it!"

"Is that so? Then what about the man who becomes an apostate out of sheer perversity?"

"Well, I'll grant you something there. That kind of man is absolutely beyond me. It's as if you were to pick up an ax and split your own head open."

"Heathens! Villains! Time-wasters! I'll split both of your heads!" The woman's agonized voice is so close, so loud, that even the two philosophers are startled out of their debate. They spring to their feet. "It's Mother! It's Mother!" They snatch up their coats from the sand and run like hunted hares up the river bank.

48

The sketch is autobiographical in respect of Peretz's early absorption in moral philosophy, but not in respect of his relations with his mother, who was a gentle, pious, loving, and understanding soul. He has chosen, here, to smile at his boyhood earnestness, but in his autobiography he recalls it as a painful phase of his growth. He recounts how, one Friday, he wandered about the fields of Zamoshch from morning to evening, communing with himself, and turned up for synagogue service in muddy shoes and in his weekday hat. His father, by nature a mild and thoughtful man, was beside himself at the desecration; and when the two of them got home he slapped the boy's face (something that happened only twice in Peretz's life) and ran into another room. The shocked mother permitted herself a protest; she murmured (not in her husband's hearing, of course): "As if a child hasn't its own childish sorrows!" And Peretz adds: "That my sorrows were by no means childish did not occur to my mother."

If consistency is the test of maturity, the sorrows of young Peretz were certainly not childish. His manner may have changed with the years, but not his interests; he found in boyhood one of his primary tasks. There came a time when, as we have seen, he could look back ironically on the portentous moods of his boyhood; but he never relinquished the pursuit of the moral absolute.

The consistency went deeper. Peretz acquired a wide if unsystematic knowledge of the modern European world of thought. The manner in which he acquired it was characteristic of his Jewish world and is worth more than passing mention. Secular education, as we understand it, was forbidden to pious Jews. I say "as we understand it" because the religious or Talmudic education did contain an immense though fragmentary and disconnected range of secular information and misinformation: on law, dietetics, geography, astronomy, ritual, morals, psychology, history, mathematics, commerce—all in the framework of Talmudic text and commentary, and shot through with poignantly beautiful legends and aphorisms and obiter dicta of all sorts. But modern secular education was anathema, and those who thirsted after it—as Peretz and thousands of his generation did, in the towns and villages of east-European Jewry—could slake their thirst either by an open break with the Jewish community, and that meant ostracism, or by stealth. The devices to which the sinners were driven in the second case were often as comical as they were pathetic.

Zangwill tells us somewhere how one such sinner used to go to synagogue and read a Hebrew edition of the *Pickwick Papers* during the service. Who would dream of examining the text of his prayer-book? It is to be assumed that the "worshipper" stood up and sat down in the right places, and punctuated the adventures of Mr. Pickwick and Samuel Weller with skillfully timed genuflections and silences. It must have been a rather grim business. Chaim Weizmann is fond of telling how a teacher of his, in the tiny village of Motol, came across a chemistry textbook in Hebrew and was so enchanted with it that he risked life, limb, and livelihood—not to mention his immortal soul— by permitting some of his older pupils to read in it after regular hours. But to deflect suspicion, the text—which lost none of its fascination for teacher and pupils for being entirely unintelligible to them—was *chanted,* so that a passer-by, seeing the light in the window and hearing the traditional melodic rise and fall of the Talmudic *recitativo,* would nod delightedly in the darkness and thank the Lord for the continuing miracle of the Torah. It is not easy to imagine what went on in the minds of the teacher and pupils, what pictures or ideas formed there, as they sang, in a heart-breaking minor key, the Hebrew of "Two H plus O equals H_2O." But it is proper to add that from these astounding introductions there sometimes resulted— or at least they were followed by—fruitful and lifelong scientific careers.

Peretz's contact with the "outside" world was not quite so grotesque. A lonely old musician of Zamoshch had taken a fancy to young Peretz and before dying left the key of his library to the fifteen-year-old boy because he was, according to report, something of a genius. In that disordered roomful of books Peretz, safely withdrawn from observation, began to plow his way through the cultural records of the modern world, or such of them as the old musician (himself no doubt a frustrated soul) had collected. Some Polish Peretz already knew; also a little German. But no French. There were German and French and English books in Polish translation and many in the original. Peretz's system was the simplest and most obvious. He decided to read *through the library*, beginning on the right as he came in, and working his way round until he had finished on the left hand side of the door. And he carried the program out! Does this sound insanely impossible to the reader? That is only because he does not know the wild longing for knowledge that tormented those Jewish youngsters of the ghettoes of eighty, ninety, a hundred years ago: has no concept of the furious mental and spiritual energies that they had inherited; has no notion of the number of Minkowskys and Einsteins and Freuds and Bergsons who were latent in east-European Jewry a hundred years ago—or who gasped out their unrealized souls in the chambers of Maidanek and Oswiecim yesterday.

Of course he sometimes did a little skipping—at first the French books, for instance, since he did not know a word of the language. But later he came across an Ollen-dorff's *Grammar and Lexicon of the French Language* and learned it by heart from cover to cover. The knowledge so acquired he used for perusal of the French books on the last shelves, and then forgot French completely. Some of the German books he piled up on one side for later reference. But whatever he found in Polish, whether original or translated, he stuck to like a limpet. The order of the volumes was irrelevant; if volume five of the *Collected Works* of Victor Hugo followed volume three of the *Collected Works* of Eugène Sue, he felt no incongruity; *Toilers of the Deep* and *The Wandering Jew* were on the same level—they were modern culture. Everything else belonged in the same way—physics, chemistry, philosophy, sociology, poetry, drama, and romance.

He came across the *Code Napoléon* in the Polish translation of Sawadski. Wonderful! He read and understood—or thought he understood. Joy laid hold on his soul. Why, here were laws and regulations in the abstract, with no mention of "Reuben and Simon," the John Does of Talmudic instance: just generalizations and no personalities. Even Maimonides hadn't reached that stage. And right after the *Code Napoléon*—traveling always counter-clockwise along the library walls—Buckle's *History of English Civilization*. Hm—not bad at all: smacks of exegesis and commentary. Next to that, a textbook of physics. Good God, can he believe his eyes? Not the bedcover warms *him*, *he* warms the bedcover. What's more, there are ways of producing artificial snow. Devoid of any mathematical training, he skips the funny little arrangements of letters and figures which are the formulas. Napoleon, Buckle, and physics yield to the straggling remnants of Hugo, Dumas, and Sue; he plows through these and emerges once more into natural history: the human body, the bodies of animals. Not very interesting! But when it comes to *ways* of living, adaptation of life to environment, habits, nest-building, food-gathering, care of the young, the wooing of females by males—he reads like one in a trance. God, how great is Thy world! How full of spirit and intelligence!

We may well ask ourselves how it was that Peretz did not become completely addled. Many a young Jew in similar circumstances did. One thinks with horror of the Niagaras of intellectual energy that ran to waste in that one small human area, and of the souls that were carried to destruction by the torrents. Peretz crossed those rapids in safety. As the years passed, the wild confusion of facts shook down into systematic divisions. Peretz the auto-didact became in turn a capable teacher; his nonfictional writings show an intelligent grasp of popular science; he conducted classes in sociology and evolution. Moreover, we see reflected in some of his pages the crystallized influences of Heine and Goethe. The material he had absorbed so unsystematically rearranged itself in his mind without conscious effort on his part.

I have said that Peretz's consistency went deeper than his abiding interest in the moral absolute. It extended to his material. All of his enduring work is Jewish, folkloristic, Chassidic. Lovers of Peretz have taken this for granted: where, they ask, was Peretz to get the material for his moral researches if not from the Jewish traditions? The answer is: he might very well have got it from his general reading. Besides, he had a sound knowledge of Russian law. From his twenty-sixth to his thirty-sixth year he was a successful lawyer in his native town of Zamoshch. If we grant that while the thinker in him drove him to the moral problem, the artist in him drove him to the fable, it still did not have to be the Jewish fable; and even the Jewish fable does not have to be steeped in Chassidic and east-European Jewish folklore.

There's a catch in the last paragraph. It was the *thinker* in Peretz that chose the fable. With all his admiration for the moderns, all his longing to be European, all his socialistic leanings, he did not believe that science had probed as deep into the heart of man as had the Chassidic rabbis. He could not accept the moral interpretation of economic determinism. He would not let the sinner plead: "I'm not to blame—it's the capitalistic system." He felt profoundly that in the secret places of the heart there are small but decisive freedoms, tiny possibilities. What we do with these possibilities depends on our awareness of them. And so, when he probed into the mysteries of man's behavior, he turned from Buckle and Mill and Marx to the Baal Shem and the Rabbi of Kotzk and the Rabbi of Nemirov and the Rabbi of Berditchev.

There is a charming little fable—whether Peretz invented it or merely reworked it I do not know—which illustrates both his method and his faith.

ALL FOR A PINCH OF SNUFF

Satan, the Evil One, the Enemy of Mankind, the Tempter and Destroyer, sat one day in his private office, idly examining his account-book. He sat at ease, one leg dangling over the other, a kindly, complacent smile on his lips; and his fingers turned at random the leaves, which bore the names of all the living souls on earth.

And then suddenly his complacency vanished and he clapped his palms together: he had come upon the page bearing the name of the Rabbi of Chelm, and it was as blank as blank could be.

At the sound of the clapped hands a host of demon

54

flunkeys came running and crowded about the door, their tongues hanging out while they waited for a word of command.

"Send someone up," said Satan, "and find out whether the Rabbi of Chelm has many years to live."

The demon flunkeys vanished as swiftly as they had come. A quarter of an hour later the report was handed in from the upper chamber. The days of the Rabbi of Chelm were numbered, the thread of his life, worn thin to invisibility, was about to snap. It might happen tomorrow, it might happen the day after.

"Send for the Recorder."

Enter the Recorder, a bald-headed little goblin, light-footed and merry-eyed. A bow, a scrape, a smirk, and he seated himself cross-legged, Turkish fashion, on the sulphur-smoldering floor; from one side he drew a bottle of blood-red ink reeking of sin, and a new crow's feather; from the other a sheet of parchment made from the skin of an atheist. The Recorder spat in his palm and threw a submissive look at his master. "Ready!"

Satan uncrossed his legs and leaned forward in his armchair. The Recorder stuck out a fiery tongue, the quill flew over the parchment, a report and claim were indited to the court of heaven:

"Whereas we are told in Holy Script: 'No man liveth who shall do good and no evil': and whereas there is among the living the Rabbi of Chelm, who stands with one foot in the grave, and the debit side of his ledger is blank; therefore, in order that the Torah of Moses shall be true and shall remain true, let the Rabbi of Chelm be delivered into the power of the Evil One. . . ."

Back came the answer: "See Book of Job, Chapter One."

That case Satan remembered without difficulty: it meant he could do whatever he wanted with the Rabbi of Chelm, save that against the man's life he could not put forth his hand. Such as the Rabbi's days were, few or many, they had to run their course.

But how was he to do with the Rabbi of Chelm what he once had done with Job? For Job had been a mighty man of substance—and the Rabbi of Chelm? A widower, alas, his children married out; and it is written in Ezekiel: "The fathers shall not die in place of the sons." Nothing doing there. As for "flocks of sheep and herds of cattle"—the poor man hadn't even a goat for milk. Nor could Satan afflict him with boils—he had them already. What trials and torments could you visit on a Rabbi of Chelm?

"Some little lust of his," muttered Satan, licking his chops. "Some tiny desire, some obscure appetite!" He stretched out his hand, lifted the bell, which was made from the skull of a sophist, and rang. The room filled with demon flunkeys.

"Whom shall we send to tempt the Rabbi of Chelm from the true path?"

"Me! Me! Me!"

The competition is fierce, and no wonder: promotion waits for the demon who can pull this one off. There is almost a riot. Finally they draw lots; a couple of minor imps get the lucky numbers, and they are off amid a chorus of "*Mazel-tov!* Good luck!"

The sun shone bright that day on the market-place of Chelm, crowded with Jews who had nothing to do. They stood about in groups, buying and selling the skins of rabbits and hares that hadn't been caught yet, cases of eggs that hadn't been laid, timber from trees that hadn't been felled. Suddenly the earth beneath their feet began to tremble, a crack as of near-by thunder split the air, and a wagon burst into the market-place, scattering Jews right and left. A strange and unknown wagon—and stranger still its behavior. High up in front stood the driver, a ragged cap on his head, a red girdle about his loins, pulling like mad at the infuriated horses; behind him stood the passenger, in decent black gabardine and fur cap, holding the whip in his right hand and cracking it over the heads of the horses. The driver pulled the horses back, the passenger urged them on! Now and again the passenger drove his left fist into the driver's back; now and again he put his fingers to his lips and emitted a piercing whistle, which made the horses start as if they had been shot.

And meanwhile the driver was wailing at the top of his voice: "Jews! Have pity on me! Save me! Jews!"

But before anything could be done, the wagon had passed through the market-place, followed by a stream of sparks. The onlookers stood paralyzed, murmuring: "God have mercy on us!"

The wagon drew near the slaughterhouse, and the huge dogs that hung about the place sprang at the horses' throats; the muscular butcher-boys came running out, grabbed the reins, and were on the wagon in a trice. The crowd drew near.

What's the meaning of it all? Nothing much—just a little difference between the men on the wagon. The "passenger" in the decent black gabardine gasps that the driver has gone mad. He wants the horses to dawdle and graze when it's a matter of life and death to get to the next market-town without delay and sell the package of diamonds. At the mention of "diamonds" the crowd falls back respectfully. But the next instant confusion returns. The "driver" begins to yell that he is not the driver at all. The other man is the driver. They've come a long way. In the middle of the night the real driver put a knife to the real passenger's throat, forced him to give up the package of diamonds—and here they are! The "passenger" denies every word of it! He *is* the passenger; the other man *is* the driver.

Who's to make head or tail of it? The crowd pulls the wagon round and leads it with "passenger" and "driver" to the Rabbi's cottage. Let *him* find out.

And the Rabbi of Chelm interrogates each man separately and privately. The plaintiff first, the man dressed like a driver. And he talks like a driver, too. And looks like one. Coarse, massive, ignorant. A man of the woods. A voice that no *cheder*-chant has ever tempered.

But that is not enough for the Rabbi of Chelm. He cross-examines.

"What's the value of your package of diamonds?"

"Rabbi, don't ask *me*. I'm an ignorant man. Can't sign my name, can't add up a column of figures. But God has been good to me, and so I'm a dealer in diamonds."

"How much money is there in the bag the other man took from you?"

"Rabbi, I never count my money. You know—it's bad luck."

The man is sent from the room. *He* a wealthy merchant? Unbelievable! But the Rabbi of Chelm sighs a heartbroken sigh for the wickedness of the world and asks that the other man, the "passenger," be sent in. And what a difference! From top to toe the man of learning. The Rabbi feels him out with half-quotations; the man caps them instantly, Talmud and commentaries. "Rabbi!" cries the man, "what's the good of all this? I'm in a hurry! Here!" and opening the bag he pours out on the table a heap of diamonds mixed with gold coins, blazing diamonds and flaming gold. "Half yours and half mine, if you say it's all mine."

A faint scream from the Rabbi's lips: "Robber!"

The crowd breaks in the door. Where's the "driver," where's the "passenger," where the diamonds and the coins? Gone like wisps of smoke! And all Chelm mutters: "Magic! Or a nightmare! God have mercy on us all!"

Meanwhile, below, Satan is furious:

"Imbeciles! Clumsy dolts! Maybe he's not beyond being bribed, but not that way. Not in the open, with a chance of being found out. Do you take him for an idiot?"

The two stupid imps are sentenced to a year of their own sulphur and brimstone. A second meeting is called. This time there is less enthusiasm. No yelling of "Me! Me! Me!" An elderly demon with a clear head and a long record accepts the assignment.

Autumn days in Chelm, between the New Year and the Day of Atonement: the penitential days, the time of the soul's reckoning and of decisions in heaven. The mud lies knee-deep in the streets of Chelm, the skies above are disconsolate. And a beggarman, all skin and bones, God help us, comes into the town limping on crutches and drags himself from house to house, from shop to shop. At every tenth door he gets a crust (and he has no teeth), and at every twentieth door a battered and faded kopeck, which almost slips out of his palsied fingers. Not that Chelm is uncharitable; but it is amply stocked with paupers of its own, paupers of standing, respectable paupers, the kind that starve in silence, widows and orphans of rabbis, relicts of teachers and beadles and saints.

The newcomer crawls from house to house the first day, the second, the third. The cold and wet go through and through him; the soaked and dripping lining sticks out of his tattered coat; his eyes sink deeper and deeper into their sockets. And then, suddenly, he falls down right in the middle of the market-place, foaming at the mouth.

A crowd gathers about him. One dashes water in his face, a second brings a cup of raisin wine, a third brings a knife to force between his teeth. Meanwhile there are some who scream: "Chelm is Sodom and Gomorrah!" and the beggarman is obviously dying.

God in heaven! They can't let him die in the street! On the other hand, who's going to take him in? Householders shrink back—every room in every house is overcrowded. And just then the Rabbi comes up. And you have just one guess where the beggarman winds up.

So they carry him into the Rabbi's one-room cottage, and there he lies, in a trance. The Rabbi sits at the table, a sacred book open before him. Every now and again he casts a glance at the sick man. Outside the cottage a number of Jews linger uneasily—who knows whether help will not be needed? Night draws on, the Rabbi is about to begin the evening prayer, when he hears a stirring in the bed. He bends over the sick man compassionately, ear to lips.

"Rabbi," the sick man breathes, "I have been a great sinner. I cannot die without confessing."

The Rabbi makes a gesture as if to call in witnesses. The sick man stops him. "God forbid. Just we two."

And he tells the Rabbi that all his life he has been a mendicant—and a fraudulent one: he begged for bread in the name of wife and children, and never had wife or child; begged for dowries for the marrying off of aging daughters; collected funds for Talmudical academies and for institutions in Palestine, but not a kopeck of that money was ever seen by a poor scholar or by a needy resident of the Holy Land. He peddled Palestine soil, which the pious put under their heads in their own coffins, and he had dug it up under the nearest hedge.

And he draws from under his ragged capote a linen

bag, saying: "This is what I've collected and saved!" He opens it: wads of banknotes. "Take it, Rabbi! Distribute it among the poor. Do with it as you think fit."

The Rabbi of Chelm leaps to the window with a joyous shout. He is suddenly fifty years younger. "Jews! Charity money! Come in and count!"

But when the Jews enter, the beggar has vanished. So has the sack of money. Magic again! Another nightmare!

Down below, Satan mutters: "This time it was not in the open; no chance of being found out."

The black folk are in despair! Then Lilith, the demon-woman, springs to the front. "I'll bring him in: the old ways are the best."

So it came to pass one day that the Rabbi of Chelm, feeling some disturbance in his health, sent the beadle for the healer, thinking that it might be well to do a little bloodletting. Meanwhile the hour arrived for the afternoon prayers, and the Rabbi was stationed at the Eighteen Benedictions, which the worshipper must repeat standing motionless and facing east. The door opened and a young woman came in carrying a fowl. Obviously a ritual question. Is the fowl kosher or is it un-kosher? The Rabbi is absorbed in his prayers; the young woman will wait. And waiting, she begins to hum to herself, absent-mindedly as it were. And what a voice! The voice of womanhood itself! Need I tell you that the Rabbi of Chelm doesn't even hear it? So the young woman, seemingly bored, sits down and begins to rock herself in the chair. The rocking and the humming fill the room. What of it? If a snake were to enter the room and bite the Rabbi of Chelm, do you think that his attention would be deflected from his prayers?

The Rabbi finishes the Eighteen Benedictions, takes the three ritual steps backward, spits out ritually on idol-worshippers, repeats the closing prayer, seats himself at the table, and says in his quiet, leisurely, good-humored way: "Let's see the fowl."

The young woman leans forward to put the fowl in his hand; in the same good-humored voice the Rabbi says: "Put it on the table. A grown-up Jewish girl should know better than that." She begins to tell him where and how she got the fowl and makes a long story of it; can't sit still, and begins to wander about the room as she talks. The voice fills every corner with music; the white teeth flash, the white body shines through the dress, her sleeves are rolled up, a perfume as of precious spices rises from her flesh. She stands behind the Rabbi and leans over; she breathes on him. And it's all wasted. The Rabbi listens, examines the fowl, puts it back on the table, and says: "Kosher! And you, young woman, had better see about getting yourself a husband."

Maid and fowl disappear through the window. The Rabbi smiles. He knows all about it.

Again an assembly of the black folk below. Some say this and some say that. A young and untried demon, without a feather in his hat, without a tooth dangling from his neck, asks:

"But hasn't the Rabbi of Chelm a single weakness?"

"Stripped clean of weaknesses," is the answer.

"No enjoyments?"

"Maybe the ritual steam-bath on a Friday afternoon."

The young demon persists. "But hasn't he some special custom of his own, some harmless habit or trick—like rolling bread-pills after a meal while he says grace?"

"Nobody's seen him eat. Probably has no such habit."

But then suddenly Lilith recalls that when the perfume

of her body assailed the nostrils of the Rabbi, he took a pinch of snuff.

"That's it!" exclaims the young demon, and vanishes.

Every Friday afternoon, having bathed for the Sabbath, the Rabbi of Chelm used to go for a walk in the woods. He always took the same path, between a wheat-field and a corn-field; and as he walked he repeated by heart—as pious Jews are wont to do on Friday afternoons—the Song of Songs. Now, knowing himself to be an absent-minded man, and fearing that some Friday afternoon he would wander out too far and fail to return in time for the Reception of the Sabbath—a grievous transgression—he had created, for his own protection, a special device. He had measured the distance against the time it took to repeat the Song of Songs and had found that halfway through the prayer he reached a certain tree. There he would sit down, treat himself to a hearty pinch of snuff from his goat's-horn snuffbox, rest awhile, then get up and return, saying the second half of the prayer. Thus he would get back exactly in time for the Reception of the Sabbath.

One fateful Friday, just before the Rabbi of Chelm set out for his walk, a spindly-legged little fellow, dressed like a German in derby hat and green-striped trousers, appeared on the scene, uprooted the tree above mentioned, and carried it out farther into the woods; he replanted it and sat himself down on the farther side.

The Rabbi, meanwhile, arrives on the spot where he has always found the tree. He is halfway through the Song of Songs, and the tree, he perceives, is quite a distance off. He is shocked. Obviously he has been repeating the prayer mechanically, rapidly, without absorption and contemplation—also a grievous transgression. He will do penance at once. He will refuse himself that pinch of snuff until he has reached the tree. His nose itches for the grateful tickle of the snuff, his heart is faint with longing—but no! Not until he has reached the tree. His limbs are feeble, his steps are tottering. It takes him a long time to get there. And all the time there is this itching and longing, so that he can hardly see. And now, at last, he reaches the tree; he sits down and snatches the snuffbox from his pocket; but his hands are all atremble, and just at that moment a wind begins to blow from the other side of the tree (it's that miserable little German, of course, blowing) and the snuffbox falls out of the Rabbi's hand. He reaches for it. The wind grows stronger and the box rolls away. The Rabbi crawls after it on all fours, his body crying out for the strong taste of the snuff. The wretched little German grins, and blows harder. Then suddenly he uproots the tree again and replants it in its proper place. The Rabbi looks up, wondering what has happened to the tree. He perceives that it is night, the sky is studded with stars! The Sabbath has begun! The sun has set, and he has not even noticed it, so furiously has his heart been set on the pinch of snuff.

But wait, my friends. The sin of the Rabbi in failing to appear for the Reception of the Sabbath was the lesser of the two sins into which his lust for snuff led him that evil day. For the demon kept blowing, the snuffbox kept rolling, and the Rabbi, crawling after it in anguish, went out beyond the limits of a permissible Sabbath walk.

The brilliant young demon, returning to the nether regions, was at once entrusted with another highly important mission.

Addressing the mephitic assembly before his departure, he said:

"Gentlemen, nobody ever stubs his toe against a mountain. It's the little lusts that bring a man down."

CHAPTER VI

"Thou Shalt Not Covet"

❁

O F THE probing, moralistic, psychological folk tales I shall present only one more, and this one, again, I choose to retell, interweaving my own comment with the narrative, for reasons that will be explained in the closing chapters of the book. To those chapters I also refer the offended Peretz-lover who thinks my intrusions unwarranted. Here I will only say that between leaving Peretz unintelligible to "outsiders" (as would be the case if I translated him by brute force) and remodeling him into intelligibility at the risk of some evaporation, I have chosen the second course.

Peretz begins this story by reminding the reader that it is incumbent on every Jew to fulfill all the commandments of the Torah. And in this connection the word *Torah*, which I have described rather than translated as indicating the body of Jewish law and consecrated knowledge, means also the divinely uttered or divinely inspired code of Jewish behavior and worship. And though, more narrowly, *Torah* is applied only to the Pentateuch (and also to the physical parchment scroll, in its velvet mantle and gold or gilt crown, kept in the Ark of the synagogue), it includes by extension the interpretations of the law by more recent teachers than Moses. It is incumbent, then, on every Jew to fulfill all the commandments of the Torah; and if a Jew misses out on certain commandments in one incarnation, he must return in another incarnation to straighten out the account.

"Incarnation?" Is not this somewhat esoteric? What is it doing in a folk tale? The fact is that the Hebrew-Yiddish word *gilgul* (reincarnation) is no more esoteric among most Yiddish-speaking Jews than the word *potato-pudding* is in English. *Gilgul* means both reincarnation in the abstract and some particular reincarnated soul. One would not expect a New York taxi-driver to say of someone he does not like: "That guy? He's the reincarnation of a dog." A Yiddish drayman would say it, and not sound miscast.

On the other hand, reincarnation is neither an article of faith among Jews, nor even widely respected as a theory. It is merely spoken of; it is a familiar outlook, spread by mystics; it is part of the everyday vocabulary, and yet appears nowhere by implication in the prayers.

At any rate, here we are, talking about reincarnation, and Jewish souls that must make the earthly cycle over and over again until they are purified, have fulfilled all the commandments, and are ready to return to their home near the Throne of Glory. Some souls there are which in their first descent into a human body are lucky enough to find a perfect combination—whence a saint is produced. And he, fulfilling the entire Torah perhaps even before he has lived the normal span of years, ascends to heaven before the allotted time. Great saints, in other words, need only one incarnation—perhaps two. An ordinary, everyday soul may, God help us, suffer a hundred and one incarnations; and some there are which go from incarnation to incarnation endlessly, and will perhaps do so until the end of the human generations. And they will have to appear, with their blots and imperfections, to be judged in the Valley of Jehoshaphat or the Valley of Jezreel.

The point of the story that Peretz sets out to tell with this introduction is, once more, the small beginning of much evil. It is the story of a little sin, the merest trifle, by reason of which an otherwise perfect soul was forced into an additional reincarnation, whence a whole cycle of reincarnations was born.

It came to pass on a certain day that the brief cycle of a certain saint was drawing to a close. The soul was ready to take its flight to the eternal home from which it had been exiled, for it was pure as purity itself. And in the heavenly regions a reception committee waited to welcome it. The committee, alas, was doomed to disappointment.

In his last incarnation the saint in question had fulfilled himself in the character of an ascetic. However, not an ascetic as this word is generally understood among non-Jews. The Hebrew for it is *mistapek bemuat,* "contented with little," with emphasis on the contentment. Another word for it is *gam-zu,* "this too," which, as every Yiddish-speaking Jew knows, is a brief reference to the phrase "this too is for the best." Whatever happens to one who is contented with little, he says, cheerfully: "This too is for the best." And "this" may be anything from a broken leg to an unbroken fast.

The saint we are telling of ate little and studied much. He lived a life apart, devoted to God's wisdom and to pious contemplation. The consequence of which, alas, was an extremely difficult death. For the body was furiously opposed to releasing the soul from the unequal partnership. The body argued: "What kind of life has he led me? What have I had out of it?" And every limb and organ had its own complaint and fought it out with the Angel of Death. The heart said: "I've felt nothing." The hands:

67

"We've possessed nothing." The eyes: "We've seen nothing." The legs: "We've been nowhere." And the Angel of Death had to contest every inch of the way, from the crown of the head to the soles of the feet. The death agony was therefore so protracted and so painful that in the very last moment, after he had already made confession, the saint uttered a moan. It was a moan of envy; he envied those whose death was easy. He coveted an easy death.

No sooner had he uttered this moan than soul and body were parted. There was not time enough for him to repent his transgression—for he had transgressed against the commandment: "Thou shalt not covet." It is forbidden to the Jew to covet even an easy death.

The committee in heaven dispersed, the gates of heaven were closed against the sinful soul; it had to return to earth to make good the defect.

There was naturally a great deal of pity in heaven for this particular soul. Certain members of the court voiced considerable indignation with the behavior of the Angel of Death. He could at least have held off for another minute or two and have given the saint a chance to bethink himself and to repent, which would have been enough. Now it was too late; nothing could be done except to make it easier for the saint in his next incarnation. And it was decided to make his life so pleasant, so full, that he would have nothing whatsoever to envy in others—not even an easy death.

Satan, below, hearing this decision, smiled to himself. They had reckoned without their host.

So the saint was reincarnated and became on earth Reb Zainvelle of Purisov. And if that affectionate diminutive, Zainvelle, followed by the dignified "of Purisov" (as it were *von* Purisov, or *de* Purisov, God forgive me), conveys nothing to the reader, here is a description of the man.

68

All the graces and virtues compounded, with good fortune thrown in. Nothing lacking. Reb Zainvelle is a greater scholar than the Rabbi, a sweeter singer than the synagogue cantor, a more impressive reader of the sacred text than the best teacher in the locality—and he a specially imported Litvak. Reb Zainvelle's wife is more precious than rubies, his children are perfection. Reb Zainvelle is, needless to say, a man of substance; his house is the finest in town; from that same house come the biggest charity gifts, and against that house is built, year after year, the loveliest tabernacle on the Festival of Tabernacles. And who, for that festival, has the noblest citron for the ritual blessing? Reb Zainvelle. Who has the most magnificent spice-holder in town for the Sabbath valedictory? Who is the best counselor, who the most honest arbitrator? The same Reb Zainvelle. And why should Reb Zainvelle want to be one of the trustees of the synagogue when every trustee does exactly what Reb Zainvelle wants?

There he sits, Reb Zainvelle, giving his days to sacred study and to good deeds. The eyes shine under the vast forehead like the eyes in the pictures of great sages of old. And when Reb Zainvelle opens his lips, a river of pearls issues from between them. As for his person and his bearing—royalty itself. A big, white curling beard, a huge fur headgear with silver threads, a satin gabardine with silver hooks. What more can we say! Torah and worldly greatness in one, as the ancient saying goes.

Would you not be certain that the soul of Reb Zainvelle was making its last earthly sojourn? That never again would it need incarnation? And so it would have been if there had been no Satan.

His Satanic Majesty disguised himself one day as a Jewish traveling salesman: a youngish fellow, modest-like, with a bit of a hump on his back, a man obviously of no importance, coming from God knows where and going to the same place. He arrived in town one evening just between prayers, and sat himself down by the stove in the Study House. Reb Zainvelle, naturally, approaches him after prayers and invites him to supper. Reb Zainvelle is always on the look-out for traveling Jews. And the modest little fellow with the bit of a hump goes to Reb Zainvelle's house and the meal is served. And as you'd expect at Reb Zainvelle's table, the conversation between courses is learned and edifying. And one of Reb Zainvelle's sons-in-law propounds a difficult problem from the Talmud and gets stuck in the exposition, and all eyes turn to Reb Zainvelle to unravel the argumentation. Reb Zainvelle smiles, and when the meal is done, honors the guest by asking him to lead in the grace. That being ended, Reb Zainvelle begins to handle the problem, and what he says is so lucid, so obvious, that it is as if a wide road were being laid down, a wide and shining road that everyone can tread. And the menfolk at the table drink in the wisdom of Reb Zainvelle as if it were the wine of the sixth day of creation. But the little man with the bit of a hump, the wandering guest, smiles a thin, bitter smile. Which Reb Zainvelle sees and, having finished the discourse, he asks: "Don't you agree?" To which the other says, impudently: "By no means!" "Why?" asks Reb Zainvelle.

The hunchback begins to explain, and a dispute ensues.

And our little hunchback takes down a couple of volumes of the Talmud and turns the pages; and he quotes and comments and adds and explains, sentence crackling after sentence like explosions of sulphur, name after name sparkling on his lips, all with such swiftness and fury that the listeners are taken aback; and the hunchback seems to take on stature, seems to tower over the other men in

the room; the words become fierier, they surround Reb
Zainvelle as with a blazing hedge, and Reb Zainvelle feels
his breath coming short: no escape, backward or forward,
by retraction or proof. The sons and the sons-in-law sit
paralyzed; they want to help Reb Zainvelle but cannot
open their lips. A burning hedge seems to be closing in on
him; it becomes physical; it threatens to sear his flesh. He
feels faint, his heart is in a vise, he cannot breathe. Somehow he manages to rise to his feet; he wants to go to the
door, catch his breath, regain his wits. For all the time
Reb Zainvelle is certain that *his* interpretation was the
right one, and the deadly hunchback has only trapped him
with ingenious misquotations and misapplications of the
Torah; a trickster, a charlatan—one has only to get the
key to his method, and in an instant he will dissolve, all
that fury of hail will turn into a thin drizzle of water.

Reb Zainvelle managed to flee from the house. It was a
winter evening, and when he stepped out of doors the
market-place was carpeted with new-fallen sparkling snow;
and in the skies above, innumerable stars twinkled. Reb
Zainvelle drew free breath. His thoughts cleared, and all
at once he perceived beyond all doubt where it was that
the wretched hunchback had trapped him, where the first
false step had been permitted to pass. He saw the blazing
hedge fall to pieces in the carpet of snow. He also saw that
the hedge had never been whole; there had been gaps in
it, lacunæ; and at every gap there stood one of the great
teachers of old, and they beckoned in friendly wise to Reb
Zainvelle, saying: "Zainvelle, it was a delusion; come here,
Zainvelle, and we'll lead you through the fiery hedge; we'll
lead you out and set your feet on a wide path."

And Reb Zainvelle smiled, and it seemed to him that he
actually saw a wide path, and at the end of it a wide world

beckoning to him. He began to remember: this or that
sage had laid down this or that rule to guard this or that
truth; here it was Rashi, there it was another. And Reb
Zainvelle was filled with immense joy. It seemed to him
that the whole universe of the Talmud lay open before
him, and he was free to linger in it, to wander over its
wide and radiant surface. *Now* he will show that impudent
guest of his. . . . Why, everything is as clear as the snow
beneath and the stars above. And Reb Zainvelle does not
perceive that while his thoughts wander about in the
upper world, his feet wander about in the lower; that he is
being drawn across the market-place and out of the city,
that he has left all the houses behind, that he is in the
open fields, in the white and clear spaces of his vision.

Suddenly Reb Zainvelle stopped and trembled.

A black, ponderous cloud had covered the heavens; the
stars were extinguished; an immense shadow lay on the
snow. And Reb Zainvelle was wandering not only with his
feet but with his mind too. He was back in the labyrinth
of the Talmudic problem.

Then his eyes fell upon a little wisp of smoke in the
distance, and since it was a sign of life, he made in that
direction. His body was tired, his spirits were low. He
plodded on until he came to a dilapidated little country
inn. He entered and found himself in a smoky room. He
stood at the door, unnoticed by anyone. And as he stood
there he saw the old peasant woman at the counter, half
asleep over her supply of drink and food. Outside the wind
howled, a bitter, wet and penetrating wind. But within,
the stove blazed, filled with faggots. Frozen half to death,
Reb Zainvelle thought of drawing near the stove, but he
noticed that all the places were taken. The drunken
peasants made a closed circle, and each of them held in one
hand a canister of whisky, in the other a piece of salt

herring or pickled cucumber. They drank and ate, their faces shone, their eyes were full of affection and happiness; and now again one peasant embraced another, and they drank together.

And in that moment Reb Zainvelle, who was a greater scholar than the Rabbi of Purisov, a sweeter singer than the synagogue cantor, and a more impressive reader of sacred text than the town's best teacher: Reb Zainvelle, whose wife was more precious than rubies, whose children were perfection, whose advice was the sagest: in that instant Reb Zainvelle could not restrain an impulse of the heart. In that instant Reb Zainvelle, standing in that miserable inn, with his coat freezing on him, with the wind blowing on him, envied the peasants who sat round the blazing stove, each drinking from his can of whisky, biting on the piece of herring or pickled cucumber, and exchanging obscene pleasantries with his neighbor.

And there began for the soul of the saint a new series of reincarnations.

CHAPTER VII

The Simple in Heart

✷

Nₒᴛ all of Peretz's folk tales are scrutinies of human motivations and lessons in the subtle temptations. Some are merely wondrous incidents woven round humble and lovable figures. They do not contain specific analyses of egotisms. They are so to speak songs to the virtues of modesty, forbearance, patience, gentleness, incorporated in people of no worldly importance. They differ from the Chassidic tales that are given in the third section of this book in the absence of the spirit of joy and personal intimacy with the Almighty. But like the Chassidic tales they draw their material largely from the most oppressed layer of human society, the lowest level of the pyramid.

Of the four folk tales which follow, "Silent Bontche" by far the best known, has been translated many times. In two of them ("Silent Bontche" and "The Three Gifts"), as in "Devotion unto Death," part of the scene is laid in the court of heaven, at the trial of a dead man. This theme recurs again and again in Peretz. It is Jewish enough, and is true to the constant preoccupation of the tradition with the Last Judgment. Peretz may have been specially inclined to the theme because he was for many years a practicing lawyer; and he may have·derived a special and private pleasure from the contrast between the irrelevancies and chicaneries of Russian and Polish courts of law and the simple fundamentals of the *Bes Din shel Maaloh,* the court of heaven.

[1]

SILENT BONTCHE

Here below, on this earth of ours, the death of Silent Bontche made not the slightest impression.

For that matter, you could not have found anyone to tell you who Bontche was, let alone how he died—whether because his heart burst, or because his strength gave out, or because his back broke under an unusually heavy load. He may have died, for all anyone cared, of simple starvation. Had he been a streetcar horse his collapse would have roused more interest. There would have been a notice in the newspaper, some hundreds of people would have turned aside to take a look at the carcass; some would even have come later to look on the scene of the accident.

Bontche lived silently and died silently; he passed like a shadow through this earth of ours, here below. At his circumcision, when he was eight days old, no glasses clinked, no wine was drunk. He delivered no sermon on his thirteenth birthday, marking his admission into the responsibilities of Jewish manhood. . . . A grain of sand among millions of its like on the seashore. When the wind came and whirled it across the water, there was no one to take note.

While he lived, the wet mud erased the marks of his footsteps; when he died, the wind uprooted the wooden marker over his grave. The gravedigger's wife found it and boiled a pot of potatoes over it. Three days after

Bontche's death the gravedigger himself hadn't the slightest idea where he was buried. A shadow! No image of him remained in anyone's mind or heart; gone without a trace.

Were there less of a human hullabaloo, someone, somewhere, might have heard Bontche's backbone cracking under the loads he carried; were the world in less of a hurry, someone, somewhere, might have had the time to notice that in Bontche's frightfully sunken cheeks two eyes still glimmered, and that even when he carried no pack he walked with his head bent earthward, as though already looking for his grave. Were there as few human beings as, say, streetcar horses, someone might have been moved to ask: "What's become of Bontche?"

When they carried Bontche off to the hospital, his corner among the pack-carriers did not remain empty; there were ten others like him to buy it out. When they took him from his hospital bed into the morgue, twenty sick paupers were waiting for his place; and on the day when he was carried out of the morgue twenty corpses, pulled from under a collapsed building, were brought in. Who knows how long he will remain quietly in his grave?

He was born quietly and lived quietly, he died quietly and they buried him quietly.

In the other world things were altogether different; there the death of Bontche produced a sensation.

The great trumpet of the Messiah pealed through the seven heavens: "Bontche is dead!" Wide-winged angels swept through space carrying the news: "Bontche has been called to the hosts of the blessed." A tumultuous joy ran through the bowers of Eden: "Bontche is coming! Bontche! Bontche himself!"

Young angels with dazzling eyes and golden wings, with silver slippers on their feet, went out in a gay company to greet him. The clattering of their slippers on the floors of heaven, and the happy laughter of their young, rosy mouths floated up to the Throne of Glory, so that God Himself knew that Bontche was coming.

Abraham our Father stationed himself at the gate, his right hand extended in a hearty welcome, a gentle smile playing on his old face.

What is that rolling noise?

It is Bontche's throne, which two angels are rolling into paradise for him.

What is that sudden glitter?

It is Bontche's golden crown, set with precious stones. All for Bontche!

"What? Before the trial and the judgment?" ask some of the saints in astonishment, and not without a touch of envy.

"Oh, that!" answer the angels. "It'll be the merest formality. Even the prosecuting attorney won't be able to think of a thing. The whole business will last five minutes."

It was Bontche, Bontche himself.

When the young angels caught Bontche up into the air and played a song for him; when Abraham our Father shook him by the hand like an old comrade; when he heard that his throne was prepared in paradise and that his crown waited for him; when they told him further that there would be no charges against him in the heavenly court, Bontche was silent—with terror. His heart turned to water; he was certain that this was a dream, or a gross error.

He was familiar with both. More than once in his earthly life he had dreamed he was picking up coins that lay in huge heaps on the floor, and had awakened as great a pauper as ever; more than once someone had smiled at him by mistake, then turned away and spat out.

"That's how it is with me," he thought.

He was afraid to lift up his eyes, lest the dream vanish and he awake to find himself in a cave among snakes and scorpions. He was afraid to open his mouth, to utter a sound, lest he be recognized and hurled down into the depths of hell. Trembling, he did not hear the compliments of the angels, did not say "Good morning!" He was beside himself with fear.

His terror became greater when, unwittingly, he looked at the floor of the court. Purest alabaster set with diamonds! "And I'm standing on it with my feet!" He was paralyzed. "Who knows what rich man, what rabbi, what saint, they take me for! He'll turn up in a moment, and that'll be the end of me."

In his terror he did not even hear the president of the court call out distinctly: "The case of Silent Bontche," or see him hand the file to counsel for the defense, adding: "Read, but make it short."

There was a rushing in Bontche's ears; everything about him was turning. Gradually, and ever more clearly, he heard the voice of counsel for the defense, sweet as a violin.

"His name fitted him to perfection, as a dress made by an artist tailor fits a slender body."

"What is he talking about?" wondered Bontche, and he heard an impatient voice break in:

"No similes, please."

The sweet voice resumed: "He had no complaint against anyone, not against man, not against God. Never did a gleam of hatred awaken in his eyes, never did he make demands on heaven."

78

Again Bontche was completely lost; and again the hard voice broke in:

"No rhetoric, please."

"Job did not hold out, but Bontche was tried more sorely."

"Facts, please, bare facts," put in the president, impatiently.

"When he was eight days old he was circumcised—"

"But no realism, please."

"The clumsy *mohel* who performed the operation could not stop the flow of blood—"

"Get on with the case!"

"He took everything in silence; even when his mother died and, at the age of thirteen, he was presented with a vicious, heartless stepmother—"

"No detraction of third parties," said the president, sharply.

"She begrudged him every bite . . . mouldy bread . . . leavings of meat . . . she drank coffee with cream . . ."

"Get to the point!" cried the president.

"But she used her nails and fists on him ungrudgingly; through his tattered clothes you could see the black-and-blue marks on his flesh. In the cold of winter he stood barefoot in the yard and chopped wood for her; his hands were young and weak, the logs were thick, the ax was blunt. More than once he sprained and twisted his arm; more than once he half froze to death. But he was silent. Even before his father—"

"That drunkard!" interrupted the prosecuting attorney, with a coarse laugh. Bontche turned cold from head to foot.

"He would not complain," counsel for the defense went

on. "And always alone; without friend and without school; without decent clothes, without a moment's free time . . ."

"Facts, please," demanded the president.

"He was silent later on, too, when, on a wild winter night, his father took him by the hair and flung him out of doors. He only picked himself up quickly and ran blindly away. He wandered for a long time, for many days; but in the moments of keenest hunger he only begged with his eyes. One confused, rainy spring evening he came to a big city and was at once arrested. He was silent, asked for no reasons. Released, he went in search of the hardest work. If the work was hard, finding it was harder. Drenched in cold perspiration, bent double under heavy packs, suffering the cramps of hunger, he was silent. The feet of others bespattered him with mud, their spit stained him; carrying his load, he was pushed off the sidewalk and among the carriages and horse-cars; death stared him in the face at every moment. He was silent.

"He never stopped to calculate how many hundredweights of load he carried for each kopeck, how many times he fell on an errand, and how many times he had to spit his soul out collecting what he had earned. He never compared his lot with any other man's. Nor did he claim his wages audibly. He only stood at the door like a beggar, and in his eyes there was a doglike supplication. 'Come back later!' He vanished like a shadow, and returned as silently to beg his due. He was silent when they beat down his miserable wages and paid him in counterfeit money. He was always silent."

"So they do mean me!" thought Bontche, relieved.

"Once," continued counsel for the defense, after a drink of water, "a change came into his life. Bontche happened to stop a carriage. The horses had gone wild and had thrown the driver from his seat, killing him. Eyes blazing, jaws foaming, hoofs scattering sparks, they dashed on. In the carriage a man sat, more dead than alive. Bontche flung himself at the horses and stopped them.

"The man he rescued happened to have a generous and charitable soul. He did not forget Bontche. He gave him the dead driver's job. He did more. He provided Bontche with a wife. He even went so far as to provide Bontche with a child, too. And still Bontche was silent."

"They mean me," thought Bontche, with more assurance. But he still lacked the boldness to look at the heavenly court.

He heard counsel for the defense continue: "He was silent when his benefactor went bankrupt and did not pay him his wages. He was silent when his wife ran away from him and left him with a suckling infant. He was silent fifteen years later when the child had grown big enough and strong enough to throw him out of the house."

"Yes, it's me, it's me," thought Bontche, happily.

"He was even silent," counsel for the defense resumed, in a melancholy voice, "when that benefactor of his came to an accommodation with all his creditors, and left Bontche out. And he was silent again when the man, riding again in a noble carriage drawn by fiery horses, ran him down in the street. He was silent; he did not even tell the police who had smashed him up.

"He was silent in the hospital, where complaints are frequent and loud. He was silent when the doctor would not approach his bed because he could not pay the fifteen-kopeck fee, and silent when the attendant would not change the linen because he had not five kopecks for him.

He was silent in his last agony, and silent in the moment
of death. No word against God or man.

"Dixi!"

Again Bontche trembled from head to foot with fear.
He knew that counsel for the defense would be followed
by the prosecuting attorney. And what would he have to
say? Bontche remembered little of his life on earth. Down
there he had generally forgotten what happened from one
moment to the next; only counsel for the defense had
brought it back to him. What would the prosecuting attorney recall to his memory now?

"Gentlemen!" began a sharp, piercing voice, and
stopped.

"Gentlemen!" it began again, but somewhat softer, and
stopped again.

Finally there issued from the same throat a voice that
was almost friendly:

"Gentlemen, he was silent! I will be silent, too."

Not a sound! Then, from above, a new voice, soft and
tremulous:

"Bontche! My child, Bontche!" It called him like the
strings of a harp. "My beloved child, Bontche!"

Bontche's heart melted in him. Now he would have
opened his eyes, but that they were blinded by tears. He
had not known such a sweetness of tears—"My child, my
Bontche"—since his mother had died.

"My child!" went on the Supreme Judge. "You endured everything and were silent. There was not a limb
in your body, not a bone, which was not broken, not a
spot which was not wounded; there was no part of your
soul which did not bleed. And you were silent.

"Down there on earth they had no understanding for
such behavior. Perhaps you yourself did not know that

82

you could cry out, and that your cry might bring down the walls of Jericho. You were unaware of your slumbering strength.

"Down there your silence received no reward, for that is the world of falseness and illusion. Here, in the true world, you will receive your reward. The court of heaven will pronounce no verdict, pass no sentence, on you. For you no reward will be measured off and set apart. Take what you wish; all is yours."

For the first time Bontche lifted up his eyes. He was dazzled by the light that shone from all sides. Everything blazed, everything and everybody poured forth rivers of light: the walls, the vessels, the angels, the judges.

He let his weary eyelids fall.

"Really?" he asked in a doubtful, timid voice.

"Certainly," answered the Supreme Judge firmly. "I tell you, all is yours. Everything in heaven belongs to you. Gather whatever you want. You are only taking from yourself."

"Really?" asked Bontche again, but now with a little more assurance.

"Really, really, really," they answered him from all sides.

"Well, if it's really so," answered Bontche, with a smile, "then I want, every morning, a hot roll with fresh butter."

Judges and angels looked down, ashamed. The prosecuting attorney broke into a laugh.

[2]

A CHAPTER OF THE PSALMS

This story comes down from the mighty scholar, the great light in Israel, "the Sojourner among the Living," so called, like many others of his kind, after the name of his most famous work.

Early one cold and windy morning the Sojourner sat with his colleagues and pupils in the Study House. They had just finished the morning prayers, and each of them had picked up a sacred book for study. Scarcely had they settled to their tasks when they heard from without a voice proclaiming: "Charity averts death," and the ringing of a charity box—the immemorial accompaniments of a Jewish funeral.

No one was surprised, for before the prayers it had been announced that Yochanan the water-carrier had died and was being buried this morning. But what did occasion surprise was the Rabbi's response. He called for his street hat and for his cane and announced that he would attend the funeral.

If the Sojourner goes to a funeral, everyone else goes. Assistant rabbis and pupils closed their books and left the Study House. If the Rabbi and his assistants and his pupils go to a funeral, everyone in town goes; and before you knew it the synagogues were emptied, the shops closed, and the entire population streamed in the wake of the Rabbi to the cemetery.

But what is the meaning of this? How comes Yochanan the water-carrier by such a magnificent funeral? Yochanan was—God forgive us—a very ordinary person. True, most attentive to his prayers; and evenings he would distribute water free of charge among the students in the synagogue. But such a funeral? After all, he was just a psalm-sayer, and not a distinguished one, either. He could not say two lines without three mistakes; and when he came to a hard word his pronunciation was so comical that listeners had to bite their lips not to laugh. It had to be said for him, of course, that he was a man who lived by the labor of his

84

own hands and took no charity except from God. But even so!

And the Sojourner went on, street after street. The ways were slippery underfoot; a fierce wind blew. The Rabbi went on, the crowd with him. They left the town. Near the cemetery the Rabbi himself put a hand to the coffin; and in the House of the Living, as we call it, he participated in the last rites of purification. He himself, again, lowered the remains of Yochanan into the grave; then he took the spade from the gravedigger's hand and threw in the first spadeful of earth. He listened to the saying of the Kaddish and responded with a loud "Amen."

By this time it was clear to all that the matter went very deep.

The funeral took place on a Thursday. Friday is filled with preparation for sanctity, the Sabbath is filled with sanctity. When the Sabbath was drawing to a close, a delegation of godly householders came to visit the Sojourner; not, heaven forbid, in order to pry into the secret meaning of the great funeral, but just by way of courtesy. And the talk was of everything but Yochanan; Talmudic problems generally, a recent case that had set the world of Jewish scholars by the ears, and the like. And since all discussions wind up with the subject of death, the matter that tormented the curiosity of the visitors lay at hand. The Rabbi smiled, knowing what was in their minds, and the visitors confessed to it. "True, Rabbi," they said, "how else? Such a tremendous incident!"

"Gentlemen," said the Sojourner, "know that in Yochanan the water-carrier there died a Jew who had a gift of the spirit for recognizing true scholars—a gift that the Sojourner does not possess. A Jew, moreover, who was able to achieve with an ax in his rough fist what the Sojourner could not achieve with the will of his mind."

Jaws dropped in amazement. No hint of this had occurred to anyone; not a word of it had come from the Sojourner.

"It was a secret," said the Sojourner. "The man refused to be revealed while he lived. To anyone. But something happened that compelled him to come to me for help. He had me promise that as long as he lived I would not speak of it. I knew, and one more, also no longer among the living—the former beadle. He too kept the secret. Now there is no longer reason to keep it."

The visitors drew their chairs closer, pricked up their ears. The Sojourner went on.

The incident of which he told them was a quarter of a century old. He himself had only just arrived in the community; indeed, he still remembered his very first visit to the big synagogue and Study House.

He came to evening prayers and saw at the pulpit, ready to lead the congregation, a scraggy little man who, they told him, was one Yossel Dvoshe's—that is, Yossel, Dvoshe's husband, a good, honest householder. And Yossel Dvoshe's led the prayers at a gallop, to the distress of the Sojourner, who thought: "He hasn't the prayers in mind, but the hot meal waiting for him at home." He was about to protest, by rapping on his lectern, as the custom is, but bethought himself, being of a deliberate nature. And sure enough, in a very little while the voice of the prayer-leader penetrated to his heart—something was amiss. When the time came for the Prayer of the Eighteen Benedictions, the Sojourner turned east with the rest of the congregation, and there, on the eastern wall, he saw written in chalk: "Let healing and recovery come for the lad Yechiel, son of Dvoshe." Thereupon he understood that the Jew was hastening through his prayers to return to the sick boy, and he repented of the sin that he had

86

committed in the secrecy of his heart, accusing the innocent man of gross inclinations. And when he came to the
passage in the Prayer of the Eighteen Benedictions, the
Sojourner put great feeling into the words: "Heal us, O
Lord, and we will be healed," directing the power of the
prayer toward Yechiel, son of Dvoshe. That same night
the boy passed the crisis successfully.

This, however, the Sojourner only told by way of introduction, so as to fix the evening in his mind. The substance of the story followed.

Prayers being ended, the beadle made the rounds, dis-
tributing candles, one candle each for those that were remaining in the synagogue to study. And the heart of the
Sojourner swelled with happiness when he observed how
great a number of students there was. The lights burned
in the synagogue like the constellations in heaven. Would
it were so in every corner of the Jewish world!

As he sat there, waiting for the beadle to bring him a
certain Tractate of the Talmud, and listening meanwhile
to the pleasant humming and chanting that rose from the
eager students, he saw a water-carrier circulating in the
synagogue and carrying cold water to the lecterns. And
the man's behavior and manner were most edifying.
When he came to a lectern he would stand there until the
student saw him and stretched out his hand to the pail
and cup; he would never break in. When the student perceived the water-carrier, he smiled, took a cupful of water,
and made the benediction, to which the other would re-
spond with a hearty "Amen!" adding: "Thank you very
much." He would bestow a loving and reverent look on
the student and go to the next lectern.

Touched by the bearing of this simple man, the Sojourner asked who he was, and received the answer:
"Yochanan, the water-carrier." Still watching him, the So-

journer was suddenly startled by a fantastic and inexplicable incident, which no one else seemed to notice. Over against the eastern wall sat a pale young man, absorbed in a volume of the mystic Kabbalah: so much the Sojourner could perceive at a distance, from the diagrams on the printed page. Yochanan the water-carrier made as if to approach this student, too, but seemed unable to reach him! It was as if an invisible hedge surrounded the student. A most extraordinary thing. In his deliberate way, the Sojourner kept his counsel; and when the beadle brought him the Tractate he asked who the kabbalistic student was. The beadle answered, not without pride: "Ah, Rabbi, that is our *porush,* our recluse. A great kabbalist: a great one for fasts and self-mortification; and always studies alone." To which he added, in a low voice: "He lives outside the town, in an old ruin. At night strange voices are heard there, and strange melodies."

What was the Sojourner to think? No doubt the kabbalist was lifted, during his studies, to such spiritual exaltation that the simple water-carrier could not break into the charmed circle. But then another astonishing thing happened. Yochanan gave up the attempt to give the recluse water and went his way with a strange, unfriendly gesture. A little while later there came another water-carrier, quite unlike Yochanan: he too served the students, but without love and reverence; he did not listen to their benediction or answer with "Amen"; his face and manner were coarse; his motive in the performance of the good deed was low. Yet this water-carrier succeeded where Yochanan failed. He had the power to break through; he approached the lectern, spoke to the recluse, and gave him the water, which the latter drank so quickly that the Sojourner could not even tell whether he had uttered the benediction.

Very strange indeed, he thought. Perhaps Yochanan had a hidden hatred of the recluse, and this hatred prevented him from performing a kindness toward him. Who could tell? The Sojourner meditated on all this awhile, then other, weightier matters drove the incident from his mind and he forgot about it until another strange thing happened.

One day, preceding a new moon, the Sojourner arrived at the synagogue before the hour of prayer. The upper windows were open, and the swallows darted in and out. Down below near the pulpit stood a solitary figure, Yochanan, absorbed in the reading of the Psalms. The Sojourner passed by him, but so sunk was Yochanan in devotions that he did not notice him. Standing at a little distance from him, the Sojourner heard Yochanan's quaint mispronunciations of the Hebrew words and was himself tempted to smile, when suddenly he became aware that the words issuing from Yochanan's lips, mangled and distorted as they were, were alive! It seemed to him further that the words ascended from Yochanan's lips to the rafters, and that the drawings of King David's musical instruments up there responded to the contact; an echo came from a flute, from a drum, from the string of a violin, but so softly that only the ear of the spirit could catch it. From the rafters the words floated to the windows, and there the swallows caught them on their wings and carried them heavenward; other swallows, returning, brought other sounds and words with them.

This time the Sojourner was so troubled and puzzled that he made up his mind to get to the bottom of the mystery.

He did not speak with Yochanan there and then; but late that evening, on returning home from prayers, he sent for him.

"Yochanan," he said, "I wish to speak with you." And he motioned him to a chair.

Yochanan would not sit down in the Sojourner's presence.

"I command you to," said the Sojourner, and Yochanan sat down on the edge of a chair.

"Yochanan, I heard you at your recitation of the Psalms today."

Yochanan sighed, and murmured that he wished he could read Hebrew better. The words were said so simply, so unaffectedly, that the Sojourner wondered whether he had not been under a delusion in the synagogue. But he remembered the incident with the *porush,* or recluse, too vividly.

"Yochanan," he asked, "what is there between you and the *porush* that you do not serve him water?"

Yochanan turned pale, his manner became confused, and he did not answer.

The Sojourner repeated the question, and Yochanan answered hoarsely:

"Rabbi, I may not tell you. It is a secret."

"But if I command it?"

"Then I'll have to."

"Then I command it."

"Rabbi," began Yochanan, "I must tell you first that the Lord of the world, in His unending goodness, blessed me with a gift of the spirit, a kind of sense of smell, with which I can recognize a true scholar and a pure-hearted student of Holy Writ. I myself am no student, I am an ignorant man. But this gift of the spirit tells me at once, and from a distance, if a student is impure of heart."

"How did you come by the gift?"

"As long as I can remember, Rabbi, I have made myself a servant of the wise. It is the purpose of my life. But I was always afraid that I might, in my ignorance, make myself useful to one whose wisdom was false and corrupt. I therefore prayed to God that He save me from this kind of error, and my prayer was found acceptable. From that time on there is in me this gift, to perceive the essence and the inner spirit of the student. There are some scholars from whose study a fresh odor arises, as of new-baked bread; that is a simple student, innocent in heart; and there are some of higher degree from whom a perfume comes of new apples; and still others who remind me of the flowers of the field; and the highest are like precious spices."

"And what comes to your spirit from the *porush?*"

"Pitch! The burning pitch of hell!"

Unable to believe, the Sojourner was silent. Yochanan continued:

"Rabbi, perhaps it is best after all that you should know. You are the teacher of this community. Some day you will need me, and you will find me useful."

The Sojourner was dumb with astonishment. Later, when Yochanan had withdrawn, after asking permission, the Sojourner reflected: "This must be looked into"; but again he let the matter slip from his mind.

Then, after a time, it returned to him; and one evening he decided to make a test. He came into the synagogue after prayers and found the students already bent over their books, with the recluse, as usual, isolated in his corner. The Sojourner passed that way and observed that the man was occupied with the study of practical or magical Kabbalah. The Sojourner went so far as to brush the lectern. But there was no effect.

The Sojourner was plunged into doubt. How could such a thing be—that Yochanan the water-carrier should perceive something in the vicinity of the student, and that he, the Sojourner, should be aware of nothing? Surely there was a mistake. So thinking, he sat down to study, but studying was impossible. He went home to eat, but eating was impossible. So after washing his hands he ate one mouthful of food, to justify his benediction and his grace after the meal. Then, feeling some confusion in his mind and uneasiness in his body, he said his night prayer and lay down to sleep. He fell asleep toward midnight and was visited by a frightful dream.

He dreamt that someone was waking him, and on opening his eyes he saw his dead father standing over him, saying:

"Your congregation is in flames, and you do not put the fire out." And therewith the dead man vanished.

This time he really awoke, and jumping out of his bed, he ran to the window. In the distance, beyond the town limits, and in the direction of the ruin that, according to the beadle, housed the recluse, he saw flames arising and bending over townward. It seemed to him, also, that one fiery tongue reached as far as the roof of the synagogue; sparks were flying over the houses. The vision lasted awhile, then vanished. The Sojourner was seized with trembling.

Now he understood that the vision was a signal to him; some dreadful evil was being perpetrated in the ruin, and he was being called upon to take action. Perplexed as to what was expected of him, he bethought himself suddenly of the words of Yochanan the water-carrier: "Some day you will need me, Rabbi, and you will find me useful." Very quietly, so that his wife should not hear him, the Sojourner slipped into his clothes and tiptoed down to the room where the beadle slept. Three times he had to ask the man where Yochanan the water-carrier lived, so strange did the question sound. Finally the beadle came to, picked up a lantern, and conducted the Rabbi through the tangle of lanes to the hut of Yochanan. They approached the window, to knock on it, but the door opened suddenly and Yochanan came out.

"I was waiting for you, Rabbi," he said. "It is time to put out the fire."

At that moment the clouds overhead were split, and by the light of the moon the Rabbi saw that Yochanan was carrying an ax. "Yochanan," he said, "what is that for?"

"It will be needed," answered Yochanan.

They made for the ruin where the recluse lived, and when they drew near, the Rabbi was aware of a smell of burning pitch; and the closer they drew, the thicker the fumes became, till they were almost suffocating. Light shone through narrow cracks in the walls; and wild sounds reached their ears, women's voices singing, a playing on musical instruments, the rhythm of feet on boards.

The beadle shook like a leaf. "Hold on to my girdle," said the Rabbi to him. But the beadle was so far gone in fear that his knees gave under him and he collapsed in the street.

"Rabbi," said the water-carrier, "leave him there. Let us hurry into the ruin, or we will come too late, God forbid."

The Sojourner asked him if he knew where the entrance was, and Yochanan answered that he would find it with his sense of smell.

"What shall we do there?" asked the Rabbi.

"Each of us will have his task," answered Yochanan. "You, Rabbi, will use your brain and your will-power; I will use my ax. You will hold them off with your conjurations—and the rest you will leave to me."

At that instant he found the door and opened it. And this is what they saw:

The interior of the ruin was ablaze with light, and some fantastic wedding ceremony was being celebrated. The four walls were adorned high up with skulls, from the eyesockets of which darted red fire. At one end of the room stood an orchestra, playing on black instruments, and the sounds that issued from the instruments were accompanied by flames. Naked wenches, their black heads crowned with red poppies, danced in a circle, and streams of sparks flew out from under their goat's-feet. They sang, and the voices that issued from their lips were accompanied by flames.

A wedding jester sprang up from somewhere, crying: "Sabbath! Sabbath!" And in the middle of the circle of naked wenches there was a bridal dance. The dancers were the recluse and the demon Lilith, bridegroom and bride; they held the opposite ends of a white kerchief, and the bridegroom, singing: "Come, my bride, come, my bride," drew Lilith nearer and nearer, till soon they were dancing hand in hand.

"Sabbath! Sabbath!" cried the wedding jester. The instruments played ever more loudly, the dancing became wilder and wilder, the flames fiercer; and just as Lilith was about to fall on the bridegroom's breast, they all became aware of the Rabbi and the water-carrier standing at the door, and for an instant all life and motion was suspended. Then tumult, screams of rage, grinding of teeth—and the assembly broke and turned with clenched fists on the unbidden guests.

But the Rabbi, by the power of his conjurations, held them off, so that they stood with uplifted goat's-feet outside of the invisible circle of four paces. Their faces blazed with hatred, their fists were stretched out, but they could not break through.

"Help! Help!" screamed Lilith, calling to the world of demons.

They came, like a storm wind; they circled the ruin, seeking an entrance; the old walls trembled; a million voices filled the air. But the door and the walls held, and the demons could not enter, because of the conjurations of the Sojourner. The place filled slowly with incantations and the air became unbreathable for the demons, so that their tongues began to protrude from their mouths. Step by step the demons drew away from the Rabbi, shrank into corners, withered, and crumpled, and fell.

Then Yochanan lifted his ax and let it fly; it found its target, Lilith, and split her in two, from the head downward. In that same instant the recluse collapsed, face forward, the winds died down, the instruments burst asunder, the demons vanished, the skulls crumbled into dust, the lamps went out. Silence, then a sound of wings, and a black figure lifted the recluse and vanished with him through a window. Outside the dawn was breaking.

"Thus it was, gentlemen," said the Sojourner with a sigh. "The recluse, the false student of sacred lore, disappeared. Who knows whether it was granted him to be buried in Jewish soil? Here, in the town, it was believed that he had gone forth to take on himself the vow of exile and homelessness.

"We went out and found the beadle where he lay. We brought him to and led him home. Not a living soul had seen us. My wife knew nothing; she had not seen me leave, she did not see me return. And Yochanan made me promise that the incident would remain a secret.

"Now you may see that a simple Jew, with his gift of the spirit, can perceive that which the Sojourner cannot perceive. And that which the Sojourner, with his learning, his will, his pure purposes, cannot achieve, the simple Jew, ax in hand, can achieve, aiming without hesitation and finding his target.

"All this with the power which is in a chapter of the Psalms."

[3]

A Bass Viol for Heaven

In the village of Tomashov, hard by the Polish-Galician frontier, there began to appear at the doors of the houses a young man, a beggar, of whom no one knew where he lived and whence he came.

A strange and inoffensive creature, he accepted neither coins nor any kind of food except bread; and because he was so modest and so unimportunate, the villagers paid little attention to him at first. They only noticed that he always had a faraway look in his eyes, and that his ears always seemed to quiver slightly, as though he could hear something when to all others the world was as quiet as is the synagogue on the Day of Atonement, the moment before the blowing of the ram's horn. If a word was addressed to him, he started, as though he had been recalled from another world. If something was asked of him, he would become confused, a sweat would break out on his face, and he would answer with difficulty.

As he became a more familiar figure, a householder or a goodwife would, now and again, try to make use of him, by sending him on a simple errand. But they soon gave up, for, entrusted with a message, he would disappear for several days and then come back with an answer that was quite meaningless; and this not from laziness or ill will, but from sheer absent-mindedness. It would turn out that he had gone about delivering the message, but on the way he had stopped to play with a field-mouse; and then a bird had called to him, and he had followed; and so he had forgotten, for a few days, where he was going and with what message. Then he had come back, quite innocently, to beg a piece of bread, and, being reminded that he should have brought back an answer, it would appear that he had in fact remembered the message at last and had delivered it, but so twisted that it was without meaning—as the answer also was, naturally.

One summer day, when the village was quiet and the shopkeepers sat at their doors waiting for customers, the young man happened to pass down the street. A shopkeeper, weary with the emptiness of the day and having nothing better to do, called the young man over for a cross-examination.

First he invited the youth into his shop, but the youth shook his head, whereupon the shopkeeper sat down on the threshold of his door and began to question the other.

"What's your name, young man?"

"My name? My name," repeated the youth. "Ah—Abraham—yes—Abraham."

"Aren't you sure?"

No, he did not seem to be quite sure. There were so many things—how could one be sure?

The shopkeeper grinned.

"And your family name?"

"Family name? What's that?"

"A family name. There are lots of Abrahams. Which Abraham are you? Whom do you belong to?"

"My father."

"And what's your father's name?"

"Father."

The man's smile broadened. "Where does your father live?"

That seemed to be a difficult question. After a while the youth pointed heavenward. "There!"

"And have you no other father?"

"No."

"Have you no mother?"

"What for?" asked the youth, and then, as the shop-keeper laughed aloud, added: "Can I go now?"

"Soon, soon. Tell me, where did you come from?"

"A village."

"Which village?"

That he could not answer. He did not know the name. And when he was asked how he came to Tomashov, and how long it took him, he said: "I walked and walked and walked," and went on endlessly, but he did not know how many days he had walked.

"Can you *davven*, can you say your prayers?"

That he did not understand; but after a lengthy explanation he broke out with: "Oh, speak with Father?"

"That's right."

"I can say the 'Hear, O Israel.' "

"And where did you learn it?"

That the young man could answer. In one of the woods lying between the villages he had met an old man, who had told him who and where his father was. He had also taught him to speak with his father, and to repeat the Hebrew of "Hear, O Israel." It appeared also that he did not know the meaning of the words, but the old man had told him that the father did, and was pleased when they were addressed to him. In this way he spoke with his father twice every day. Also, he played whenever he spoke with his father.

"You play? On what?"

Well, sometimes he played on reeds; and then someone had taught him how to cut himself a whistle; someone had also given him, once, a clay flute, and he had learned to play on it.

"And suppose someone were to give you a fiddle."

Red spots suddenly appeared in the young man's cheeks. A fiddle! If someone were to give him a fiddle! He wanted a big one, he said, a very big one, the kind they carried with a strap.

"Well," drawled the shopkeeper, immensely amused, "maybe someone will buy you a big fiddle. But let's see first what kind of musician you are."

Without waiting for a second invitation, the young man drew from under his tattered shirt a clay flute and blew on it. Hardly had he begun to play when the birds gathered overhead and flew in circles round the ascending music. But the shopkeeper did not look up or mark anything. The young man stopped playing, smiled, and put the flute back under his shirt.

"Tell me," said the shopkeeper, "what did you live on in the woods?"

"Mushrooms."

"And in the villages?"

There he lived on whatever the good people gave him.

Aha, thought the clever shopkeeper; now he had caught the youth out.

"Who gave you things?"

"Everyone. The peasants, and even the priests."

"And you ate everything they gave you?"

No, he had thrown everything away except the bread. He had lived only on bread; the other things were for the birds. He said that the old man in the woods had also asked him what he ate, and when he told him that he loved only bread, the old man had been very pleased.

That was why he had taught him how to speak with his father. He had come to love the old man with all his heart, because he had taught him the 'Hear, O Israel.'

"And suppose this old man were to tell you to steal."

Then he would steal, said the youth.

"Or to kill someone."

The old man would not do it; he was good.

"Still, if he told you to kill someone."

Then he would kill.

"And wouldn't you be afraid of your father?"

Why should he be afraid, asked the young man, more with his eyes than his lips.

"Because he would punish you."

For the first time the young man laughed outright.

"You're making fun of me. A father doesn't punish."

At that instant the time for afternoon prayer was announced, and the shopkeeper went to the synagogue to tell everyone of his witty interrogation of the young man.

The community of Tomashov had an orchestra—God save the mark: two fiddles, a flute, a clarinet, a tambourine, and, as the usual additional noise-maker, a bass viol. It was a melancholy little orchestra, used for local weddings or at the occasional performances given by strolling players; it was also called in, from time to time, by the neighboring landowners when they could not get anything better for their dances.

One winter morning the Tomashov orchestra was returning from a ball. The men were hungry—they had not dared to eat anything in the gentile home, for all the food there was un-kosher—but they had, according to the custom, taken a few drinks; they went along the road arguing, singing, cursing, and quarreling over their accounts. A snow had fallen, and the bass-viol player, an old man

staggering under the weight of his instrument, kept lag-
ging behind, crying out to the others not to leave him.
They paid no attention to him. Meanwhile it came on to
snow again, and the men walked faster and faster. When
they arrived in Tomashov they scattered to their homes,
tumbled into their beds, and slept like the dead. But not
for long. In a little while the bass viol's wife was making
the round of the houses, screaming for her husband.

A search party was sent out, and returned empty-
handed. For several days the hope lingered that the man
had taken refuge in a peasant house by the roadside and
was snowed in. But on the following Friday afternoon,
when the storm had died down, a peasant cart drove into
the market-place, and on it lay the frozen body of the lost
player. They buried him with the utmost haste and barely
managed to be through with the ceremony before the on-
set of the Sabbath.

The next day the widow interrupted the services—
according to the immemorial tradition that had grown
up for such purposes—and would not let the prayers continue until the heads of the community had promised to
make provision of some kind for her and her five orphans.
That evening a meeting was held, with all the musicians
present. There was no community chest in Tomashov; it
was therefore proposed that the orchestra should do without a bass viol, and that whatever pay would have been
given to the bass viol should now be given to the widow.
The musicians objected: an orchestra without a bass viol
was no orchestra. They might manage at Jewish weddings, in view of the circumstances, which would be pro-
claimed by the heads of the communities; but no gentile
would ever hire for a dance an orchestra without a bass
viol. Whereupon the Rabbi observed that the sustaining
of a Jewish family was more important than a bass viol,

and the musicians replied that the Rabbi—if he would forgive them—just didn't know anything about music. Which greatly offended the Rabbi, but brought the matter no further forward.

Then suddenly the witty shopkeeper who had interrogated the young man with the clay flute smote the table and cried:

"Gentlemen, I have an idea!"

And he proceeded to tell them of the joy which the young man had manifested at the possibility that he might some day get a bass viol. Now, would it not be an excellent idea to marry the young man to the widow with the five children, give him the dead man's instrument and his position, and thus take care of the family without the community being one kopeck out of pocket?

Perhaps he meant it by way of a sorry jest, but the meeting caught at the idea, and the Rabbi was deputed to make the suggestion to the widow. He found her willing enough; and Abraham the beggar had no objection. So within a month they were married, and all unexpectedly Abraham acquired a wife, five children, and a bass viol complete with bow.

The arrangement worked quite well. The couple got along nicely. Abraham never set foot in the house; he passed his time as he had done heretofore, no one knew where. When he became hungry, he knocked at the door, his wife handed him out a piece of bread, and he disappeared with it. When he was needed for a performance, he turned up in time, strangely enough, and was taken along. The neighbors asked the erstwhile widow what kind of life she led with her new husband. She laughed and answered that it was perfectly wonderful. What did an elderly woman need, after all? This husband of hers ate practically nothing, drank not at all, and never said a harsh word to her—and hardly any other kind, for that matter. She did business direct with the orchestra and got her husband's pay intact. It was perfect.

Abraham, too, was quite content. At first he had his troubles with the orchestra. He learned to handle the bass viol well enough, but he paid very little attention to the music. He seemed to play all for himself, or as part of an orchestra that nobody else could hear. He would go on playing when the others had finished, and had to be stopped forcibly. In time the difficulty was overcome, however; not that Abraham adjusted himself to the orchestra: it was the orchestra that adjusted itself to Abraham. At Jewish weddings either they knew what the situation was or else they thought that besides being a bass-viol player Abraham was a bit of a buffoon, and his solo playing when the rest of the orchestra had ended occasioned much merriment. At gentile dances the musicians simply snatched away his bow as soon as a piece came to an end.

With his musical instrument Abraham acquired a new habit. Three times a day—mornings, evenings, and midnight he used to play the 'Hear, O Israel' on his bass viol. The sunrise and sunset worship he offered up by the river bank in the meadow outside the village; but at midnight he came into the village and stationed himself in the market-place. The melancholy tones of his instrument would melt into the night and steal through the doors and windows into the hearts of the sleepers. And there was something so earnest and simple and insistent in the deep *loo-loo-loo* of the bass viol that many sleepers whom the knock of the beadle had failed to waken for midnight prayers would start up at that sound, listen awestruck for a while, then light a candle and hasten to the synagogue.

A wondrous affair came to Tomashov, such an affair as the village might expect only once in a hundred years. And this was the manner of its coming:

The president of the community of Lublin, that mighty city and mother in Israel, and the Rabbi of the community of Cracow, a city not less illustrious in Jewish annals, were making a marriage alliance. Since neither city would yield to the other the privilege of witnessing the wedding, it was decided that the ceremony should be performed at a point equidistant from the two. This point was occupied by the townlet of Tomashov.

The president of Lublin was the host; and the first thing he did was to have a barrelful of gold coins rolled up out of the cellar, for the wedding costs. Could he do less to signalize the honor he had achieved? To have married into the family of the Rabbi of Cracow! Well, he would delight the Rabbi and the Lublinites and Cracovites with a wedding that would be talked of for generations.

The cooks and servants and waiters and attendants invaded Tomashov to make the arrangements. There would be guests from Cracow and guests from Lublin: merchants, scholars, high synagogue dignitaries, rabbis, and simple householders; and the inhabitants of Tomashov would be invited along with the outsiders, because their townlet had been privileged to occupy the point midway between Cracow and Lublin. Three orchestras would play: one from Cracow, one from Lublin, and the one from Tomashov. The wedding would be held in the big barn outside the village. The ordinary use of this barn was to house through the winter the logs of the timber merchants who floated their rafts down the Vistula to Danzig. For its new, exalted one-time function it was transformed into a palace; the walls were painted and decorated with pictures; costly hangings were brought from Lublin, and innumerable paper lanterns; two immense tables were laid along the length of the barn, one for the men, the other for the women, to accommodate a total of forty quorums; that is to say, of four hundred guests. There were to be separate entrances for the men, for the women, for the waiters, and for the musicians. The main door, or rather gate, a mighty affair on which was painted the crown of the Torah, was reserved for the Rabbi of Cracow and a few other distinguished guests.

The day of the wedding arrived, and with it the hundreds of guests, who were accommodated in the homes of the Tomashovites. Tomashovites so honored were happy and proud to give up their best rooms to the visitors. In the evening visitors and Tomashovites streamed to the transfigured barn, which presented a glorious scene. For when the guests were all seated, and the lamps were all lit, and the precious stones twinkled in the earrings and on the kerchieves and on the stomachers of the women, and the hall was filled with the light of the Torah and the dignity of rabbis and scholars—the magnificent Rabbi of Cracow presiding over all—it was like a vision of another world.

The long rows of waiters wound in through their door, carrying the plates of fish; there was a happy tinkling of silver knives and forks, against a background of happy conversation; up at the head table a learned discussion developed, led by the Rabbis of Lublin and Cracow. And then there broke in the mingled music of the three orchestras. The flames in the lamps danced with joy, the precious stones took on a fresh sparkle, the voices became gayer; and the Rabbi of Cracow leaned his head on his hand and listened happily. It was known that he was a great lover of music.

The orchestras passed from a merry piece to a pastoral, from a pastoral to a religious melody. A violinist from Cracow dominated the music; the tones melted the hearts of the listeners; the orchestras strummed softly while the melody soared and fell and rose again. It was as though a river were flowing through the hall, as though the Vistula had spread its waters between the tables and moved, rocking and murmuring, among the guests—a tribute to bride and bridegroom and to the Rabbi of Cracow. And above the river a bird floated wondrously, and from its beak poured delicious and melancholy music, one religious theme after another, themes from the Sabbath service and from the services of the High Holy Days, the Days of Awe. The mood of the guests alternated; there was great joy for the occasion, for the gathering of learning and piety, for the marriage of the young couple; then would come the recollection that Jewry was in exile, and the Divine Glory was in exile, and it was unbecoming to feel too happy. So for a moment a reflective sadness would descend on the guests. But a moment later the pride and exaltation of the occasion would sweep away the touch of melancholy, and a riot of gay voices went up, carried on the waves of music which poured inexhaustibly from the orchestras, so that players and guests alike were transported into upper regions where all was light and bliss.

Suddenly the music stopped, as if every string had burst and every instrument fallen apart. In the silence that followed was heard the *loo-loo-loo* of Abraham's bass viol, proceeding all alone, as if it did not belong to the place and occasion. The astonished guests turned and saw him seated with his face to the wall, fiddling away peacefully, the only hand still in motion, *loo-loo-loo*.

The musicians had arranged this little comedy for the amusement of the guests at Abraham's expense. Somehow

the trick did not take. The musicians waited for the public to burst into a shout of laughter—but the public stared
first at Abraham, and then from Abraham at the Rabbi
of Cracow. The musicians had miscalculated: the guests
would not permit themselves to laugh at anyone in the
presence of the Rabbi of Cracow. Not that they were not
so inclined; their lips were already twitching; but they
looked at the Rabbi, and they saw that, leaning his head
on his hand, he had closed his eyes. Had he perhaps fallen
into a doze?

Meanwhile the bass viol played on, *loo-loo-loo,* and an
uneasy feeling spread through the hall.

Suddenly all eyes turned from the Rabbi toward the
central door or gate, which had been reserved for the
most important guests. Something was happening there.
Footsteps and voices were heard; attendants, clustering
round the door, seemed to be thrusting back a throng;
and the guests heard a frightened whispering:

"No, no, not here. There will be a separate banquet for
the poor."

Beggars, it seemed. . . . The Rabbi opened his eyes
and was about to say something. Doubtless he was about
to order the attendants to admit the poor guests—what
else would a Rabbi of Cracow do?

But before he could speak, the door sprawled wide
open, and the astonished assembly saw an old man in tattered headgear and tattered gabardine, an old man with
unkempt beard and earlocks, a beggar, one would have
thought, like all other beggars, except for the majesty
that shone from his eyes and informed the gesture of his
hand. The attendants had fallen back, involuntarily, and
involuntarily they made a pathway for him. The old man,
in rags from head to foot, a mendicant if ever there was
one, but possessed of the presence of a king, advanced

down the hall, followed by a company of beggars as ragged as he. He came down to the center, in front of the Rabbi's throne, and paused there, his company clustered behind him. The wedding guests looked on, dazed, the Rabbi not less than the others. Those nearest the beggar had turned round and were leaning over; others, at a distance, had stood up silently. Only Abraham, face turned to the wall, went on playing; the trembling hand moved back and forth unceasingly, the bass viol gave forth its sad, earnest tones: *loo-loo-loo-loo-hoo.*

The old king in beggar's garb opened his lips and uttered a single phrase:

"The midnight prayer."

Then, after a pause, he went on:

"Rabbi of Cracow, Abraham is playing for the midnight prayer. You do not understand or believe, but soon you will. It will be granted you to hear and understand the midnight prayer of Abraham. And it was in order that this privilege might be conferred upon you that the marriage was arranged between your family and the family of the president of Lublin, so that you might come to Tomashov, which is midway between your cities. And for your sake the other guests will hear and understand, but none so well as you, Rabbi of Cracow, who are a lover of music."

Loo-loo-loo-loo-hoo the bass viol went on, and the assembly listened as in a trance. Then suddenly the old man lifted his right hand in a signal to the roof, and the slopes of the roof moved, parted, and swung open slowly, one slope to the right, one to the left. Above the heads of the wedding guests the midnight sky appeared, set with a million stars. The old man made a second gesture, and the sky itself divided, as the roof of the hall had done; and up in the deep beyond the deeps a light trembled, and out of the light came music. The hosts of the blessed were intoning the midnight prayer, the orchestra of the angels played, and the melody of Abraham's bass viol mingled with the heavenly melody and was part of it; and Abraham's song ascended and became one with the song that trembled in the midst of the light in the deeps.

The wedding guests sat in awed silence.

Again the old man made a signal with his right hand. The music from above died out, the heavens closed, the shimmering light was replaced by the twinkling of countless stars. And once again that gesture, and the slopes of the roof swung back slowly and shut out the heavens.

Loo-loo-loo-loo-hoo sang the bass viol.

Suddenly the bow fell from Abraham's hand. He rose, turned toward the assembly, and recited the prayer of the dying Jew: "Hear, O Israel, the Lord thy God, the Lord is one." He recited it to the melody which had sounded in the heavens and to which his viol had played the accompaniment. And having ended the recitation, he fell to the ground in a faint.

The old man went over to him and lifted him in his arms.

"Carry him to the charity house," he commanded some of the attendants, and handed the body of Abraham to them.

When they had left, he turned again to the Rabbi.

"Rabbi of Cracow," he said, "it was not for a wedding that you were brought to Tomashov, but for a funeral. Abraham has been called to the orchestra of the hosts of the blessed. They were short of a bass viol."

And the old man vanished, together with his company.

Abraham died the next day, and the Rabbi of Cracow and the wedding guests attended the funeral.

The old man, they say, was Reb Levi Yitzchok, the Compassionate One.

[4]

THE THREE GIFTS

Once upon a time, generations and generations ago, an obscure, unimportant Jew died somewhere, and when the body had been consigned to the earth, and the first Kaddish had been said over it, the soul mounted to heaven, where it was brought to immediate trial. The court was assembled, the scales stood ready on the table, the prosecuting attorney and the counsel for defense were prepared for their roles.

The latter carried with him the bag that contained the good deeds of the dead man, the former the bag that contained his wicked deeds. The bag with the good deeds smelled as of spices, and the light of its contents shone through the cloth; the bag with the wicked deeds stank of tar, and the filth oozed through the texture.

The prosecuting attorney emptied the contents of his bag into the scale at the left; counsel for the defense emptied his into the scale at the right. The disembodied soul stood there, looking on in astonishment. It had never imaged that there was such a difference between good deeds and bad deeds; down there, on earth, it had often failed to distinguish between them and had more than once taken one for the other.

The scales rose and fell slowly, almost imperceptibly; now the right scale descended, now the left. The pointer trembled, moving conversely left and right. And always by a hair's breadth, not more. The soul had belonged to a very ordinary Jew; no great villain and no martyr; just tiny little virtues and tiny little sins; dust, almost; some of them hardly visible to the naked eye. Still, the pointer kept moving, a little bit this way, a little bit that way. And every time the scale with the virtues sank, there was a joyous response in heaven; and every time it was outweighed by the other scale, there was a sighing and sadness audible as far as the Throne.

The angels poured out the contents of the bags with great attentiveness and deliberation; one pinch of dust after another; like poor householders at the synagogue service bidding kopeck by kopeck for the honor of carrying the Scrolls of the Law.

But if a well can be drained in time, how much more a little bagful of human deeds? The angels stopped pouring.

"Is that all?" asked the court clerk, an angel like the others.

Attorney and counsel took the bags and turned them inside out. That was all! Then the court clerk approached the scales and examined the pointer: was it on the right or the left? He looked and looked, scarcely believing his eyes: for here was something that had not happened till that moment since heaven and earth had been created.

"What is it there?" asked the presiding officer. "Why is it taking so long?"

The clerk stammered: "Dead even! The pointer is at dead center!"

The good deeds and the bad deeds counterbalanced exactly.

"What, exactly?" asked the presiding officer.

The clerk looked again and answered: "To a hair."

The court retired for consultation and came back with the following sentence:

"Inasmuch as the sins of this soul do not outweigh the

good deeds, the soul cannot be sentenced to hell. And inasmuch as the good deeds do not outweigh the sins, the soul cannot be admitted to paradise. Therefore it has been ruled that the said soul shall wander about in space until such time as the Lord of the universe shall in His compassion bethink Himself of it and call it to Himself."

The clerk of the court conducted the weeping soul to the exit.

"Why do you weep so?" asked the clerk. "True, you have been excluded from the bliss of paradise; on the other hand, you will know nothing of the torments of hell. You're even!"

But the soul would not be comforted. "Better the most frightful torments than nothingness! Nothingness is unbearable!"

The clerk of the court felt a twinge of pity, and said: "I have good counsel for you. Fly downward toward earth and keep close to the living. Do not look up at the sky. For what will you see from the other side of heaven but the stars? They are creatures of light, but they are cold; they know nothing of pity and they will not intercede for you; they will not remind the Lord of the universe of your existence. Only the saints in heaven will remember and take thought for an unhappy wandering soul. But listen carefully to what I say: even the saints in heaven need little reminders; they are very fond of gifts, beautiful gifts. Alas," and the tone of the clerk became somewhat bitter, "they've picked up that habit from latter-day arrivals in heaven. So do this: fly down to the world of the living, and watch closely. And should you come across a strange and exceptionally beautiful deed, snatch up the evidence of it and fly to the gate of heaven. That will be a gift for the saints in paradise. Hold fast to the gift and knock at the gate; tell the angel in the keeper's lodge that I told you to report to him. Hand him the gift. And I promise you that when you will have brought three acceptable gifts, the saints will intercede for you, and the gate will be opened."

The First Gift

Downward across space flew the sad little soul, downward toward the world of the living, to seek gifts for the saints in paradise. When it was low over the earth, it flew back and forth, over fields and villages and cities, pausing at every Jewish settlement. In the summer it flew among the blazing rays of the sun; in the rainy season among the glistening drops and between the slanting needles of water; in the winter among the innumerable snowflakes. And always on the alert, always watching, till it was faint from watchfulness.

Whenever it saw a Jew it descended hastily and stared him in the face, wondering if he was about to sanctify the Name of God with some deed of holiness. At night, always sustained by the same hope, it would peep in through the shutters of Jewish homes: perhaps in one of them it might perceive, growing quietly, the flowerets of God, hidden deeds of virtue. Alas! More often than not the soul started back, horrified.

The cycle of the seasons passed, and cycle followed cycle, year followed year; the soul almost yielded to despair. Cities turned into cemeteries, cemeteries became plowed fields. Forests were cleared away, rocks were worn into sands, rivers changed their beds, thousands of stars fell, millions of souls ascended; and God had not remembered the wandering soul, had not sent a single wonderful deed of goodness in its direction.

It meditated sadly: "The world is so poverty-stricken, the souls of men are such gray mediocrities, their deeds

113

are so small! What do they know of the strange and wonderful? I shall be a wanderer and an outcast forever and
ever."

But as it meditated thus, there came suddenly a flash of
red light, a red flash in the darkness. The soul swooped
down. The flash had come from a high window. Peering
in, the soul saw a rich room, and in it masked robbers.
An old man was there, obviously the owner of the house.
One of the robbers held aloft a flaring torch. A second
pressed the point of a shining dagger against the owner's
breast, saying, over and over again: "One move from you,
Jew, and you're a dead man! One move, and this dagger
goes through you!" Meanwhile the other robbers ran-
sacked the chests and cupboards.

The Jew stood there calmly and watched; not a flutter
of his eyebrows, not a motion in the long white beard
which reached to his waist. It was all no concern of his.
The Lord giveth, the Lord taketh away, blessed be the
Name of the Lord. He had not been born with this wealth,
he would not have taken it with him into the grave.

Thus he stood, watching peacefully, while the robbers
opened the drawers of the last cupboard and took from
it sacks of gold and silver, boxes of jewelry, precious plate.
Not a word escaped him. From the tranquillity of his
bearing it might even seem that he was relinquishing all
claim to his possessions, so that the robbers might be free
of the sin of theft.

Then, suddenly, one of the robbers, reaching into the
last corner of the last drawer, drew forth a little sack,
hidden behind all the others, and apparently the most
precious of them all. At that moment the old man forgot
himself; he trembled from head to foot, his eyes flamed;
he lifted his right arm and cried:

"Hands off!"

And at that moment a red stream burst from him; the dagger had done its work; his heart's blood spurted out and stained the sack in the hands of the robber.

The old man fell to the floor, and the robbers flung themselves on the little sack. This was beyond a doubt the big find.

What a bitter mistake! They had shed blood in vain. There was neither gold nor silver nor jewelry in the little sack; there was nothing in it of any value in this world. All that the sack contained was a handful of earth from the Holy Land, which the merchant was saving to put under his head in his coffin. This was the only possession he had sought to save from the robbers—the one for which he had forfeited his life.

The soul swooped down, picked up a pinch of the precious, bloodstained dust, and flew up with it to the gate of heaven.

The first gift was accepted.

The Second Gift

"Remember," called the angel after the descending soul as it closed the wicket. "Two more gifts."

"God will help me again," answered the soul, in high spirits.

The high spirits did not last. Again the seasons and the years passed and the soul found nothing. Again it was assailed by melancholy thoughts.

"Like a living stream the world broke forth at God's command and set out on its path; and the stream, pouring onward, gathers sand and silt; the waters become darker and ever more unclean; very few are the gifts to be found in it. Men become smaller and smaller; their virtues are nothing but fragments, their sins are clotted dust. Their deeds are too tiny to be perceived."

And the soul meditated further: "If God were now to take the whole of the earth and weigh the virtues against the sins, the pointer of the scales would lie in the dead middle again. The earth can neither rise nor fall; and like me, it is an outcast and a wanderer between the bright heavens and the nether darkness. The prosecuting attorney and the counsel for the defense would dispute the possession of the earth forever, as darkness and light, heat and cold, life and death, dispute its possession. The world rocks, but it neither ascends nor descends; therefore there will be forever marriage and divorce, births and burials, love and hate, forever and ever."

Again something broke at last into the soul's meditations.

A pealing of horns and trumpets!

The soul descended, and beheld a German city of the olden days; sloping roofs encircling the magistrate's square, crowds in multicolored dress, numberless faces at windows, spectators clustering on towers and balconies. . . .

The court is arrayed before a table covered with a green cloth, from whose corners hang rich golden braids and tassels. The magistrates are clad in velvet robes and fur headgear crowned with white feathers held in place by silver buttons. The president sits apart at the head of the table. A lean, hungry eagle is perched above him.

At one side of the square stands a Jewish girl. Near her ten grooms hold in rein a wild horse. The president of the court rises and, turning toward the center of the square, reads forth the sentence:

"The Jewess standing before us is guilty of an abominable crime which God, for all His infinite mercy, cannot forgive.

"On the occasion of our last sacred festival she stole

116

out of the ghetto and polluted with her footsteps the streets of our noble city. She defiled with her shameless glances the holy images that we carried in procession to the sound of music. Her accursed ears drank in the hymns sung by our white-clad, innocent children and the sound of the sacred timbrels. And who knows whether the unclean demon who is concealed under this exterior of a Rabbi's daughter did not actually lay a defiling hand on one of our sanctities?

"What did this demon in lovely human form desire? For it cannot be denied that the disguise is a lovely one. She is beautiful to behold, as only a demon can be. The wanton, impudent eyes flash under cover of the silken lashes; the alabaster cheeks have not been withered by her imprisonment; her fingers are slender—the light shines through them. What did this woman desire?

"Only this: to distract a soul from its sacred preoccupation, to turn its attention away from the high purity of the moment; and therein the demon succeeded. For the sake of this demon in woman's guise a knight left the procession, a son of one of our noblest families.

"But this insolent triumph was perceived, and the halberdiers closed in at once on the temptress. The demon in her did not even seek to defend herself. How could she? At that moment the soldiers were purified from all sin, and the devil had no power over them.

"Therefore I pronounce the following judgment on the Jewess in whom the demon lodges:

"Her long demon's plaits shall be tied to the tail of the wild horse. Then the horse shall be released and shall drag her like a corpse through the holy streets which her footsteps have defiled. Let her blood wash clean the stones which her feet have besmirched."

A wild cry of joy issues from the throats of the assembled; and when the wave of sound has passed, the condemned woman is asked if she has a last wish to express.

She answers quietly: "I have. I want a few pins."

Out of her wits with fear, is what the magistrates think, and they say something to that effect.

"No," she answers calmly. "That is my last wish and request."

They grant her request.

"And now," the president commands, "the sentence!"

Halberdiers tie the long plaits of the Rabbi's daughter to the tail of the horse, which the ten grooms can scarcely hold in check.

"A pathway!" commands the president again. The throng stirs and presses backward against the walls. A pathway is cleared. Hundreds of hands are lifted, and in them are whips, goads, rods, to urge the wild horse on. Faces flame and eyes flash; a panting rises from the mob. In the tumult and excitement none of the bystanders notices that the condemned woman has bent down and is fastening the hem of her dress to her flesh, driving the pins in deep, deep, so that her body may not be exposed when the horse drags her through the streets.

Only the invisible wandering soul has observed it.

"Release the horse!" comes the order from the president.

The grooms spring back, and with one wild bound the horse leaps forward, while at the same moment a wild cry leaps from the throats of the onlookers. The whips and goads and rods whistle in the air, the terrified horse dashes across the square into the streets and through the streets to the open country.

The wandering soul draws a bloodstained pin from the body of the condemned woman and flies heavenward with it.

"Only one more present!" says the angel at the gate, comfortingly.

The Third Gift

Again the soul descended earthward, this time in search of the last gift. And again the seasons and years rolled by. Again a deep melancholy settled on the wanderer; for the world seemed smaller than ever, and smaller than ever the deeds of men, their evil deeds no less than their good.

"Such deeds cannot alter the balance," thought the soul. "They are utterly without weight. Forever and forever the pointer will stay dead center."

But it had been decreed that the wandering soul was to be redeemed, and after many years it was awakened out of its dark mood by a sound of drums.

The time and the place were unfamiliar to the wanderer. It saw an open space before a prison wall. The heavy iron gratings on the windows threw back the sunlight; and sunlight fell, too, on the stacked arms of the soldiers, who, instead of arms, now carried knouts. The soldiers were drawn up in two long lines, with a lane between.

Who was to run the gantlet? The wandering soul beheld the little figure of a Jew, his gaunt body only half concealed by his tattered shirt. This was the culprit! For what crime was he about to be punished? Theft? Murder? Or was it—who could tell, in that world, in those far-off days?—a libel and a false accusation?

The soldiers were grinning. They seemed to be asking: "Why so many of us? He won't last half the course."

The wretched little man was thrust forward till he stood at the head of the lane. Then the blows of the knouts began to rain on him; and he walked on and on, without stumbling, without turning. The knouts whistled, the blows fell on his flesh, and he endured.

A mad anger seized the soldiers. The lashes hissed in the air like furies and wrapped themselves round the man's body like serpents. The blood started out on the flesh.

"Hu-ha! Hu-ha!" panted the soldiers.

And then it happened that one soldier aimed his blow too high, and the skull-cap fell off the condemned man. He continued for two or three steps without noticing the loss, and then observed it. His head was bare! Like a heathen's! Like an unbeliever's! He paused, as if he were reflecting. Great God! He would not permit himself to be bareheaded! Calmly the man turned round and walked back to where his skull-cap lay in the dust. He bent down, picked it up, replaced it on his head. Then he turned again and continued the course tranquilly, blood-bespattered from head to foot, but with the skull-cap covering him, according to the commandment. So he went until he fell.

And when he had fallen, the wandering soul descended, snatched the bloody head-covering from under the feet of the soldiers, and flew with it straight to the gate of heaven.

This gift, too, was found acceptable; and the saints intervened for the wandering soul, which was admitted to Paradise.

And the saint who on earth below had been the famous Rabbi *Urim ve-Tumim,* so called from the name of his book, said:

"Really beautiful gifts! Of no practical value, to be sure, but as gifts altogether wondrous."

CHAPTER VIII

The Divided Man

❀

IF IN the retelling of the story of Reb Zainvelle ("Thou Shalt Not Covet") I have succeeded in maintaining a tongue-in-cheek note, I have, I believe, done justice to Peretz's intention. For Peretz even in his capacity as folklorist—that is, quite apart from his Europeanized self—occasionally displayed an ambivalent attitude toward Jewish life.

In this, however, he was specifically Jewish. The self-critical spirit of the Jews is one of the strangest phenomena in history. I will not examine its expression in Biblical and first post-Biblical literature. That is sufficiently well known and is, besides, outside the scope of my subject. Of its expression in the exile after the destruction of the Jewish State, it is enough to say, I think, that we cannot find an instance of another people which, having been driven from its soil by peoples at least as bad as (actually much worse than) itself, should wander about the world saying: "It served us right. We lost our homeland because of our sins."

This the Jews did for about two thousand years, with irrelevant results. For the nations among which they sojourned, not given to much self-criticism, and having a lower moral standard than the Jews, naturally thought:

"If they call themselves bad, what extraordinary villains they must be!" Public confession is not a good thing. Listeners are shocked by the catalogue of the sins, not edified by the moral standard that the confession bespeaks.

In the Yiddish-speaking segment of modern Jewry the self-criticism took the form of irony. A deep belief in the fundamental ethos of Judaism was accompanied by a subtle disrespect for Jews in high places. Modern Jews did not take seriously the view that God had arranged a two-thousand-year chastisement for His people. But they did feel that somewhere, somehow, something was wrong with the Jews. Perhaps that something was only Jewish moral aspiration, the desire to be better than others. And perhaps it was a consciousness that on the whole Jews *were* actually better than their host peoples, and in their negative mood they did not want to be. It was not comfortable; good people are seldom liked before they have been safely buried.

Occasionally the ironical attitude passed over into the savage and tormented. If one sometimes looks upon Jewry as the saint among peoples, one must sometimes hate it as well as love it. We react with a confused love and loathing toward the saint, who is as sensitive as a genius and as patient as a spittoon. Peretz was tied to the Jewish people with all the fibers of his heart. In certain moods (as in "Devotion unto Death" and in "All for a Pinch of Snuff") his love was whole and untroubled. In other moods (that of "Thou Shalt Not Covet," for instance) the note of sardonic self-deprecation is audible. And in more extreme moods it drowns out everything else.

Typical of this last is Peretz's bitter little essay on Purim. Now, Purim is a jolly half-festival which celebrates the rescue of the Jews from the plot of Haman to destroy them. It is secular in spirit and was never taken

too seriously in the religio-historical consciousness of
Jewry. Queen Esther was a beautiful woman, her uncle
Mordecai was a good Jew, Haman was a villain, and King
Ahasuerus was an ass; and the story of the palace intrigue
that brought about the rescue of the Jews and the down-
fall of Haman was always treated with high good humor,
and even with a touch of buffoonery. On Purim young
people went masquerading, dishes were sent from house
to house, older people took a drink or two, fiddlers were
hired, an hour or two was taken off the working day.
Peretz saw a deeper meaning in Purim. He wrote:

"There is a proverb: 'Purim is no festival, fever is no
sickness.' There's little to envy in a man shaking in the
grip of a fever, there's less to envy in a people that makes
of Purim an occasion for rejoicing. And that is not because our rescue was affected by divine intervention
rather than by ourselves; we do not have to be ashamed
of Deborah, Jael, and Judith. But to Queen Esther we
are beholden for the first victory we ever carried off not
against a foreign oppressor, but *under* him. Purim is the
birth-day of the first *Schutz-Jude,* the first Jewish toady
to foreign royalty, the first Jewish informer, and the first
Jewish procurer for a royal bed. It is a festival for beggars,
fiddlers, and masqueraders, and for a people made up of
these! Dance around the nuptial beds of others, wretched,
tattered, beggarly soul! Dance on the grave of your one-
time glory! Drink and forget—if you can!"

Which is the "real" Peretz? That question is itself un-
real. It is more pertinent to ask: which is the dominant
Peretz, or the enduring Peretz? Certainly he of the folk
tales and of the Chassidic tales. Why, then, mention the
other one at all? Because I believe that though such pieces
add nothing to Peretz's literary stature, a knowledge of
them gives us a glimpse into the heart of the man, and

I am concerned here with a man (even though as a type) as well as a literature.

The folk and Chassidic tales were his dominant and enduring mood; but in recurring fits of self-contempt he resented the idealizations that those tales embody. When the two moods overlapped, he wrote such things as "Thou Shalt Not Covet." When the negative mood triumphed he wrote as follows:

"Once upon a time, in the good old days, there were imps in all garrets, demons danced in back yards, souls from the world of fantasy chopped logs in the forests; old ruins were haunted, and spirits there crowed like the most gifted roosters. . . . Those were the real, romantic days, when angels' visits were everyday things. They always came in time to wipe away the widow's tears, conduct a virgin in safety across the slippery ice. . . . They even used to appear to the wicked in dreams and warn them not to fill to overflowing the cup of their sins. Besides which Elijah the Prophet was pretty active, too; he would appear out of nowhere to rescue a come-down Danzig merchant and throw a sack of gold in through his window, or to finish a piece of work for an ailing and bedfast working-man. . . .

"The Jews lacked nothing in those days.

"The question: Who will give us meat? never arose. Under every bridge there was a herd of bewitched calves. Money? Every cellar had its treasure-trove of churchly gold. . . . And anyway, wasn't the Messiah always in the offing? Before you knew it the paper bridge of the prophecy would be there to conduct the Jews across to eternal bliss, while the iron bridge would break down and cast the wicked into eternal damnation.

"When life was so easy, writing was easy too, even if one never got paid for it. Every writer had one foot in this world, the other in kingdom come. And in kingdom come we Jews were of course the people with the strongest claim. All other nations had only their special genii or angels; our 'angel' was the Lord God Himself. And with the help of God everything ended happily."

Whom is Peretz making fun of here? Or, to use a juster word, whom is he sneering at? Himself. Himself in the dominant role of the weaver of fables and legends. He himself brings in Elijah the Prophet providentially in "Devotion unto Death" and many other stories. How, in fact, could he write Jewish folk stories without the stock character of Elijah, the universal saint-errant?

Peretz was a master of the story with the God-given happy ending, and he sometimes disliked himself for it. Now and again he wrote a short story in which goodness did not get its reward on this earth. He even has a sketch that shows a saintly soul refusing the offer of heaven with the remark: "I would rather go to hell, where I can be of some use." Predominantly, however, the good triumphs in his tales, and he knew that from one point of view this is not true to life. For that matter, he knew also that the function of good is not to be rewarded; it is, simply, to be good. He knew that the innocent must suffer with the guilty, if only by definition; for if they did not, they would not be innocent, they would be merely shrewd.

Because he did not always stick to this truth, Peretz wrote pieces like the one above. Now, there is a curious streak in some artists which on the surface resembles a venal defect. Just as there are some writers who produce pot-boilers for money and are later disgusted with themselves, so there are writers who make the good triumph out of love for the good—and they are also disgusted with themselves. Perhaps they plan a story with an "honest" sad ending; then a bitter protest rises in them. They simply will not give evil the satisfaction of triumphing. Also, they have an irrational feeling that evil cannot triumph in the long run. So their seeming venality is really another kind of intellectual integrity; being true to another aspect of themselves, they revert to the happy ending. This has nothing to do with the ordinary commercial motives for the happy ending. But the revulsion from this concession can be as violent as from the other, the worldly one.

But is that feeling of the ultimate triumph of good irrational? Were the Hebrew Prophets sentimentalists when they preached that goodness alone can save the world? We, in the closing fifth decade of the twentieth century, can at least testify that evil will not. It is only a pity that a world blown up by atomic warfare will not be able, like the Jews in exile, to look back and say: "Serves us right." That virtue leads to life was certainly deeply believed by the Jewish people for the Jewish people as a whole; thence the belief was transferred, perhaps falsely, to the individual.

There was another source of self-repudiation in Peretz, and it was also part of his "honesty." I use quotation marks because intellectual honesty is not a simple business. "Know thyself" and "to thine own self be true" are superficial directives. One of Peretz's intellectual honesties led him away from his Jewish association. He even protested once against the limitations of the Yiddish language. In any case, he had spasms of desire to get away from the stifling disciplines of a people out of touch with the contemporaneous European world, away from the taboos and superstitions, the mumbo-jumbo, and the insularity. That side of his honesty is expressed in the sketch that makes up my next chapter. It is a sketch that I have translated closely, not reworked; for with the introductory remarks here provided, it is wholly and beautifully intelligible in any language.

It deals with a Jewish unbeliever, or *the* Jewish unbeliever, who differs from other unbelievers, as I shall show.

For the unbeliever generally, for him who rebels against his early faith, the issue seldom remains settled. Having said no, does the no remain forever? As Browning's Bishop Blougram asks:

> *And now what are we? Unbelievers both,*
> *Calm and complete, determinately fixed,*
> *Today, tomorrow and for ever, pray?*
> *You'll guarantee me that? . . .*
> *All we've gained is that belief,*
> *As unbelief before, shakes us by fits.*

And when this happens, when one is shaken by a fit of belief, then (perversity of human thought!) the intellectual dishonesty consists in being afraid to admit our·condition. What? Can those impossible people whom we have repudiated have been in the right after all?

Complete intellectual honesty consists in admitting that intellectual honesty is not everything.

It is not all a matter of the brain. Intellectual honesty would be a much simpler matter if we did not have an emotional investment in certain truths. In such truths we are not merely seeking the answer to a problem in calculus: we are seeking those values to which we may legitimately attach our lives; our emotions, too. And what if the emotions are not so docile? What if they can't be led by the nose—least of all by a Jewish nose—whither the intellect leads?

The story of a man's break with his people's traditions has been told over and over again. It is properly one of the standard themes of literature, and should remain so forever. Each well-told story with that theme at its center is a special and helpful instance of a majestic and cruel law of growth: that traditions may be born, traditions must die; that peoples may be created, peoples must die out. But the act of dying, for a people or a tradition, is always full of pathos—and sometimes of ugliness, too.

The death of a Jew to his people and his faith is (perhaps I say it because I am a Jew and know more about this instance) singularly tragic. I do not speak here of Jews who have been brought up without a tradition to overcome, but of those who were in the heart of the tradition and were compelled by "intellectual honesty" to break away. I cannot think of a parallel to the tragedy. A Jew leaving the faith under those circumstances leaves everything.

Not so, let us say, an Englishman who breaks with a church-going family. He remains an Englishman—in an English land. He lives in an atmosphere suffused with familiar values. He has rejected certain articles of faith; he has not rejected a civilization and gone away to adapt himself to another.

The traditional Jew, of the closed Jewish life of old Europe, rejected all the instruments of his former life when he rejected his faith. He was like the unhappy village Kaffir who goes to work in the compounds of the gold mines of Johannesburg—except that the latter does not go from intellectual choice. Nothing of his old life is about him. The ceremonials, rewards, disciplines, ritual, the cycle that filled the days—all is gone, together with father, mother, friends. It is like a bloody rebirth.

The parallel is faulty, but useful. It suggests something of the tragedy. The Kaffir has this disadvantage: unlike the Jew, he cannot enjoy the values of the world into which he has been forced. But the Jew has this disadvantage: he goes into a world hostile to his own people without having been forced into it. Unlike the Kaffir, he becomes by moral neutrality one of the persecutors. And because he did it of his own free will, because he identified himself in important respects with the persecuting majority, he must often loathe himself for his new associations. The misery of conscious treachery mingles with the misery of homelessness.

And when, at stated seasons, there come round the days that are deeply implicated in the patterns of his life's responses, the anguish of his separation may become unbearable. Not to be home for the Passover ceremony of the seder, for instance. How shall I convey that? Let me compare this man with a Christian who has repudiated all the "superstitions" of his faith, and all the symbols associated with it; but a Christian in whose childhood the Christmas tree, the family reunion, the presents, the laughter, anticipation, loving-kindness—all the tenderness of a great, overriding redemptive idea—were living things. He too has made himself homeless by an act of the intelligence; for him too (let us assume) the personal, the religious, the artistic warmth of his early life is gone forever, never to be recaptured because it is of the essence of its enjoyment that it shall never have been challenged, never stained with a repudiation.

For the Christian thus self-exiled the reminders of the season, in windows, in streets, in public squares, and in shops, pursuing him all day long and all through the evenings are painful in the extreme; this is the price he pays for remaining in a familiar world. But his case is still happier than that of the disbelieving Jew self-exiled from the Passover seder, that unique family gathering, round the dinner table, of the first and second nights of the festival.

129

There is no way of comparing the hold of the seder on a Jewish child's memory with that of Christmas on a Christian child's; and the attempt would be tasteless, as well as pointless. But let it be said that the seder ceremony has been specially devised by generations of pedagogues to appeal to children. Its ritual is charming, ingenious, and powerful. Its folkloristic texts—historical and devotional—are of exceptional beauty. Some of them are deliberately amusing. The child who has sat through a few seders carries into later years an unforgettable Passover nostalgia.

Yet this is not the point. For if a "renegade" Jew is homesick for the Passover as the "renegade" Christian for Christmas, and the two are in these respects equally miserable, there is a particular torment reserved for the Jew at Passover time. He too is surrounded by reminders, but they are of a terrible and ambiguous character. The Passover coincides with the time of the Christian Easter; and in certain lands Easter is the season for whipping up vengeful emotions round the death of Christ. Then the Jew must feel rising all about him that ancient, recurrent annual flood-tide of fury against his people. Let us assume that he has not accepted the Christian faith—he has lost only his Judaism, not his self-respect. Still he must feel he has betrayed someone. For the sake of "intellectual honesty" he is not there, in the beleaguered citadel. For the sake of intellectual honesty he is on the outside, living with safety (at least transient) among the armies of the besiegers.

And then he remembers incidents out of the past. There mingle in his mind poignant recollections of his own childhood seder and the seders of neighbors: the solemnity and the fun, the divinity and the earthliness; parents, brothers, sisters. His mind casts back to the antiquity

of the ritual. He thinks of seders in other climes, celebrants in other costumes; and, with the seders, he remembers the lowering, threatening world outside.

The legend of the seder has to do as much with the
Jewish exile now as with the liberation from Egypt. The
ritual began in Palestine; it has taken on colorings, memories, associations, in the two thousand years since the
Jews left Palestine. Passover! It is the time particularly
chosen among Christian peoples for the revival of the
blood libel against Jews! The Jews have killed a Christian
child to use its blood for the preparation of their matzos!
Let their houses be searched! Perhaps a corpse will be
found—a child's, a man's. Perhaps it can be arranged that
a corpse shall be found there (that is part of the theme of
the sketch in the next chapter). Easter and Passover and
blood! The blood from the wounds of Christ has flowed
across the centuries through a million Jewish homes; and
the seder is a ceremony with many strange, unacknowledged meanings.

The celebrants sit at table in street dress, prepared at
any moment—symbolically—to get up and leave the exile
for the promised land. They also sit prepared—and this
time literally—to get up and have the house searched for
the corpse. Here is one unacknowledged double meaning.
A second lies in the ritual opening of the door at a certain
point in the prayers. Ostensibly it is to invite in the invisible and incorporeal Elijah, the Prophet. Actually it is
also to invite in very visible and very corporeal Christians
to see that no human blood has been used. Christians have
of course accepted the invitation more frequently than
Elijah. Nor have they waited for the invitation.

What deep, burning irony there is in the prayer which
is uttered when the door has been closed in that part of
the ritual: "Pour forth Thy wrath upon the heathen that

know Thee not. . . ." A sensitive and ethical modern religious movement (Reconstructionism) has excised from the Passover ritual that prayer; it is offensive to the Jewish spirit. So it is. But the removal destroys the three-dimensionality of the seder. The two-dimensional façade of the obvious alone remains; the unspoken-historical, the resonant deeps of experience, the suffering which has given point to the survival of the Jewish character—all that is gone.

I turn now to Peretz's sketch of the young Jewish intellectual who has renounced, in the name of honesty, participation in and even sympathy with the forms and rituals and beliefs of his people. It is written in the third person—but there is much of Peretz himself in it.

CHAPTER IX

"Stories"

✿

H E STROLLED along the bank of the Vistula, thinking: "Today she will come."

And so thinking, he saw it all in the most vivid colors:

He is sitting on the bed in his room, in the darkness, waiting. Every sound on the stairs makes his heart beat faster, and he asks himself: "Why? I'm not in love with her, am I?"

And then it is really she: he recognizes the light, swimming step. He gets up and kindles the lamp on the table. She, meanwhile, pauses on the other side of the door. She is catching her breath; the flight of stairs is a long one. She is putting her hair in order; she stops and peeps in through the keyhole. Then she taps with one finger on the door, almost inaudibly.

"Come in."

She opens, and asks from the doorway: "Got any stories for me?"

"Yes, I have."

If he hasn't, she turns back. She doesn't like *him,* she says. In fact she's frightened of Jews. But she loves his stories.

Their acquaintanceship began in Warsaw's Saxony Park, in a downpour of rain. She stood under a tree. She wore a thin white blouse, and she had no galoshes on. The tree afforded little protection, and she kept glancing up through the sparse branches, her face expressing mingled fright and hope. As he was carrying an umbrella, he went up to her and offered his assistance. She hesitated. He pleaded earnestly with her, and finally she yielded. She excused her hesitation: there are so many bad people about. . . . But his voice, she said, gave her confidence. Encouraged, he offered her his arm; still hesitant she took it and gave him her address.

As they walked along the streets—he had not the money for a droshky—she told him she was a seamstress. (Right. He had noticed that her fingertips were pitted with tiny holes.) And she learned from him that he was a writer. Does he write songs? No, stories. Stories! Oh, she loves stories! To which he answered that he could tell her no end of stories. Would she let him come to see her? No. She had no father, and her mother was mean. When she said this her voice trembled a little. The idea! A man coming to visit her—and a—a Jew at that. She did not use the word *Jew* easily; she blushed and threw a comical sideways glance at him. "How do you know I'm a Jew?" The eyes, the hair, the way he spoke, and—well—the nose. She giggled. Her voice was pure and childlike; and yet the forehead was already wrinkled.

During the summer they used to meet in the Saxony Park. During the winter she would steal up to his room, at rare intervals, for a story. When she planned to do that, she would leave a message for him in the morning with the janitor. This very day he had received such a note from her. Her Polish was illiterate—a dozen mistakes on every line: but so childishly warm.

"Jew, have a story ready for me. But a happy one, with a princess. Life is so sad. And you mustn't dare to touch

134

me. I'm not interested in *you*. You are so ugly. If you touch me I shall scream and run away. Do you hear?"

And yet he had ways of softening her: the story he is telling takes on a mournful tone; the king's son and the queen's daughter are in danger. . . . The lovers have been driven apart by a terrible slander, the work of false people. And if he feels like it, he can throw the queen's daughter into a dungeon, while somewhere else, in an alien land, the king's son is being led to the gallows. They're the victims of a horrible frame-up. And then the listener throws herself on her knees before him and catches his hand; or she strokes his face in sheer pity for the unfortunate lovers. Then, for one kiss on the lips, he conjures away the dangers and brings prince and princess together to the strains of the wedding march.

Why does he do that? What does he want her kiss for?

He is sorry for it every time it happens—and yet there is something that draws them to each other. Both are filled with longing for happiness; both have missed it; both are willing to be deluded for a few minutes. Two lost, desolate souls.

Once he asked her: "Does your mother hit you ever?"

She turned pale and her eyes flooded. "I won't tell you. I'd rather hear your stories." And he stroked her brown hair and went on.

Now, as he strolled along the river bank, he felt that he had no story for her. His mind was confused and restless, like the water dashing up against the bank. His thoughts wandered vaguely, like the formless clouds overhead.

What obscure thing was it that was eating at his heart?

He remembered suddenly that he had not yet eaten that day.

There had been a sort of restlessness, a running about and a rummaging in his lodgings. The sun had unexpectedly broken through the clouds that morning, and, getting out of bed, he had left the house without even drinking a glass of tea. The streets, too, were oddly agitated. What the devil was it all about? Now and again passers-by had jostled him. He had barely managed to make his way down to the river bank, where it was his habit to stroll mornings. By now he was quite faint. He felt in his vest pocket. Yes, he still had some change. He turned and made for the restaurant where he usually took his lunch; there he sat down by a window that looked out on the Vistula.

The restaurant was empty. "Yellow-face" sat behind the food-laden counter, dozing. She woke as he came in, and greeted him sleepily. Still half asleep, she served him, then went back to her perch to doze again. He ate meditatively: there *had* to be a story of a king's son and a queen's daughter. She, the queen's daughter, would have to be asleep somewhere on a mountain peak. A magician or a witch would have to be guarding her. Today he would add something—there would be a serpent at her feet. He'd given her so many queens' daughters—the serpent would make a special impression. And the mountain peak would be a very lofty one. He had never seen a high mountain, but he would say: "High, very high, very high up . . ." and she would lift up her eyes and follow his forefinger. Below the point where the queen's daughter slept, he would draw about the mountain a circlet of clouds, and to make it prettier, the clouds would be edged with crimson. Down in the valley no one knows about the queen's daughter; the clouds conceal her. Right through the year the circlet hangs there. That too is a piece of magic. But high up, 'way above the sleeping princess, there is an eternally blue sky; she lies between cloud and heaven, the serpent at her feet.

He finished his meal. A king's son would have to be found on the way home. Meanwhile he had to pay the check. Yellow-face still dozed.

He tried to waken her in his old, approved fashion: he would make bread-pills and flick them at her long nose. One in twenty would hit the target, and Yellow-face would start out of her sleep, frightened. "I beg your pardon, sir. Is that your idea of a joke? What did you have, sir?" He would smile good-humoredly, tell her, and pay.

This time it didn't work. He aimed countless bread-pills, never hit Yellow-face. Meanwhile he kept thinking of his prince.

He clawed out a soft lump of bread, rolled a few pills, forgot to aim them. The prince! He saw him suddenly. There he was, marching across field and forest. A raven, which he had once rescued from certain death, had told him the secret of the sleeping princess. . . . The raven flies before him, showing him the way. But of course it won't be as simple as all that. One can't let the prince reach the happy end of the story in a single chapter. For when the story is ended the listener goes home, and he is left alone with his agitated nerves and his incomplete thoughts. Well, then, he will bring in a wolf; and after that a river. So the prince will uproot a tree and float himself across the river on it. After that an impassable mountain will confront the prince; whereupon the raven will take him on its wings and fly him over. No, not the raven, but an eagle, the raven's uncle. And then—and then—well, after that the prince will simply start feeling hungry. The banal and the commonplace always have to come in. Even a king's son can become hungry in the midst of his adventures. The raven sets out to get food for him, but it's a long way to the nearest village, and the raven does not return. The sun blazes overhead; the barren fields stretch in every direction. If only wheat grew hereabouts; he would forget his dignity as a king's son and tear a few ears from the stalks. But nothing grows here except bitter herbs, and before flying away the crow warned him: "Don't touch them. They are poison." That's the work of the magician who guards the sleeping princess; for now we are not far from the mountain, and more than one adventurer has eaten of these bitter herbs and been poisoned.

How hard, how frightfully hard it is to wait for the raven. The prince's heart faints in him. His eyes burn. Meanwhile a peasant girl passes, carrying a loaf of bread; fresh, odorous bread; the smell of it fills his nose tormentingly.

"Peasant girl," he calls out in a weak voice, "a piece of bread."

"Pay," she answers curtly.

"I have no money."

"Those that have no money don't eat."

"I am a king's son. When I return to my home I will send you a king's treasure."

"Tell it to the wind. . . . Debts written in water. . . ."

"I am dying of hunger."

"What's new about that? It's happened to your betters."

She walks on a little space, then turns back.

"I'll tell you what. I like you. Marry me and I'll give you bread."

"I can't. I'm in love with the queen's daughter."

"And you want to eat?"

"I'm hungry."

"Marry me and you'll not be hungry."

The peasant girl was obstinate, hunger gnawed at him, and he had to yield. He pledged her eternal faithfulness.

A hare ran across the field, and they called him to witness the marriage. The king's son snatched a piece of bread and followed the peasant girl toward the village.

Yellow-face opened an eye and closed it again. The story wove itself on.

For a long time the prince lay sick in the village; the fresh bread had been too much for him. Then he became better and married the peasant girl. And since he could neither plow nor sow nor reap, but could read and write, he became the village teacher. Their married life was peaceful. . . . The peasant girl used to call him, lovingly, "my little loony," and he would smile foolishly. But he kept the queen's daughter in a secret place in his heart. Who knew? The peasant girl used to work with the nobleman's automatic reaper; some day something might happen, then he would renew the quest. . . . Of course he never clothed the thought in words . . . quite possibly he was not even aware of the thought. The hope found a hiding-place in an obscure corner of his heart, and he kept the secret to himself.

But nothing happened to his peasant wife. Indeed, she became sturdier and stronger from day to day. Not so with him. It may have been the coarse peasant fare, and it may have been the vain-longing in his heart; in any case, he aged early. And when he observed that his beard had turned gray, that his eyes were dimming, that his forehead was wrinkled, he called his pupils to him and, weeping, revealed to them the secret of the queen's daughter. They broke into laughter: teacher had taken leave of his senses! And yet . . .

He became aware that the light had changed. Darkness had fallen. He looked out through the window; the weather, too, had changed. A wet snow was falling. He felt a contraction of the heart. Hastily he picked up a bread-pill and threw it. This time he hit the target, and Yellow-face started up.

"Come here, Yellow-face, I'll tell you a story."

"What do I want stories for?" she asked.

"It's a pretty story, all about peasant boys in search of a princess."

"That's silly."

"No, it's not silly. The princess is asleep on a flower-bed on the summit of a mountain. The village teacher told them to look for her."

"Not a bad idea."

"Sure it's not a bad idea. The princess is good and beautiful and clever."

"Quit making fun of me. You'd better pay and go."

"Sure, sure. But the youngsters of the village armed themselves with wooden swords and wooden spears. . . ."

Yellow-face yawned.

"Are you tired, Yellow-face?"

"God, what weather!" And she added, irritably: "Whenever there's a Jewish holy day there has to be bad weather."

"What sort of holy day do you mean, Yellow-face?"

"It's their Easter."

So that was the meaning of the running about in his lodgings, the restlessness in the streets! Passover!

He paid and ran out.

In the street he burst into laughter.

Somewhere in him a reincarnated soul was stirring: a grandfather's, or a great-grandfather's. What a pang of homesickness! Every man is a carrier of reincarnated souls.

The first year he was away from home he nearly went

out of his mind with homesickness when the night of the seder came round. The family where he lodged had been invited out for the seder, and he had had the run of the house to himself. He went to bed early, having nowhere to go. But he had forgotten to pull down the shades and the moonlight woke him. He came to with a painful beating at his heart. He lay there a long time, wondering what it was. Then he remembered. Suddenly he sprang up, tore the sheet off the bed, wound it about him like the white ceremonial garment his father wore at the seders, and ran from room to room bellowing the seder prayers at the top of his voice, by heart. The second year, terrified by the recollection of his homesickness, he sold his overcoat and made a trip home for the Passover. On the way home he kept repeating to himself that he was going to give in, give in completely. And, indeed, he went with his father to synagogue, came home, let his mother prepare the seat for him at the seder table, with the ceremonial cushion; and at the right moment he asked the ritual "Four Questions" of the seder. But when it came to that part of the ceremony which rehearses the Ten Plagues visited on the Egyptians, he could not stand it any more. He simply refused to follow the hallowed custom of flipping a drop of wine out of his glass at the mention of each plague. And farther on in the service, where the sages of old discuss the manifold character of the plagues—the plagues within the plagues, as it were—he almost ran from the room. It was all his mother could do to keep him there. But on the third day of the Passover he left, without saying good-by to his father. His mother waited for him outside the city.

He mounted the stone stairway from the river bank.

He was sorry for that incident now. What sense had

there been in hurting them so? In those days he used to justify himself by saying: "For the sake of the truth." Was there such a thing as truth?

His thoughts ran on: "We, the younger ones, must suffer. Our pains are creative; they drive us to new work, the production of new forms. But the pains of the old people are fruitless; they only end in futile tears, but at least the heart does not become petrified."

He traversed the Krasinsky Park. The milk institute was deserted. Belated people hurried along the walks. He drew near the hillock that looked out over the Nalevki Street. He was tired, but it was still too early to go home. He sat down on a bench facing the little hill.

On its lower slope the hillock was bare, as if a barber had shorn it; higher up there were tufts and patches of grass and thorns; here and there a bush or even a clump of trees. Birds could nest and sing there. *She* was very fond of birds. Once she used to work in the country, and whenever she heard birds singing, the tears came to her eyes and she couldn't hold them back; it was as if her soul wept, she said, it was so sweet.

And there were times when she talked in such a strange, wonderful way. . . . She would play with the tips of her long white fingers, with their needle-scars; or she would touch the tips of her even whiter teeth. She would use expressions like "soul-star." . . . Where had she picked it up? Perhaps she too was a concealed princess; her mother, with her washing-bales, was no mother, but a witch, watching over her to see that no stranger prince approached and woke her up.

Well, if that was so, *he* wasn't the prince. The prince had to be pure from sin.

A nurse with four little charges hurried by. The boys turned aside and began running toward the hill. Boys armed with swords and spears—"they ascend the mountain." The nurse became angry; it was time to go home; their parents would be worrying . . . it was a festival day. The boys pay no attention: "To the princess!"

He closed his eyes and saw the village schoolmaster's pupils mounting the hill to the princess, their wooden weapons in their hands. . . . A cloud is spread between the "rescuers" and the princess. They do not see her; they only believe in her. Shall he let them reach her?

And here the old witch comes swooping down through the cloud, riding on her broomstick.

She takes one of the boys by the hand.

"Where are you going, little one?"

"To the princess."

"What have you to do with her?"

"I want to waken her."

"What for?"

"I want to marry her."

"What do you want to marry her for?"

"She's so good! Our teacher told us. And she's clever and sweet. Teacher knows."

"Sure he does! And you, of course, like good, sweet things."

"You bet I do. Mamma calls me 'Sweet-tooth.' "

"Well, you silly little boy, what's the sense of crawling all the way up the mountain and getting all tired out? I can see you're a noble and delicate child—"

"What's that got to do with you?"

"You silly little fellow, don't you see I'm your auntie? Don't you know me? I'll give you all kinds of sweet things."

She waves her broomstick in the air. Hocus-pocus! And right at the boy's feet falls a basket full of the loveliest things: almonds in their yellow chemises, pressed figs.

143

bunches of raisins, flaming oranges, chocolates, and other tempting things that the boy didn't even know by name. He uttered a cry of glee and fell on his knees before the lovely basket.

Meanwhile the other three went on. Against them came the magician, old, white-bearded, with heavy white eyebrows, and big blue spectacles on his nose.

He heard the creaking of the park gate and opened his eyes. The nurse and her charges had disappeared. He got up from the bench and hurried out into the almost deserted Nalevki Street. Meanwhile the story went on weaving itself in his brain.

The old magician stops one of the three.

"Where are you off to, young man?"

"To waken the princess. I want to marry her."

"What for?"

"Teacher told us wonderful things about her. She's so clever."

"You want to learn from her how to be clever?"

"Sure I do. A man ought to be clever. If you're clever you get money and medals."

"Well, well, I can see that you're quite clever already. And if you want, you can become as clever as can be, without the princess."

"How?"

"Very simple. Here!"

The old man takes out of his inside pocket a little book bound in white leather and edged with gold, and hands it to the boy who is quite clever already.

"Sit down and read. When you'll have read one page through, you'll be cleverer than Daddy and Mamma; after the second page you'll be cleverer than everyone in the village; and by the time you're in the middle of the book you'll be as clever as three professors."

The youngster snatches the book and sits down to read.

The last two have meanwhile gone on. Suddenly the snake blocks their path. One of them runs away; the other remains, paralyzed with fear.

But the snake doesn't bite him. It draws its tail across its fangs and asks in a snakish-friendly voice:

"Whither away, young man?"

Well, he's going to the princess, to wake her up and marry her because teacher said she was beautiful.

"Do you like beautiful things?"

"Of course."

"Then come with me. Do you see that crystal palace over there? It's full of little dolls; they wear sateen dresses and slippers of white silk. . . . They have cherry-red lips and eyes that flash like precious stones. . . . You'll choose the doll that you love best, and look, you won't have far to walk; it's close by, no climbing."

But what about the fourth one, the one who ran away and returned? What's to be done with him? Let him reach the princess? That would be a pity. He would be the unhappiest of the boys. He would be left without anything —he would not even have a vain-longing to look back on and self-reproaches to cling to.

And yet for her sake he must do it. He must let the boy reach the princess.

After which, a wedding ceremony, music, dancing, a honeymoon trip, a stroll in the hanging gardens.

And *she*—she will close her eyes blissfully, and she will be so moved that she will let him put his arms round her and draw her on to his lap, and he will wonder what he is doing it for. She will put her hot cheek to his, he will feel her sweet breath, he will kiss her, and inwardly he will say to himself: "Swine!" She will jump up from his lap, terrified, and she will start crying brokenly, and he will throw himself at her feet and implore her pardon; and in his heart he will say to himself: "Clown!" And she will forgive him at last, but for a long time she will not come to see him again. . . .

Somebody elbowed him aside; he slipped and almost fell down on the wet pavement.

The staircase lay in shadow—only one oil lamp for two flights. He had no matches. His neighbor on the same floor had an electric torch, but he didn't envy him that: the man's wife was so ugly. Whenever he passed their door he trembled lest she show herself. Ugliness is the greatest of all sins. And if the woman was ugly, the servant girl was even uglier. He shuddered, partly out of revulsion, partly with the cold. He had forgotten that his spats were torn and he had stepped into puddles. In the night he would cough and perhaps run a temperature. The doctor would come and threaten him again with tuberculosis. Who cared? Let it be tuberculosis, as long as something happened.

He stood stock-still in terror.

There in the dark corner of the stairway a picture had suddenly risen before him. A seder table, a snow-white gleaming tablecloth, three red engraved wine-beakers, gleaming plates, silverware, candles in three tall, wrought-silver candlesticks: Mother stands there, saying the benediction over the candlelights. . . . She has her back to him. . . . Her shoulders tremble. . . . She is weeping into her hands . . . weeping for him. . . . Where is he? Where is he now?

"Ha! It's beginning!" In a rage he dashed up the remaining steps three at a time. And then suddenly he regretted the rage and the hurry. His mother might have turned round to him. What did she look like now? She wrote that she lay awake through the nights. . . . She'd sent him four pairs of socks a little while back. "Do be careful and keep your feet warm."

"Bah!" He shook himself. "A man must be a man."

He entered his room with firm footsteps; with firm hand he lit the lamp. He didn't like the dark. He looked round. "What poverty!" Cobwebs in the corners; but, as against that (he smiled bitterly), at least no scrap of the forbidden leavened bread. Well, tomorrow someone would invite him out; he would hang around the German synagogue at service time; he knew a certain teacher. . . .

He sat down on the bed. The lamp smoked a little; he got up to fix it, and forgot himself. What was it he had got up for? He sat down again, drew his feet on to the bed. His eyes fell on the mirror hanging by the bed. He took it down and examined himself.

He smiled. "I'm not as ugly as she makes out." He hung the mirror up again. "Yes, rather dark, like a Tatar; but what eyes!"

He is proud of his eyes. Few women can look at them and not be moved. . . . When he becomes intimate with a woman she always kisses him on the eyes. His lips—well, they were a little too full . . . too ready to kiss, dangerous. Even in the old days, when he lived at home. . . .

The thread breaks. What's happening at home just now? Has Father come back from synagogue service?

He hears his father's greeting: "Happy Festival!" He hears his mother's answer. No happiness in the voices. How can there be, God help them? An only son, and he far away.

He tries to shift his thoughts to other matters, but without success. The seder refuses to be conjured away. This is the fifth year.

He gets out of bed and walks over to the window. The

wet stones in the courtyard below throw back in flickering ribbons the festive lights in the apartments opposite. He *will not* lift his eyes to the windows above. But he must. . . . He lifts them slowly, but halfway to the first floor he stops again, as if again paralyzed. Another picture:

A seder table, utensils of gold and crystal. Is it a family? No, it must be a gathering of several families. The women are in strange habit, fashions that have passed away many generations ago. Men in white, embroidered ruffs under their white covering garments. . . . Golden circlets, gold-embroidered skull-caps. . . . What part of the seder service are they at? A murmurous *recitativo*—

Then, suddenly, a knock at the outside door.

The men become rigid; the women tremble; a girl faints away, and a young wife falls on her husband's neck.

From outside a voice: "Open in the name of the law!"

Ha! The blood-libel!

The patriarch of the family cries out: "Quick! Look under the table." A few men bend down. Horror of horrors! A dead child!

The patriarch of the family stands up and issues commands in a tense but firm voice.

"Put it on the table and cut it up."

It is done. The banging on the outside door becomes more insistent. Footsteps. Ring of steel on steel.

"Everyone take a piece on his plate."

It is done. The intruders are now banging at the inner door.

"Eat!"

The pieces are eaten up. Police and soldiers burst in then. They look everywhere in vain. They go out raging. And when they are gone the furious cry of the prayer goes up from the assembly of celebrants:

148

"Pour forth Thy wrath upon the heathen that know Thee not. . . ."

"Not for me," he thinks. "That needs a stronger pen than mine."

Better, then, to lie down on the sofa, with closed eyes.
His strength is gone, eaten away by moodiness. . . .
There are easier pictures to paint.

For instance: the famous seder where the Master of the Name, the Baal Shem, the founder of Chassidism, presided. No—that isn't it, either. The seder he is thinking of was celebrated in the house of a rich Jew who was actually a *Misnaged,* an opponent of Chassidism. The Baal Shem humbled himself and sought an invitation to the man's seder. Couldn't get it so easily, either.

That was at the synagogue service before the seder. The Baal Shem *asked* for the invitation, saying humbly to the rich Jew: "Let me come. You'll find me useful."

The rich man consulted the Rabbi. Was it permissible to have a Chassid at one's seder? The Rabbi answered yes; besides, it was a sin to shame a man by a refusal.

And the Baal Shem sits quietly at the seder. The first part passes—the Four Questions; and then the passage beginning: "Slaves we were unto Pharaoh." And suddenly the Baal Shem speaks up and asks that an additional prayer-book be brought, and an additional praying-robe. Laughter breaks out at the table. The tone of the Baal Shem changes: "I command it!" What's this? An hour ago he was begging for an invitation, and now he's issuing commands at table! The master of the house stares at him; the eyes of the Baal Shem are blazing. Fear takes hold of the host. He orders the prayer-book and the robe brought and placed before the Baal Shem. Then the Baal

Shem kicks at something under the table and says: "Yantek! Stand up!" And from under the table there crawls forth and rises to his feet a young peasant lad, his face bloodless; a corpse with closed eyes, and across his throat a cut. The guests start back.

"Yantek! Open your eyes!"

Yantek obeys.

"Yantek, put on the robe, tie up the girdle, put on the skull-cap."

Yantek obeys.

"Give him a chair. Yantek, sit down!"

Yantek sits down in robe and skull-cap.

"Open the Hagaddah and say the prayers with us."

The celebrants tremble and murmur the prayers, and Yantek murmurs with them.

Suddenly the door is broken open. It is the old story. They have come to look for the corpse they planted under the table. . . . No sign of it. . . . The intruders withdraw, baffled and ashamed. . . .

The Baal Shem turns to the resurrected corpse:

"Yantek! Close your eyes again, and go to the cemetery and bury yourself. And because it has been your privilege to wear a Jewish prayer-robe, and say a Jewish prayer, your resting-place will be the Jewish cemetery. And when you meet Father Abraham you will say to him . . ."

A light tap on the door.

"Come in."

"Got any stories?"

"All kinds."

CHAPTER X

"Ah, Sinful Nation"

❊

T o THE anonymous young man who is the hero of
the last chapter I shall give the mathematical notation P_1.

He is an aspect of Peretz, his revolutionary and assimilationist self. And what a wonderful illustration "Stories"
is of the indivisibility of style and content! P_1 hungers for
the modern European world—and his manner of telling
a story belongs to the modern, sophisticated European
school. It has no connection with the folk tales. It might
have been written by Gide: the writer watches himself
tell a story and notes the effect on himself. Nothing could
be further from this artistic egocentricity than the naïve
(or seemingly naïve) objectivity of the chronicler of Reb
Chiya.

It is P_1 who is the author of that brutal piece on Purim
(page 123) and the caustic description of the Yiddish senti-
mental fabulists (page 124). What makes P_1 so angry? Is
it only the moral unsavoriness of the Esther episode and
the intellectual dishonesty of the Yiddish romantics? I do
not think so. He is also angry because he is condemned to
write in Yiddish. And "Confound it!" he must say to himself, "I produce the best effects in the story, the shattering
climax, by reverting to purely Jewish material that cannot be presented to non-Jews without footnotes!" In "Sto-

ries" P_1 has lost both worlds, the European and the Yiddish. The great climax lacks, for non-Jews, the necessary directness, the simple evocativeness that makes explanation unnecessary. And for Yiddish readers the body of the story has no appeal; "Stories" is hardly ever mentioned by Peretz-lovers!

P_1 is a tragic figure, for is not tragedy the fatal clash between design and destiny? But suppose P_1 had been a whole person instead of an aspect of a person, and suppose he had had a son, whom I will call P_2; and suppose P_2 had been brought up without a Jewish education and had picked up only tiny scraps of Jewish association from his father; suppose further that P_2 had "assimilated" into a world that did not want Jews. . . . Should we then have another tragic figure? No—P_2 would not be tragic, he would only be pathetic. He would be Leopold Bloom in James Joyce's *Ulysses*.

Leopold Bloom has neither designs nor a destiny; he is therefore pathetic, which also means comical. Leopold Bloom cannot have designs because he has no will; he has only the desire to have a will. He has no destiny; he has only reminders of a destiny. He thinks of himself as the complete Irishman, and is pulled up externally and internally at regular intervals by his incompleteness. In Barney Kiernan's saloon the Irish citizen taunts Bloom with his Jewishness, to which Bloom answers hotly with: "Mendelssohn was a Jew and Karl Marx and Mercadante and Spinoza. And the Savior was a Jew. . . ." Is not that Stock Answer No. 1 (or "Letter to the Editor") of the Jew who knows very little about Jewish things beyond those names and, knowing so little, has nothing else to fall back on? But Leopold Bloom is pulled up internally too. In his waking dreams of self-aggrandizement he sees himself as the savior of Ireland, and then: "A streamer bearing the

legend *Cead Mile Failte* and *Mah Tov Melech Israel*
spans the street. . . . A fife and drum band is heard in
the distance playing the Kol Nidre. . . . The chrysele-
phantine papal standard rises high. . . ." No wonder
someone asks of him: "Is he a Jew or a gentile or a Holy
Roman or a swaddler or what the hell is he?" Alas, P_2—or
Bloom—is not even P_1, his father. P_1 was somebody and
wanted to be somebody else; P_2 is nobody and *thinks* he
wants to be somebody. I say *thinks,* for how can he who
has never been a somebody entertain the very concept of
a somebody else?

Joyce has given us in Leopold Bloom the most penetrating study ever made of a Jew assimilating into the
non-Jewish world (that is not, of course, all of *Ulysses*),
and it is a matter for great wonder that this should have
been done by a non-Jew without a sympathetic understanding of Jewishness. The focal characteristic of Bloom,
the source of the high hilarity to which he moves us, is
his lack of a focal characteristic. He wants, in a driveling
and fatuous way, to be an Irishman; but—as he reveals
time and again, but particularly in the Mabbotstown
scene—he is ready to be anything. He is even ready to
be a mother! Now, a man who wants to be everything
actually wants to be nothing. He expresses only escape;
and the point of the joke is that what he seeks to escape
from is also—his nothingness!

P_1 too wants to escape; but it is from something very
definite and into something equally definite. As we see, he
fails. He is forced to return to the Jewish theme for the
climax of "Stories." I have suggested that this frustration
found its way into Peretz's biting criticisms of the things
he loved. It was the pious and traditional Jewish world
that touched him most deeply and furnished him with the
material and the motivation of his greatest work; it was

also the pious and traditional Jewish world that stung him to his fiercest revulsions. We have here a curious mixture: the old, traditional, prophetic castigation of the sins of the Jewish people ("Ah, sinful nation, a people laden with iniquity, a seed of evildoers, children that are corruptors," etc., etc.), the hostility of the rationalist and modernizer to the mystic and traditional, and the frustration of the individual. One advantage P_1 enjoyed by virtue of the fact that he wrote in Yiddish for a closed audience: he was freed from the dilemma of the modern Jew who, writing about his people in the language of a gentile nation, must always bear in mind that his strictures are going to be read by the wrong people and may turn up in anti-semitic pamphlets. One sometimes wonders whether the Prophets would have been so outspoken if they had been prophetic enough to foresee that their denunciations of the Jewish people would be translated into every language in the world.

I have chosen, as my first illustration of Peretz in the role of Jewish-traditional satirist and castigator, a sketch called "Mendel Brainnes." Its subject is a well-known type of the traditional Yiddish world: the pious and unworldly scholar whose life is fixed *al Torah v'al avodah*— on the pursuit of divine wisdom and the practice of good deeds. That Hebrew phrase occurs often in Peretz's stories. He had a deep reverence for the man who withdrew from the struggle for gold and glory, and even for bread —such a one was, for instance, Reb Chiya. But when a man does that, someone has to feed and clothe and shelter him. He who withdraws completely from the worldly struggle without actually leaving this world does not diminish the volume of the struggle; he only lets his share be taken over. In the case of Mendel Brainnes the share was taken over by his wife. Happy the Jewish woman who is privileged thus to serve a husband who is a saint and scholar! Blessed is she in this world, and thrice blessed in the world to come!

MENDEL BRAINNES

They called him Mendel Brainnes—that is, Brainne's Mendel—after his wife, for this was in the days before Jews were compelled to find themselves surnames. He was what they call "a tent-dweller," like our forefather Jacob (in contradistinction, that is, to Esau, the rough and uncouth huntsman)—which means a fine, quiet, studious example of a Jew. No great scholar, to be sure. Not for him the subtle disquisitions and problems of the Talmud. He was content with the simpler passages, the legends, the aphorisms of the sages, the morality books, and the Psalms. To these he gave his heart—to these and to pious deeds. His house was always open to the homeless traveler; no morning passed but what he dropped a coin into the charity box for scholars who have settled in the Holy Land; and no benevolent enterprise could get under way in the town without Mendel's name on the list. Perhaps a preacher would come to town; Mendel would put him up; perhaps a collection would be started, for matzos, for potatoes, for firewood, for anything at all concerning the poor: Mendel would don his gabardine, pick up his big walking-stick, and accompany the Rabbi from door to door. Mendel considered it a special merit to carry the box with his own hands, even though the synagogue beadle was in the procession.

His days were filled with activity from dawn to dusk. There were psalms to be recited, a page of the Mishnah to be studied, morning prayers to be said, good deeds to be done, the midday meal to be eaten, grace to be intoned, then afternoon prayers, and evening prayers, and prayers before falling asleep, and midnight prayers. . . .

Mendel Brainnes was not what you would call clever. When he was a boy in cheder they used to call him Mendel Loony. Then, when he grew up and married, the description was softened down to Mendel Simpleton. Later on, when he had finished the traditional years of "keep" to which a young husband is entitled from his father-in-law, when he set up house for himself, and his wife opened a grocery store and made lots of money, he was promoted to Mendel Brainnes. And since he never got in anyone's way, never uttered a mean or angry word, and was always doing something for somebody, people were willing to forget what they once called him; and nobody laughed out loud when he used to ask, at every other sentence: "I'm not foolish, am I? In fact, wouldn't you say that I'm quite clever?"

Brainne was a devoted and loving wife to Mendel. She had but one ambition: to serve as his footstool when he sat upon the throne that was surely waiting for him in paradise. In the meantime, on this earth, nothing was too good for her Mendel—the daintiest foods, the finest clothes. Brainne worked like a donkey to support him and to feed and clothe the children, of whom there were four, two sons and two daughters. Pending her translation to paradise she asked for nothing save the sight of her Mendel occupied in the fulfillment of his pieties. Her heart swelled within her when she looked out from the door of her store and saw her Mendel in dignified procession down the street, the charity box in his left hand, the big walking-stick in his right. Brainne had had a wonderful seat of her own in the women's gallery of the synagogue; she had sold it for next to nothing and had paid a

huge price for another seat, in a much less distinguished
place, only because from there she could watch her Mendel at the Sabbath service and see him when he was called
up to the pulpit for the reading from the Scrolls of the
Torah. Bliss welled up in her when she saw her Mendel
leaning over to the cantor, murmuring into his ear, telling him to announce to the congregation that he was do-
nating eighteen times eighteen kopecks to the synagogue
for the health of his wife, Brainne. Is not eighteen de-
noted in Hebrew by the two letters *chet* and *yud*? And do
not these two letters also make up the word *chai,* which
means "life"? And what bliss it was to go with Mendel on
Sabbaths and holy days to the synagogue! When they
reached the synagogue steps and had to part company, he
to proceed to the men's section, downstairs, she to the
women's gallery, she would take leave of him and then
turn round to see her Mendel lift his legs from step to
step. And after service she would wait for him on the same
spot, and when he approached and uttered his hearty
"Good Sabbath" she would blush for happiness, for all
the world as if they had just come out from under the
bridal canopy.

Brainne knew well enough that her Mendel was no ex-
pert in the trashy nonsense which is called "worldly wisdom." There in the synagogue Study House, among the
pietists, he was the big man; but the everyday world was
her domain. And so when Mendel used to propose that
they sell out the store and go to live in the Holy Land, she
would answer, sweetly:

"No, no, Mendel. One doesn't sell one's livelihood like
that. Maybe some day, some far-off day, when we'll have
married off the children, when we'll have provided our
sons-in-law with a few years of keep, when we'll have

grandchildren, and perhaps even a great-grandchild or two—maybe then we'll consider it; maybe then we'll turn the store over to the children."

And Mendel, who knew that in worldly matters his wife was nothing short of a genius, nodded agreement.

One day Mendel came home from the synagogue Study House in melancholy mood.

"Look, Brainne," he said, "a summons from the heavenly court," and he showed her a gray hair in his beard.

Brainne comforted him: "Don't talk foolishness, Mendelle. You don't understand these things. My father, God rest his soul, was gray at fifty, and yet (may his virtues bring you long life), he—"

"Bring *us* long life," Mendel corrected her.

"Bring *us* long life," said Brainne, "he lived another thirty years."

"Ah, other days, other people; we're a weaker generation," said Mendel, and looked down sadly.

Brainne talked him out of his sadness and made up her mind to feed him better than ever. That same day she ordered an extra half pound of meat for supper.

"Well, well, Brainne," said the butcher. "Important guests? Prospective in-laws? Good luck, Brainne."

"No, no," she answered. "We're a weaker generation, that's all."

And at mealtimes she would coax Mendel to take a little more. "Mendelle, taste this, it's delicious," and looking into his eyes she would think: "God strengthen him! Weaker generations, that's what we are."

Then she would add: "You need strength, Mendelle, to do all that holy studying. I don't have to eat as much as you. What have I got to do all day long but sit in the store with my hands in my lap; or maybe I'm in the kitchen, standing over the stove. And if a customer comes in, what is there to do but weigh out a pound of beans or grits or flour? And if no customer comes in, well, there's nothing at all to do. And so I don't have to eat as much as you."

And Mendel thought: "Bless my soul! She's quite right. All the things I must attend to! So many psalms every day; the prayers; a page of the Mishnah; the collection box. I do need more food."

And it made him happy to think that his good, pious Brainne had such a peaceful, untroubled life: sat all day in the store with her hands in her lap; or idled over the stove; or, if a customer came in, weighed out a pound of beans or grits or flour; and if no customer came in, well, there was nothing at all to do. At least *she* didn't have to work the way he did. God be thanked for it! And Mendel ate heartily and carefully, so that he might live long and practice his arduous and sacred duties for many years.

There was another source of happiness in Mendel's life, apart from the easy time his Brainne was having, and that was the way his children had developed. One son was already married out, to another town, and the young man was still in the first period of his keep with his in-laws. Since his departure not one letter had arrived from him, which Mendel took as a sign that everything was going nicely. People coming from that town always brought greetings. . . . Now there was another son to be married off, a youngster still attending cheder. It was Brainne who looked after the boy's education, engaged teachers, provided for their pay, managed everything. Mendel did his duty by giving the boy an examination every Sabbath. In the afternoon, of course, after the midday meal; Mendel disliked doing anything before a meal. And on the Sabbath, as everyone knows, there's a feeling of leisure after the midday meal; you settle down comfortably in your chair and listen to your son reciting the weekly portion of the Pentateuch; you can also doze off from time to time. Mendel, however, always managed to wake up toward the end of the recitation, just as the teacher—who was there, naturally—was lifting up his glass of brandy and saying: "Good health." Then Mendel would congratulate the teacher and pinch his son affectionately on the cheek.

Next to the sons there are two little girls, very well-behaved, very respectful, very quiet. And always so neat and clean—a delight to the eye. Really, Mendel never notices when Brainne washes them and mends their clothes. It's beyond him how children can be born so sweet and clever and well-behaved.

"*My* children," he thinks, proudly. "They take after me." And he thanks the Lord of the world again for having granted his wife Brainne such a tranquil, easy life. Not like some unhappy mothers he could think of, whose children drive them half-crazy. And how attentive and obedient they are! If he asks for a drink of water, and Brainne repeats it after him (that's a habit of hers): "Bring your daddy a glass of water," how the little ones run! It does one's heart good. And he has only to show himself at the door, and Brainne says: "Your daddy's here!"—and quiet falls upon the house.

Now, God be praised, there's an offer for the second son. An excellent match. Brainne is all in favor of going at once to inspect the prospective bride. Mendel thinks it a good idea. Let the poor woman have a holiday. She travels four times a year to the fair, for merchandise, and she always comes back exhausted. This will be a rest for her; and the world will see what kind of wife he has. He himself, Mendel, will only appear on the scene for the betrothal and the wedding. Or maybe only at the wedding. That was how it had been with the first son: Brainne had attended to everything.

The years pass, and the grace of God is not withdrawn from Mendel. The second son is married off; he too lives peacefully with his parents-in-law, and Mendel's days follow one another tranquilly. He hardly knows how it has all happened—it has been like a dream. Not a single day has Mendel omitted the repetition of the assigned portion of the Psalms. Never has he known the meaning of the word *headache*—except, perhaps, on the morning following the big night of prayer, when he hasn't slept enough.

Only two girls remain to be married off, and Brainne manages these things so skillfully! After that's done, they'll sell the store, pack their belongings on a wagon, and it's off to the Holy Land!

Only latterly he's not been feeling quite his wonted self. His legs bother him, and his breath comes short. But Brainne is always there to look after him; she shields him from worry; she cooks the most delicate dishes for him; she assures him that he'll live to see all his dreams fulfilled.

One day as he is sitting over a volume of the Mishnah in the synagogue Study House, he hears a terrible outcry. For a moment it seems to him that the voice is his daughter's. But no, that cannot be. A girl of her age, ready for marriage, what would she be doing in the synagogue yard? And yet—the footsteps come closer, the familiar voice wails: "Daddy! Daddy!" Yes, it is his daughter's voice. But no! It cannot be.

He must think this over. He takes a pinch of snuff from the box and is about to apply it meditatively to his nostrils when his daughter bursts in and catches him wildly by the lapels.

"Daddy! Daddy! Mamma's had a stroke! Help!"

161

And before Reb Mendel had recovered from the shock and managed to make his way home, Brainne was dead.

In a single day Reb Mendel's beard turned as white as snow. His feet swelled up, he could not catch his breath. It had never occurred to him that Brainne could possibly die before him—with such a husband, too, such wonderful children, and such an easy life. . . .

And Brainne, who had been so inconspicuous while she lived, was almost as hard to see when she lay in her coffin, so wasted was she.

In "Mendel Brainnes" Peretz gently and unobtrusively eviscerates a traditional Jewish type much respected in the old days. It might be argued that here Peretz carries out the operation not on the true scholar and pietist, but on the smug imitation. There are, however, many utterances of Peretz's that reveal a general distaste for prayerful and charitable people. The rationalist in him rejected prayer, the socialist in him saw in prayer and philanthropy class devices. It is P_1 who writes: "Prayer is a fine recipe for spreading respect for the upper classes and general tranquillity. Prayer sometimes dulls the hunger of the pauper, like a mother's finger thrust into the mouth of her starving baby. Prayer is in fact a recipe for a great many things."

And when this mood is on him he tells the story of the elderly seamstress, almost blind from years of sewing, for whose benefit a charity ball was arranged by some of the kindly families in whose service she had all but lost her eyesight.

The generosity and the dancing yielded enough to get her a husband—an old widower—for a dowry of forty-five rubles, and a second-hand wedding dress. The seamstress seemed strangely indifferent to what was going on; it was as if the arrangements were being made for someone else. During the negotiations she lay on her bed and applied cold compresses to her head.

"A dummy, a stone image, God help us," said her friends.

"An ingrate," said her benefactors. "Hasn't even sense enough to thank us," and they wrote down the good deed in their heavenly account, not forgetting the local newspaper.

The bride came out of her stupor only when they brought in the second-hand wedding dress of faded satin and put it on her bed. She threw one glance at it, and then it was as though a demon had taken possession of her. She began to scream, to tear her hair, to beat her withered breast. It took quite a time to calm her, to turn her again into a stone image which could stand under the wedding canopy.

She knew that dress! She herself had sewn it—and she remembered for whom. She had attended the ceremony in the synagogue to see for what king's son the bride would wear the dress. And under the canopy she had recognized the bridegroom.

"That is the way of the world," concludes Peretz. "*Rich brides break in the wedding dresses for poor seamstresses, and poor seamstresses break in the bridegrooms for rich brides.*"

The threefold foundations of the world, according to the Jewish sages of old, are "sacred study, sacred service, and deeds of charity." As a final illustration of how P_1 felt toward the devout and pious, I offer a sketch of his written in the first person and, from internal and external evidence, strongly tinged with autobiography.

The Poor Boy

"Give me five kopecks for a flop."

"No," I answer curtly, and walk on.

He runs after me with doglike supplication in his burning eyes, grabbing my sleeve and kissing it. It does him no good. I say to myself: "My income doesn't stretch to these hand-outs every day."

"The poor," I add as I walk away from the charity kitchen where I'd shaken off the young mendicant so harshly, "the poor very quickly become sickening nuisances."

The first time I had seen that haggard, dirty young face, with the deep-sunken, blazing, melancholy, yet clever eyes, I had felt a stab at my heart. Even before I heard what he was saying I snatched a five-kopeck coin from my pocket and thrust it into his bony hand.

I remember clearly that my hand performed this act without even consulting the heart, as to whether it felt pity, or the mind, as to whether it was proper for a person who earned forty-four rubles sixty-six kopecks a month to hand out five kopecks on the street.

The sound of his voice was like an electric spark that flashed through me, shattering every calculation. Only later, when the boy had snatched the coin joyously and danced out of the kitchen, did the brain receive the information regarding this new expense.

Absorbed by many worries, my own and those of others, I soon forgot the beggar-boy. But not wholly, it seems. Somewhere within me there must have been a consultation of my practical instincts. For on the second evening, when he stopped me again, and his whimpering, childish voice repeated his plea for the price of a flop, there swam out of me, all prepared and in orderly array, the proper thoughts: "A boy of seven or eight should not beg, should not hang round the charity kitchen. It only makes an idler and mendicant of him. This way he'll never amount to anything."

Once more my hand flew automatically to my pocket; but I caught it there and stopped it. I was thinking: "Ah, if only I were a pious person, I might look at the matter differently. I might then ask myself: 'Is this particular good deed, which will be written down to my credit in heaven, worth the five kopecks it costs? Can't I get the same credit in heaven by putting some extra sincerity into my prayers this evening?' " But not being pious, I thought only of what was good for the boy. These five kopecks which I would give him would be bad for him, would confirm him in mendicancy.

And yet I gave him the money a second time. My hand came out of my pocket—again I was not the master—and I gave him the coin. Something hurt inside me, and my eyes became moist. Again he danced off joyously, and my heart was lighter, a smile came over my face.

The third time it lasted longer, a great deal longer. I had already calculated that my income simply did not permit me to spend this extra five kopecks a day. Yes, it was a pleasure to see his haggard young face light up, the flames dance in his eyes; it was a pleasure to know that with my five kopecks he would not have to sleep in the street; on the other hand I, with my particular income, could not permit myself such pleasures.

Of course I did not say this to the boy. I lectured him instead. Naturally.

I explained to him in much detail that with this constant begging of his he was ruining himself. He had to grow up to be a man; he had to learn how to work; work was a sacred thing; and if one looked for work one found

165

it. And I went on, telling him all the fine things I had read in books, none of which, however, could serve as a substitute for a "flop," or even for an umbrella on a rainy night.

And he stood there and kept on kissing my sleeve, kept on lifting his eyes to mine to see whether some glimmer of compassion hadn't come into them, whether his supplications were not falling on deaf ears. I, on the other hand, felt that he was not waiting in vain. A certain warmth was beginning to steal into me behind the frosty façade of my expostulations; his doglike eyes were having their effect on me; I was going to give in. And suddenly I had an idea. I would give it to him this time, but I would tell him once for all that he must never beg again. I would say it so firmly, so severely, that he would never forget it.

I gave him his five kopecks and admonished him sharply: "Here you are. But don't you ever beg from me again!"

How had those two words "from me" got into the admonition? I had not intended to utter them. I would gladly have given him something extra if I could only have taken those two words back. A chill fell on my soul, as if I had torn away her covering and left her exposed. But all this was momentary. My manner was very effective: the admonitory right hand, the left foot thrust forward, the severe metallic voice—everything. He stood there, longing to get away to the flophouse; he became paler and paler, and finally the tears began to tremble on his eyelids.

"No more begging," I repeated sternly. "This is the last time. D'you hear?"

And today I really didn't give him anything. I am not going to break my word. I'm not the kind that makes formal promises and swears things on Bibles: my word is my

word. A man must be firm, otherwise no order or system
is possible.

I think it all over, and I am filled with self-approval.
I just can't afford five kopecks a day. And yet that isn't the
most important point. The fact is that I acted on principle, for his good, and for the general good, too.

With the youngster I had spoken the simplest kind of
Yiddish; with myself I was a little more cultured. I said to
myself: "The most dangerous microbe in the public body
is mendicancy. He who does not work has no right to eat,"
etc., etc., etc.

I stepped out of the kitchen into a dark, muddy, rainy
night. A nasty wind was making the gas lamps flicker. One
might have thought they were shivering with the cold.
Their feeble, irregular light was reflected in the mud
puddles, so that one became dizzy.

A wailing, whistling wind filled my ears, like the lamentation of a thousand souls imploring redemption; or
like a thousand boys pleading for a bed in a flophouse.

Blast it! That boy again!

On a night like this one didn't drive even a dog into
the street. But it was precisely in the street that the boy
would pass the night. And yet what should I have done?
Wasn't three times enough? Wasn't it good enough if,
with my cough, and my sore throat, I'd come out on such
a night to do my share of work at the charity kitchen? Yes,
of course, I was a member of the executive committee,
but no one expected me to come out in this weather—and
without a fur overcoat, too. If at least I were pious, I
would have something out of it; I would run home
quickly now, throw myself into bed, and fall asleep; my
soul would mount to heaven and make sure that this good
deed, this valuable item, was entered on the credit side of

my ledger, and opposite, on the debit side, a big fat piece of roast leviathan, payable as soon as I was comfortably ensconced in paradise. But I had come out that evening without a thought of roast leviathan. My heart had driven me.

And thus praising myself, I began to feel a little warmer. When somebody else praises me I can't help feeling embarrassed, I can't help making little of what I've done. But when I sing my own praises I can listen quite shamelessly. I might have gone on much longer and found no end of fine attributes in myself if I hadn't stepped with my somewhat dilapidated shoes into an icy mud puddle.

A saying of the Talmud flashed through my mind. "Those who go on errands of mercy shall come to no harm." Apparently that applied only on the way *to* the good deed and not on the way *back* from it. I felt the wet cold creeping up from my feet into the rest of my body. A coughing fit would follow; and then that familiar needle pain in my chest. . . . I was terrified. I had only just spent four weeks in bed.

I dashed into the nearest teashop and ordered a glass of steaming tea.

While I was being served I picked up an illustrated comic paper and looked at one of the cartoons. It bore the legend "Who Has Too Much?" and it showed a stormy night in which two pedestrians had come face to face. One was a large, buxom, elegantly clad lady, whose only protection from the rain was a tiny parody of an umbrella; the other was a little girl in tatters, hurrying along with a pair of men's shoes under her arm—obviously her daddy's shoes being taken to the cobbler—while in her free hand she held a huge umbrella, again obviously her father's, which afforded her ample protection: and the little girl was grinning up into the face of the elegant lady. Very comical indeed, I thought, and reminded myself of the beggar-boy. *He* had no umbrella at all; no home waited for *him*. No bed. What on earth had made me think of him? Yes! I suddenly understood. It was the ten-kopeck piece that I had to pay for the almost untouched glass of tea. Five kopecks was all he had asked for.

Why had I spent these ten kopecks? Hot tea, and something to eat, were waiting for me at home. I had ordered the tea because I had been ashamed to take refuge in the teashop without ordering something.

I comforted myself with the thought: "The feeling of shame has to be paid for, too."

Outside, the storm had increased in fury. The wind tore at the roofs of the houses as if they were Jews and it an anti-Semite. The unhappy people who had to be on the streets were doubled up against the fury. And again I thought of the weak, unhappy little boy.

"If he were mine?" Would I then have hesitated for a moment? If I had to think of this mad wind carrying before it a child of mine. . . . And because he is not mine, is he the less a child? Or because those who should be looking after him are lying underground somewhere, with a headstone over them.

I simply could not go home! I had no right to! No right to my home, no right to the samovar of hot tea that awaited me there, no right to the smile of welcome. It was as though the word *Cain* or *murderer* were burning on my forehead.

"Damnation!" I cursed at myself. "Why can't I be a pious believer? How nice it would be to know that He who dwells in the utmost heights beyond the stars never takes His eye off the world, and that He has not forgotten the little beggar-boy!"

Why should he be there, like a weight on my heart?

How pleasant it would be if I could only throw him off on to the heart of the world! If I could only believe that he was secure under the gaze of the Cosmos-eye, he would not pursue me thus. But as it was, I had to turn back to the charity kitchen to look for him. It was a shame and a scandal. Exactly why a shame, and in whose eyes a scandal, I had no idea, and still have none. But turn back I did; and I did not find him. I had come too late.

I got home at an unearthly hour and hardly slept a wink. In nightmare after nightmare I wandered through the city, finding the youngster. I found him huddled on some stone stairs; I found him scurrying before the wind; I had a vision of him being used as a ball in a game between demons, who flung him back and forth; I found him frozen to death in a garbage can.

I could not wait for the morning.

When it came, I threw on my clothes and ran like one possessed to the charity kitchen.

There he was!

If I hadn't been ashamed I would have washed the mud from his face with my tears of gratitude. I wasn't a murderer!

"Here!"

I handed him a ten-kopeck piece. He looked at me with wondering eyes. He had not the faintest notion of what he had done for me.

But the following day I gave him nothing. Only this time I did not lecture him. I went away from him ashamed and dissatisfied. I was ashamed that I could not keep on giving.

Ah, it was not for nothing that my grandfather, God rest his soul, used to say: "He who is not pious lives a life of heartache and dies uncomforted."

CHAPTER XI

The Confused Revolutionary

❁

Peretz was really no revolutionary. He would have liked to be one, in all honesty; his heart was in the right place, and he did not lack courage. He spent three months in prison for his socialist views—to be sure, no great matter in Czarist Russia, where a prison term was practically routine for an honest man. He also lost his livelihood in his native town of Zamoshch because of his radical activities. But as a revolutionary he lacked doctrinaire implacability. He could not put on blinkers. Nor could he see only black and white.

"My heart is with you," he writes to the workers, "my eye never wearies of the sight of your flaming banners; my ear never wearies of the sound of your thunderous songs." But he goes on, in the same piece: "Do you not proclaim that mankind must march forward like an army, while you lead the van with your music? But mankind is not an army. There are the strong, who are in the front ranks; there are the sensitive, who feel more deeply; there are the proud, who tower above the rest. Will you not, in the time to come, cut down the cedars in order that they shall not be taller than the grass? Will you not spread out protective wings over mediocrity?"

He is afraid of the conquered who become conquerors,

even if they are the workers: "For every conqueror sins against the human spirit." And though he wrote innumerable articles in the revolutionary vein, and spoke the modern "scientific" language of revolution, he was first and last the moralist. When he mounted the political rostrum, as it were, and made his regulation speech, he was the sociologist. But his love of the oppressed, his hatred of oppressors, came from other, deeper sources. So much we learn, in fact, from his incomplete autobiography.

Once, when he was a child, a visitor came to their house in Zamoshch; evidently a very pious visitor, for when he had to wash his hands ritually he picked up the large jug, filled it at the barrel, and emptied it over his left hand and his right. This he repeated three times, using a jugful each time—which was quite unnecessary for a ritual washing. Now, water in Zamoshch had to be brought from the well, as everyone knew—including the visitor. The water-carrier to the house of the Peretzes was a sick little Jew called Eizikel. When the pious visitor had finished his extravagant demonstration, young Peretz heard his mother murmur to herself: "Pious at Eizikel's expense."

And once, when there was much excitement in Zamoshch about a call for recruits, and the Jews—who naturally had little inclination to fight for the Czar—were greatly perturbed, Peretz's father calmly advised complete mass abstention: "Don't worry! *They can't put a whole world in prison.*"

And Peretz, writing as an old man, says: "My father's 'They can't put a whole world in prison,' and my mother's 'Pious at Eizikel's expense'—these two seeds which were thrown into my young soul were not lost. They remained there forever. Quietly and secretly they have sprouted in everything I have written."

And so, fundamentally, Peretz knew that his social pro-

test did not spring from modern revolutionary or sociological theory. It was grounded in family and Jewish tradition. Political realism, with its coarse necessities, was
repugnant to him. As this sensitivity made him distrustful
of the ultimate triumph of the workers, it drove him also
from the practicalities of the Zionist movement.

In Peretz's boyhood, Zionism consisted of the old,
dreamy *Chibath Zion* (Love of Zion). To this he was at-
tracted. When Zionism became political and realistic, he
was repelled. He wrote:

"I had a beloved once. I loved her because she was
poor and in rags. I loved her because I am an incurable
romantic and idealist in this 'practical' age. . . . Pleasant
were my nights then, and sweet my dreams. . . . Time
passed, and my beloved fell from grace and became corrupted. She turned pious and wept her lovely blue eyes
out over foolish prayers; she became a busybody in the
synagogue, and the perfume of roses that once issued from
her has been replaced by the stale smell of the ritual bath.
. . . She goes from door to door with the collection box
in her hands, gathering a dowry. . . . The name of this
lady is *Chibath Zion*, and whenever I see her now my
heart contracts with pity and rage."

"Incurable romantic and idealist." It is an accurate description of him; perhaps more accurate than Peretz realized. And yet in personal matters he was a man of solid
common sense. For several years, in his late twenties and
early thirties, he was a practicing lawyer in Zamoshch,
employing half a dozen assistants and earning a large income. Those were years, it is true, when he wrote very
little. Later, when he had been denounced to the authorities as a liberal and was forbidden to practice law, he obtained a position with the Jewish Community Office of
Warsaw—in the Cemetery Bureau, of all places. He was

an excellent administrator. He kept the position for twenty-five years, until his death in 1915, his pay rising from 500 rubles a year to 2,400. In the execution of his duties he was rapid, resourceful, and quite untemperamental. Many of the heads of the Jewish Community—his employers—were assimilationist Jews, who resented his activity in the Jewish cultural national field; but against his abilities as an official they could adduce nothing. Peretz also went in for the publishing and editing of periodicals and the production of plays; he became a man of organizations, and conducted innumerable controversies, many of them quite poisonous.

In what sense, then, was he the romantic and idealist? In the ultimate sense of his life's meaning and value. His practicalities and controversies were gesticulations; the immortal part of him was not involved. The Prince lived apart, guarding his people's treasury.

Here is what he wrote about himself in his closing years:

"Toward immediate facts, when they concern my private life, I react weakly or not at all. For me the facts are for the most part too trivial; the motives are tangled and confused; the colors are too harsh, the tones too shrill, the lines coarse.

"Memory refines and purifies everything. I ask of life only one thing: that the wave shall pass. Before that happens I confront the wave with a large portion of resignation and philosophic endurance. I will not let myself be broken. I guard my inner being from even the slightest intrusion. A torrent of evil descends on me; I am not wetted inside. But these waves, once they have passed away, are renewed by my memory, and then I love them. From the chaos below the threshold of consciousness they rise again, purified and limpid."

In this same autobiography he warns the reader: "You do not have to believe what I tell you. I do not describe people, but the image they have left in me, and these images are seldom like the people themselves—that is, like the outer persons. My mind retains a dark image of a blond person if that person gave expression to a gloomy thought; contrariwise, I have a blond image of a dark person who happens to have thrown a ray of brightness into my soul."

Here is the key to his romanticism:

"The fable is always truer than the actual incident, the real fact. A human being yields to circumstance, covers his face, and does what the situation calls for. Nevertheless, the mass of the people instinctively perceives the essential character of the man, *and recounts what he would have done if he had been true to himself. . . .* Hence the saying: 'Sainthood comes only after death.' The incidentals of a man's life, the little practical devices, the dodges he resorted to for the sake of bread, the acts dictated by passing anger or a fleeting lust for triumph—these fall away, and the soul issues as it were in its nakedness, to be reclothed becomingly. This is the magic and the truth of folk tales; it is, in fact, the magic and truth of art itself."

Peretz could not have realized how accurately he was writing about himself, for he too had to wait for death and transfiguration. Yet he knew that his essential self did not belong to the tumult of the market-place; he was not for the barricades or the revolutionary councils. Nor were his editorial and theatrical enterprises of importance. For that matter, even his personal life after he had left his native town of Zamoshch at the age of thirty-six meant little to the artist in him. By the time he was ready to write he had, like Proust, all the material he needed. Thereafter he should have devoted himself to the process of externalization. For every one of Peretz's significant pieces goes back to Zamoshch and to what he had seen and felt there.

An artist of this type, an adept of memory, errs when he goes out into life after he has reached his saturation point. Life has nothing more to tell him. It can only distract and irritate him. In his early years Peretz had absorbed completely the Yiddish civilization into which he was born. He had met the individuals whom he was to exalt into his needed prototypes. He had seen good and evil; he had learned to love the one and hate the other. He had seen poverty and affluence; he had learned to pity the one, to despise the other. To re-create the values of that Yiddish world, and thereby to add to them, was his fundamental task.

This he did in the folk tales and the Chassidic tales, and these alone matter. Whatever else of him I have described in this book has been merely in deference to the record.

CHAPTER XII

Ecstasy

✿

CHASSIDISM was many things: a religious movement, a social protest, a national renaissance, and a great explosion of spiritual folk energy. But above all it was an ecstatic seizure. It was an exalted mood among the masses of the poor of eastern Europe. It was a singing, dancing, worshipping, loving approach to God and the world. It was a mighty Yea-saying. Like all such unpredictable manifestations of the human spirit, it ultimately died down into strange forms and broke up into strange contradictions. But in the days of its first joyous blossoming, a hundred and fifty to two hundred years ago, among the Jewries of Russia and Poland, it was one of those rare illuminations which break from time to time upon the somber surface of human history.

But definitions and descriptions of Chassidism, literary or historical, will not get us very far. One must listen to the Chassidim themselves. And there's the difficulty. They had a language of their own, unintelligible to outsiders. I do not mean that they used a special dialect of Yiddish or of Hebrew. Not at all. Their language was the simplest imaginable. But they infused into their talk—which was of course the mirror of their experience—such a quality of exaltation that the outsider understood all the less precisely because every one of the words was misleadingly familiar to him.

They could not explain themselves to others; their views and feelings had to be transmitted by emotional infection. Therefore it was inevitable that their foremost spokesman to the outside world should not have been one of them. Peretz was not a Chassid. As we already know, he was as far removed from the Chassidim in his beliefs and daily preoccupations as any modern Jew could be; or, let us say, in his conscious beliefs and preoccupations. But it was his peculiar gift to have caught and made accessible to us—to whatever extent it can so be made—the spirit of the Chassidic world. It is of course open to the skeptic to suggest that we have no means of knowing whether what Peretz gives us is really Chassidism. But the alternative is to believe that Peretz created the contents of a whole religious movement—that which no single person has done in the history of the world. (Skepticism often makes big calls on our faith.)

Peretz was not a praying Jew; as we have seen, he could be bitterly rationalist on the subject of prayer. He rarely if ever went to a synagogue, and he certainly never put on prayer-shawl and phylacteries at home—at least, after he left his father's house. But, as we shall see, he transmits the bliss of Chassidic prayer with an intensity that the Chassidim knew only from within. Peretz paid no attention to the dietary laws, and he never made the benediction before eating a piece of fruit or drinking a glass of water—or of brandy. But what the benediction before food and the grace after it meant to a Chassid, he alone makes the non-Chassid understand. Peretz did not use the physical symbols of the ritual, did not wear the woven fringes under his shirt, did not (except perhaps by accident) have a mezuzah on the lintel of his door, did not build a booth for the Feast of Tabernacles. And yet if we who resemble him in these matters want to understand with what intimate joy they were invested for the Chassidim, we shall do best to go to Peretz.

"Look you," says one of his Chassidic characters. "We Chassidim take a drink of brandy, and *they* take a drink of brandy." ("They" in this context are either gentiles or non-believing Jews). "Why do *they* drink? They don't even like it. They pull a face as they pour it down their throats. It's the evil inclination, the Devil's will, that drives them to drink. You can see their souls shrinking from it, their faces wrinkling up. But when *we* take a drink we make the benediction over it and invoke the name of the Blessed One. In fact, we take the drink only for the sake of the benediction. The mention of God's name is the purpose of the drink. And therefore the soul enjoys the drink, and wants to drink.

"*They* are forever proclaiming: 'Happiness! We want happiness! We want to enjoy the good things of this world!' And I tell you that happiness and the good things of life are ours alone. For He is the source of all happiness and of all good things; from Him alone they stream forth."

Another of his Chassidic characters talks of the Rabbi of Nemirov, one of the most exalted figures in their tradition.

"It is known to the whole world that He of Nemirov served the Eternal One in purest joy. Happy is the eye that was privileged to behold the radiance which spread from him and shed its light on all about him. The Jew within range of it forgot the exile, forgot all pain and tribulation; nay, he forgot himself. All the souls were poured into one soul, and that was the soul of Him of Nemirov.

179

"And what shall I say about his singing, and his sacred dances? Words and movements were steeped in the Holy Spirit. And once, in an ecstatic moment, he called out: 'I hereby do proclaim and reveal to mankind that the whole world is nothing more than a singing and a dancing before the Holy One, blessed be He. Every Jew is a singer before Him, and every letter in the Torah is a musical note. Every living soul is a letter of the Torah, wherefore all souls taken together make up the Torah— and souls and Torah are a song to the King of Kings of Kings, the Holy One, blessed be He.'

"Then he went on to say that just as there are many singing voices, so there are many musical instruments; and every melody is suited for some particular musical instrument, which alone can render it; and for every instrument there are particular melodies. For the instrument is the body and the melody is the soul.

"Every man, too, he told us, is a musical instrument, and his life is a melody, a gay or mournful melody. And when the melody has been played out, the soul—that is, the melody—flies out of the body and joins in the great melody before the Throne of Glory.

"And alas for the man, he said, who lives without a melody; for it is like living without a soul. It is no life at all."

The speaker reports further what the Rabbi of Nemirov had to say concerning the formalists and scholars, the Talmudists and men of learning, against whose icy dominion over Jewish life Chassidism was the revolt.

"Such scholars," said He of Nemirov, "whose learning, however great, is only on the surface, are like visitors to a royal palace who are permitted to see its outside, but are forbidden to enter. They have not even the courage to knock at the door, for fear it will not be opened. They see the walls, the windows, the doors, the chimneys, and the banners flying over the roof. Sometimes they see smoke ascending from the chimneys; and sometimes they even catch from afar off the voices of servants passing through the vestibules. . . . But those who let their souls sink into the spirit and meaning of the Torah are like visitors for whom the doors stand open, and they are welcomed into the King's glory."

And again, He of Nemirov likened those dry scholars, those unadmitted visitors about the palace, to workmen who know how to make a musical instrument, or how to mend it, but cannot play on it. "Their hands are often skillful, but their ears are stopped up; and when someone plays the instrument they have made, they cannot hear. Or else their hearts are stopped up; they hear but do not understand. And if there is among them an exceptionally gifted workman who does occasionally put the instrument to his lips, all he can do is imitate someone else's melody.

"I," added He of Nemirov, "am no scholar; that is, no workman. I cannot make an instrument nor mend one. But, God be thanked, I can play on all of them."

Now, concerning the "inwardness" of prayer among Chassidim, which is like the inwardness of the Torah, another Chassid described a great experience. He does not mention the name of the Chassidic Rabbi who was at the center of it; it may have been He of Nemirov; it may have been another. Nor do I know whether Peretz invented the incident or whether he found it in the tradition.

"Joy within joy" he calls the experience—a special visitation of ecstasy. It was connected with the services of the New Year—the time of the annual accounting and judgment of mortals in heaven. "And as you know," he reminds us, "we Chassidim make a happy occasion of it. We aren't like the other Jews, the Misnagdim, who are terrified by the approaching judgment. We know that we are not being haled before a foreign potentate. It is our own Father in heaven who is going to judge us; and so, after prayers, we take a couple of glasses of brandy, and we dance."

But on this New Year of which he tells, something quite out of the ordinary happened and made it the most memorable New Year in the annals of that Chassidic group.

The Rabbi stood before the congregation, leading it in prayer. And what a prayer-leader he was! All day long his voice poured out supplication and praise; for on the New Year he permitted no one to take his place. And who would have wanted to? Who would have dared? As he stood there, the messenger of Israel to the Throne, his voice was like a pathway from earth to heaven. It stretched from prayer to prayer, broad and unbroken, bearing the hopes of his people.

And then, suddenly, a dreadful pause, a break. He had reached the prayer that begins: "To God who prepareth judgment." The words rang out clearly. But those which followed: "To Him that searcheth hearts, to Him that uncovereth the deeps," were uttered uncertainly. And when he came to the words: "To Him that buyeth His slaves in the day of judgment," his voice broke completely, and a frightful silence followed.

One second, two seconds, three—and every second an eternity. Terror spreads through the congregation; up in the gallery women fall down, fainting.

And then the Rabbi comes to. A shudder passes through his body, and the tense and terrified silence is broken by a joyous cry: "Who taketh mercy on His people on the day of judgment." And the Rabbi prolongs the words in happy turns and roulades, while his feet begin to move, as of themselves, in a jubilant dance. And the rest of the morning prayers continue with renewed strength.

Between the first and the second morning prayers the Rabbi explained what had happened. A very trifling matter, you would imagine; but wait.

As we know, when a man reads from the prayer-book, the eyes run ahead of the lips. The lips say "uncovereth the deeps," the eyes are already at "buyeth His slaves in the day of judgment." And thus it happened with the Rabbi that morning of the New Year service. But there and then it occurred to him that the words made no sense! He simply did not understand them, had never understood them. What possible interpretation could one put upon these words, which declared that "God bought His slaves in the day of judgment?" And in the utter confusion of that moment the Rabbi suspended his prayer and became silent.

As you may well imagine, the break was noted at once in the Upper Circles. Our Rabbi's prayer suspended! A calamity! Not to be endured! Immediately the decision was made to reveal to him, in a vision, the meaning of the words, so that he might continue with the prayer.

And as the Rabbi closed his eyes in perplexity, the heavens were cleft before him. This is what he saw:

The chamber of the heavenly court. It is still empty. The prosecuting attorney, counsel for the defense, the judges, all are yet to arrive. The Rabbi looks around. The chamber has five doors: one in the right wall, with the sign: "Counsel for the Defense"; one in the left wall: "Prosecuting Attorney"; three doors at the back, in the eastern wall, and in front of them the table and the scales. The middle door at the back, which is closed, bears the legend: "Hosts of the Blessed"; the other two doors at the back are open. Through the one on the right the Rabbi sees the garden plots of paradise. There the Patriarchs and the sainted ones are seated, steeped in the effulgence of the Divine Light, studying the Torah. Their crowned heads are bent over the sacred texts: for them there is no judgment day. Through the door to the left the Rabbi sees the labyrinths of hell. Hell is empty and silent; on a holy day the souls in hell are given respite, there is no torment and no punishment. The fires still burn—it is "the everlasting fire which shall not be extinguished"—but the demons are occupied with a special task.

And now the door in the right wall opens, and counsel for the defense enters, carrying under his arm the records of the good deeds of mankind for the past year. Alas, a very small sheaf. A poor year it has been for good deeds. Counsel for the defense observes that the door opposite is still closed. A bad sign, that. It is taking them too long to collect *their* records. The harvest of mankind's misdeeds fills the granaries of hell. Counsel for the defense drops into a seat and closes his eyes sadly.

The door in the left wall opens, and two demons enter, staggering under the load of the first bundle. The Rabbi hears their bones creaking under the burden. They throw down the bundle and sing out loudly: "That isn't even a tithe of the harvest. The demons are still collecting— whole treasuries are yet to come."

Counsel for the defense covers his face and groans. He apparently feels that no one hears him. The court is not yet assembled, the residents of paradise are busy with the Torah, hell is empty.

Counsel for the defense is mistaken! Among the residents of paradise there is the beloved, the unforgettable Chassidic Rabbi Reb Levi Yitzchok of Berdichev, the Compassionate One. *He* hears the groan of anguish that bursts from the lips of counsel for the defense. He alone among the children of bliss has not forgotten those who dwell in darkness and the shadow of death; he alone remembers that for *them,* on earth below, there is still a judgment day. And if someone groans in heaven, it is undoubtedly for them. Reb Levi Yitzchok interrupts his studies, looks up, and through the open door perceives the crushed figure of counsel for the defense.

Levi Yitzchok of Berdichev, tenderest of all Jews, most vigilant in defense of his sinful people, rebuker of the Almighty for His severity toward mortals, Levi Yitzchok of Berdichev steals into the chamber and understands at once what is toward: he sees the slender sheaf under counsel's arm, the vast bundle on the table. It takes Reb Levi Yitzchok just one instant to decide. He bends down and, straining himself to the utmost, picks up the bundle of adverse records; he flings it through the door at the left, down into the flames of hell.

Again two demons enter, bent double under a load of records. The moment they leave, Reb Levi Yitzchok deals with this bundle as he dealt with the first. And so with the third and the fourth and the rest.

Finally it is the Ashmedai himself, Asmodeus, the Devil and prosecuting attorney, who enters, a broad grin on his face. What is this? Help! The records! Not a sign of that opulent harvest. He looks around, sees the last bundle burning in hell; looks around again, and sees Reb Levi Yitzchok sneaking back toward paradise. He runs over, grabs him by the arm, and yells:

"Stop, thief!"

The cry resounds through all the seven heavens. Patriarchs and saints start up from their studies and rush into the chamber. The center door at the back opens and the members of the court file in. Counsel for the defense starts up.

"What is it?"

Before this heavenly assembly the Devil declares how he caught Reb Levi Yitzchok red-handed. He points to the fires of hell, where the last bundle—it was the heaviest of all—is still smoldering.

Truth is truth! Reb Levi Yitzchok confesses. Justice is justice! The Devil is asked what sentence he demands. He too decides on the instant. He quotes the Scriptures—he would!—"The thief shall be sold for his theft." Let Reb Levi Yitzchok be sold as a slave publicly, to the highest bidder. The Devil will of course join in the bidding. And no matter what it costs him, he intimates, he will find it worth his while.

This is the law, and there is no appeal from it. Let the auction begin!

So they stand facing one another, the Devil on one side, the children of bliss on the other, Reb Levi Yitzchok between them. The members of the court take their seats; the bidding opens.

Father Abraham makes his offer: his heavenly credit for the priceless gem of the Covenant, the first Jewish commandment; and he adds as bonus his credits for his famous hospitality. After him comes Isaac, whose contribution is almost as large: the credits for his readiness to be sacrificed on the altar by his father. Jacob follows: his possessions are his simplicity, his devotion to learning in the days when his brutish brother Esau went hunting in the fields. Then comes Rachel, with *her* special distinction, the love-mandrakes; and after her the other Matriarchs, each contributing her own glory. And row upon row the saints follow, each putting up, for the purchase of Reb Levi Yitzchok, whatever reward he had garnered during his sojourn on earth.

But it is the Devil himself against whom they are bidding, and he has treasures beyond computation. For every addition to the right scale he throws a corresponding price into the left scale. He ransacks the earth, brings out forgotten wealth from beyond the hills of darkness, till the eyes are dazzled by the display. The saints have exhausted their stocks, the two scales stand level, and in a last flourish the Devil takes the crown off his head and flings it into the auction. He must have Reb Levi Yitzchok at any price. The scale on the left begins to sink; it falls lower, lower.

Counsel for the defense advances and throws in on the right the meager records of the year's good deeds. In vain. They are not substantial enough to arrest the downward flight of the scale on the left.

A crooked and vindictive grin spreads over the Devil's lips, and triumph flickers in his eyes. Oh, what a catch, what a haul, what a victory for hell! Reb Levi Yitzchok of Berdichev, perhaps the most glorious figure in the Chassidic world after the founder himself, the Master of the Name! Before the scale has touched bottom the Devil places a hand on Reb Levi Yitzchok's shoulder and points significantly to the door on the left, the door opening on hell. "This way, please."

Horror runs through the ranks of the blessed. What! Reb Levi Yitzchok lost? It cannot be! And yet—what is to be done?

The horror and confusion increase—until they are suddenly stilled by a Voice. It is the Voice from the Throne of Glory.

"*I* buy him!"

And again through the deathly silence: "I raise the bid! 'For Mine is the earth and the fullness thereof'—and I give the whole world for Reb Levi Yitzchok."

The Devil's face became black as thunder.

Gleefully the Chassid finishes the story:

187

"That's what the Rabbi told us in the pause between first and second prayers that New Year's morning. And you, you non-Chassidim, you Misnagdim, you unbelievers, can you understand what happiness was ours that New Year?

"First, there was the record of our sins destroyed—which means a happy and prosperous New Year as good as in our pockets. Second, Reb Levi Yitzchok redeemed. And third, to top it all, and best of all, the secret of a text at last revealed. 'To Him that buyeth His slaves in the day of judgment!' "

That was the "inwardness" of prayer among Chassidim, an intimacy of communion between man and God that made the word *Father* literal. It was part of the general mystic self-identification with divinity which Chassidism revived and popularized from the esoteric doctrines of the kabbalists, extending to the simple masses what had been the privilege of the spiritual elite.

As Chassidism grew older and developed its careerist rabbis, its wonder-workers and dynasties, it also developed its sects. The followers of Shnayur Zalman of Ladi, at the beginning of the nineteenth century, were thinkers, scholars, and ascetics. Shnayur Zalman was by intellectual equipment much closer to the Gaon of Vilna—who turned him from his door, or rather refused to open it to him—than to the founder of Chassidism. And again, the followers of the Rabbi of Kotzk did not hold with prayer; they were more for study as the expression of man's relation to the Divinity. But the original strain of Chassidism, surviving in the bulk of the movement till the present day, was interpenetrated with the ecstatic experience; for the classic Chassid prayer was the most difficult of human exercises—the deliberate daily renewal of inspiration.

188

Peretz gives us a story of the Baal Shem—the founder of Chassidism—at a seder ceremony, and puts into his mouth (though the story and explanation are of Peretz's invention) a typical Chassidic exposition of prayer.

The Baal Shem wanted his listeners to understand in what manner prayers mounted from earth to the Heavenly Throne. Not all prayers proceeded straightway to their destination, he said. The rates of ascent differed. A's prayer, offered long after B's, might register long before. It depended on the purity of the prayer. Prayer, said the Baal Shem, consists of body and soul; the words are the body, the intent is the soul. The more soul or spirituality a prayer possesses, the straighter is its upward path. But if a prayer is deficient in these lightening elements, it meanders, it rolls about, it is pushed hither and thither by the winds, it is swallowed up by fogs, drenched by rains, perhaps even forced downward, to become tangled in the growths of jungles. In the end it reaches heaven; it must, for the letters of the Hebrew words are sacred, they are of heavenly origin, and all things must return to their origin. Sooner or later, then, the prayer comes home. Thus it comes about that although Jews pray at stated hours of the day, and for longer stretches during certain days of the year, the arrival of prayers in heaven is continuous, and not intermittent. That is the meaning of the verse: "The Guardian of Israel neither slumbereth nor sleepeth." Compassion forbids that He should not always be alert to the arrival of a prayer.

Now, it sometimes happens, the Baal Shem went on, that a Jew will be standing up during the solemn prayer of the Eighteen Benedictions, murmuring the words, but thinking all the time of his purchases of grain. That prayer, God help us, is then loaded down with sacks of wheat and other gross earthly things. A prayer so handicapped may well wander about in the wilds of space for a hundred years or more before it shakes itself free of its burden and makes the ascent. Meanwhile the man has died! He is called to trial. The prosecuting attorney piles his evil deeds on the left-hand scale, counsel for the defense stands there empty-handed. "But God Almighty," screams the Jew, "where are my prayers, at least? I know I prayed." Alas, his prayers have not even started their ascent. And the court, to vindicate its reputation for justice, opens a window and lets the man look down. Far away on the earth below, somewhere in a farmyard, he sees his wretched prayers still struggling to get out from under the weight of the sacks.

As to what happens to this unhappy man until his prayers arrive, we will say nothing.

CHAPTER XIII

"And Even Beyond"

✿

THERE are some contradictions in the accounts of the Rabbi of Nemirov, illustrious pillar of Chassidism. We are told in one place, for instance, that "He of Nemirov served the Eternal in purest joy." But elsewhere we learn that he was not a stranger to sorrow and heaviness of heart; as, for instance, in the story of the Rabbi and the skeptical Litvak, which Peretz calls "And Even Beyond."

But before you listen to the story you must learn what a Litvak is, or rather what Litvaks are. You may think you know. "Litvaks," you answer, "are Lithuanian Jews." Right enough. But what are Litvaks, or what were they, in the eyes of Chassidim? The Lithuanian Jews were from the beginning the core of the opposition to popular Chassidism. The mighty Gaon (Master) of Vilna, the man with the universal mind, placed the Chassidim under a ban. How else could it be, since Vilna, the Jerusalem of Lithuania, was the very center of Jewish scholarship in those days, and learned Litvaks looked with contempt, derision, and horror on the corybantic Judaism of the Chassidim? A religion for ignoramuses, draymen, unlettered cobblers, charlatans—not a religion at all, but an impudent defiance of the masters of the Talmud, a rejection of the very foundations of Judaism, which are of the intellect, a movement of enthusiasts (the word is used in the eight-eenth-century sense, which had a suggestion of goofiness), next door to apostasy, and reminiscent of Sabbathai Zevi, may his name and memory be blotted out.

The Chassidim, of course, retorted in kind. To them the Litvaks were death's-heads, skull and crossbones, cas-uists, intellectual exhibitionists, verbal prestidigitators, dry-hearted, small-spirited, ingenious manipulators of Talmudic texts. They were learned enough, in their way, no one could deny that. But they were the visitors who were not admitted to the King's palace. Rational and pe-dantic, they knew only such truths—if such truths there be—as can be demonstrated black on white, deduced from the Talmud and its commentaries, which of course they knew by heart. But of the truths of the heart—and per-haps these are the only truths—they knew nothing. In short, they illustrated the difference between "knowing by heart" and "knowing with the heart."

And now to our story.

It was a habit with Him of Nemirov to disappear on the mornings of the Penitential Days—the days between the New Year and the Day of Atonement. He was no-where to be found; neither in the synagogue, nor in either of the two Study Houses of Nemirov, nor in any group of worshippers assembled before dawn for the special Peni-tential prayers. And of course he was not at home; the door stood wide open, people looked in—no Rabbi of Nemirov.

But where could the Rabbi be? Ridiculous question! In heaven, of course. At such a time, when the year's des-tinies were being sealed for millions and millions of Jews, when hearts were atremble in every Jewish home, do you think that the Rabbi of Nemirov could do less than mount to heaven and attend in person to the wants of his people?

So much to be asked for! Health and livelihood and peace, good matches for marriageable daughters, freedom from Satan and temptation and evil deeds—and forgiveness for the past. And up there, in the heavenly court, the Devil, the accuser, the prosecuting attorney was as busy as —well, as busy as the devil himself—lodging complaints, demanding punishment, parading before the tribunal all the sins and misdemeanors of the Jewish people. Where, we ask, could the Rabbi of Nemirov be if not up there, defending his people?

Now, a Litvak once came to town during a Penitential period; and when he heard that the Rabbi of Nemirov went up to heaven every morning he laughed. And being a Litvak, he at once showed you a verse in the Talmud which said that even Moses our teacher never went up to heaven. No, not even at Sinai. Moses, said the verse, was only permitted to approach within ten handbreadths of the floor of heaven. There's the text! Go and argue with a Litvak.

"All right, Mr. Litvak, where does the Rabbi disappear to?"

"No business of mine," he answers, and shrugs his shoulders. But, as you'll see in a moment, he did make it his business. Those Litvaks!

For that same night, immediately after prayers, he stole into the Rabbi's house, and into the Rabbi's room (the nerve of a Litvak!), and hid himself under the bed. *He* was going to find out, once for all, where the Rabbi disappeared to on the mornings of the Penitential Days.

Anyone else, you may be sure, would have fallen asleep and missed the moment. Not a Litvak, though. He had a trick: he kept awake by repeating from memory a whole Tractate of the Talmud, on the Law of Damages, or the Law of Vows, or God knows what.

193

Before dawn he heard the beadle in the street, going from door to door waking the Jews for the Penitential prayers. The Rabbi had been awake for some time—perhaps a whole hour; and the Litvak heard him sighing.

Only he who has heard the Rabbi of Nemirov sighing over the fate of his people knows how much heartbreak, how much anguish there can be in a human sigh. It made your heart run out of you like water. That is, unless you were a Litvak and had a heart of iron. He lay there and listened—he under the bed, the Rabbi on the bed. Litvaks!

Then he heard the people in the house getting up; he heard voices and footsteps, the pouring of water over hands, the murmur of first prayers, the closing of doors. Then again silence and darkness, except for the sighing of the Rabbi and the glimmer of the moon at the window.

Long afterwards the Litvak confessed that when he found himself alone in the house with the Rabbi of Nemirov, his flesh broke into goose pimples, and the roots of his earlocks pricked at his temples like needles. I should think they would! If you offered me all the wealth of King Solomon I wouldn't face that combination for one second: the Penitential Days; darkness before dawn; a lonely house; the Rabbi of Nemirov. But then, I'm not a Litvak. He lay there, quivering like a fish on the hook, and didn't die.

Finally our Rabbi, God bless him, got out of the bed. He said the awakening prayer, poured water over his hands, and dried them. Then he went over to the clothes closet and took out a bundle, which he unwrapped. The Litvak, peering out from under the bed, saw to his stupefaction a peasant's smock, coarse linen trousers, a sheepskin coat, a pair of big boots, a blouse, a heavy fur cap. These the Rabbi unwrapped and put on. From the pocket of the coat protruded the end of a rope. Having dressed, the Rabbi left the room and went into the kitchen. There he picked up an ax and stuck it into his belt. Then he left the house.

The Litvak followed, still trembling like a fish, but still as obstinate as a Litvak. Outside, in the blue darkness, the spirit of the Penitential Days brooded over the sleeping streets. Here and there the moan of a sick person floats into the night; here and there the silence is broken by the tormented voices of Jews at their Penitential prayers. The Rabbi stole along swiftly, keeping close to the walls; the Litvak followed. They swam out of darkness into moonlight, out of moonlight into darkness. Louder than the footsteps of the Rabbi the Litvak heard his own heartbeats. And thus they went on till the last street was behind them.

Just outside the townlet there was a little forest. The Rabbi, God bless him, plunged straight into it and made for a young tree some thirty or forty paces from the road. And then, to the utter amazement of the Litvak, he drew out the ax from his belt and began to cut the tree down. Stroke after stroke it went, until the tree yielded and fell. Then the Rabbi chopped the trunk into logs, the logs into faggots. Finally he gathered up the faggots, tied them into a bundle with the rope which he took from his pocket, threw the bundle over his shoulder, stuck the ax again in his belt, and turned back to the townlet. The Litvak followed.

At a dilapidated hut in a wretched alley the Rabbi stopped and knocked at a window.

"Who's there?" asked a sick woman's voice.

"I," answered the Rabbi in peasant Russian.

"Who are you?"

"Vassili."

"Which Vassili, and what do you want?"

"Vassili the wood-gatherer. I've got firewood—very cheap." And without waiting for an answer, the Rabbi stepped into the hut.

The Litvak too slipped in and saw, by the dim, gray beginnings of the morning, a poverty-stricken room, a few wretched sticks of furniture, and a bed on which a woman lay, wrapped in rags.

"Firewood?" she said bitterly. "Cheap? What shall I buy it with? A widow, sick and penniless."

"I'll trust you," said the Rabbi, still in Russian. "Only three kopecks."

"And where will I ever get the money to pay back?"

"Foolish one," answered the Rabbi, "you're poor and sick, and yet I'm willing to trust you. I know you'll pay me some day. You have a mighty God in heaven, and you won't trust Him—not even for three kopecks."

"And who'll light the fire for me?" whispered the woman. "I haven't the strength for it, and my son hasn't come back from work yet."

"I'll light it," said the Rabbi.

And as he stuffed the faggots into the stove, the Rabbi began to murmur the first of the Penitential prayers. When he applied the tinder to the faggots, he reached the second prayer. And by the time the fire was crackling cheerfully, he finished the third. Then he closed the stove and withdrew.

The Litvak who had witnessed all this became one of the Chassidim of Nemirov. And thereafter, whenever a fellow Chassid said in his hearing that on the mornings of the Penitential Days the Rabbi of Nemirov ascended regularly as high as heaven, the Litvak no longer laughed. He only added quietly: "And even beyond."

CHAPTER XIV

At Home with the Almighty

❀

I N THE Chassidic view, goodness is not a duty and a discipline; it is, on the contrary, the gayest form of self-fulfillment; it is life at its jolliest. And "to love God" is to have a good time. According to Chassidic doctrine—which is not doctrine at all, since there is no Chassidic catechism, any more than there is a Jewish—wickedness produces sadness, and sadness is a sign of wickedness. So formulated, Chassidic tradition is neither new nor interesting. It all depends on the life-mode in which it is incorporated. It depends on who says it, and how he says it.

When Dante thunders against *accidie,* or heart-heaviness, as a deadly sin, all he does is give us a sinking feeling at the stomach. Never was there gloomier exhortation to gaiety or a more depressing commendation of cheerfulness. Or, to take an altogether different instance, Spinoza's highly tenuous "intellectual love of God." There is something very real in the love of mathematical abstractions, and the simplest people have some experience of it—witness the universal popularity of arithmetical puzzles. But this complete intellectual self-identification with the universe—at least, as far as I can glimpse it in Spinoza—has little to do with the heart. "God-intoxicated," Goethe called him; to which we can only say: "a *Yiddisher shikor*"

—a Jewish drunkard—a mere theorist of drink. To talk of "love of God" as a principle brings us no nearer to an understanding of Chassidism; it is the style, the legends, and the folklore that give the phenomenon its character.

A story is told about a gay little Chassid who came home from synagogue one Friday evening in a mood of unusual religious merriment. The melodies of the service still ringing in his heart, the Sabbath spirit in the home, the candles on the table—illumination and sanctity—were almost too much for him. He greeted his wife and children, and something in him overflowed. He strode to the table, lifted up his eyes to heaven, and cried out: "Almighty Father! Do you think I am frightened of You and Your power, Your laws and commandments and prohibitions? Not a bit of it! Here!" And bending down, he blew out the Sabbath candles! Desecration of desecrations! It is a mortal sin to kindle or extinguish any fire on the Sabbath. To direct this sin against the Sabbath candles themselves is to pile a Pelion of sacrilege on an Ossa of blasphemy. It is equivalent to spitting on the host and eating pork on Yom Kippur. The little Chassid, his face irradiated, straightened up, lifted his arms to heaven again, and exclaimed jubilantly: "But, Lord of the world, I'm just crazy about You!"

They were at home with the Almighty to an astonishing degree, and interpreted His immanence not only literally but very personally. Omnipotent He was, ubiquitous, everlasting from the past into the future—He was all of that; but one thing He was not, standoffish. You could run to Him, talk your heart out to Him, argue with Him, bargain with Him (had not Abraham himself set the example 'way back?), and, in the heat of an argument, even tell Him where He gets off. Now Reb Levi Yitzchok

198

of Berdichev, the Compassionate One, whom I have already mentioned several times, was a great hand at having it out with God Almighty. Of Reb Levi Yitzchok Peretz tells us the following story.

It was the eve of the Day of Atonement in the synagogue of Berdichev. The skies were dimming outside, the tall white candles blazed within. The preliminary prayer had been uttered, it was time for Reb Levi Yitzchok to open the diapason of the *Kol Nidre*. And Reb Levi Yitzchok stood there silent.

All eyes were fixed on him as he stood in his prayer-shawl and faced the Ark, his back to the congregants. Not a whisper was heard from the men below or from the women in the gallery above. They waited. Perhaps Reb Levi Yitzchok would introduce the prayer with a few words in homely Yiddish, as he sometimes did, addressing himself to the Almighty in a friendly, brotherly way, outside the stately choreography of the Aramaic.

But Reb Levi Yitzchok was silent. Not a syllable; no motion. What could it mean? Were the gates of prayer still closed? And even if they were, was not Reb Levi Yitzchok capable of knocking at them? No sound, no gesture. He only stood there with his head slightly cocked, as if he were listening to something or for something from above. Was he listening for the sound of the turning key?

Then suddenly Reb Levi Yitzchok turned round and called: "Beadle!"

The beadle came running up, and Reb Levi Yitzchok asked: "Is Berel the tailor already here?"

The congregation could not trust its ears. The beadle stammered that he did not know whether Berel the tailor was in the synagogue. Everyone looked around; Reb Levi Yitzchok too looked. "No, he's not here," he said at last.

"He's stayed home. Beadle! Go to the house of Berel the tailor and tell him to come here. Tell him that I, Levi Yitzchok, the teacher of this congregation, call him."

Berel the tailor lived in the synagogue alley. It took but a minute to bring him. He was wearing his workday clothes; he had neither prayer-shawl nor prayer-robe. There was a queer expression on his face, half anger, half fear. He addressed himself to Reb Levi Yitzchok:

"Rabbi, you sent for me. I've come to *you.*"

Reb Levi Yitzchok smiled.

"Tell me, my dear, good Berel, why all the excitement about you up there?"—and he indicated the heavens. "The hosts of the blessed don't stop talking about you for a moment. What have you been up to? Wherever I listen it's 'Berel the tailor' and 'Berel the tailor' and 'Berel the tailor.' "

"Aha!" exclaimed Berel triumphantly.

"Have you got some sort of complaint?"

"I should say I have!"

"Against whom?"

"Against the Lord of the world," answered Berel.

The congregation was stupefied. They were ready to fall upon Berel and tear him limb from limb. But the smile on Reb Levi Yitzchok's lips only became broader as he said: "Wouldn't you like to tell us what it is?"

"Certainly," said Berel. "What's more, I'm ready to let you arbitrate the matter. Shall I go on?"

"Speak!"

"Rabbi," began Berel, "last year, all summer long I was, God save you from it, without a stitch of work. Neither Jew nor gentile crossed my threshold. I could have stretched myself out on the floor and died with my tongue hanging out."

"Now, now," said Reb Levi Yitzchok in gentle reproof.

"Are you forgetting that you live with the children of Abraham, Isaac, and Jacob, merciful children of merciful fathers? You had but to speak up."

"Not I, Rabbi! I'm not the man to speak, and not the man to take charity from my fellow men. My portion in the Lord of the world is as good as anyone else's. I'll tell you what I did. I sent my daughter out of the village to take service in the city. And I waited and waited and waited at home, to see what our Father in heaven would do.

"A couple of days before Tabernacles the door opens! Oho—He has bethought himself of me. Who should come in but the special messenger of the Baron? What is it? The Baron wants a fur-coat relining.

"All's well again! He that gives life gives bread. I'm conducted to the castle, led into a private room, given the fur coat and a number of fox pelts. But those pelts! You should have seen them, Rabbi. Gems! Beauties! From the very homeland of the foxes."

The congregation was still waiting for *Kol Nidre*. The Rabbi prodded Berel:

"So you relined the coat, did your work honestly—and then?"

"And then? Why then, Rabbi, something unexpected happened—three little pelts were left over."

"And you took them?"

"Not so fast, Rabbi. It's easier said than done. When you leave the castle, there's a lodge. In the lodge there's a guard. If he has the slightest suspicion, he searches you, strips you, takes your boots off. And if he finds anything on you, God forbid, the Baron has dogs, the Baron has whips."

"What did you do?"

"What did I do? It's not for nothing that I'm Berel the

tailor. The first thing I did was to go into the kitchen and ask for a loaf of bread."

"Berel! The bread of idolaters!"

"Rabbi, I wasn't going to eat it, God forbid! I got the loaf—a big one. I went back into the private room, made a cut in the loaf, and scooped out the insides. I kneaded the soft bread in my hands until I got the sweat all worked in. Then I threw the bread to the dog in the room, and he gobbled it up. Dogs like human sweat. Then I put the three fox pelts inside the loaf and went on my way.

"At the lodge the guard stopped me. 'Hey, Jewman, what's that under your arm?' I show him: 'A loaf.' And so I got out of the castle grounds, and as soon as I was out of sight of the castle I turned off the road and went across the fields through the cornstalks—a short cut. And I skipped along, singing. Three lovely little fox pelts. I'd get me a lovely palm branch for Tabernacles, and a lovely citron. All my own! I wouldn't have to wait my turn to use the community citron. I wouldn't have to borrow. Such beautiful little pelts!

"Then all of a sudden I felt the earth drumming under my feet, and I knew at once what it meant. A horseman at full gallop, the Baron's rider from the castle. My mother's milk grew cold in me. They'd counted the pelts, examined the coat. . . . There was no sense in taking to my heels; a horseman, and one of the Baron's horses. The first thing I did was to throw away the loaf, among the cornstalks. Then I made a marker, a very clear one, no way of mistaking it. And then I waited. Not for long.

" 'Berko! Hey, Berko!'

"The Baron's little Cossack, right enough. I'd know his voice a mile away. My insides were all atremble, my heart went up into my throat. But Berel the tailor doesn't give himself away so easy. I turned round cool-like. You wouldn't have suspected a thing. And, Rabbi, all that fright was for nothing! I'd forgotten to sew a hanger on the coat! So I got on the horse, behind the Cossack, and thanked God in my heart. I sewed that hanger on, left the castle a second time, came back to my marker—there was no mistaking it. The loaf was gone.

"It was a long time after the harvest. Not a soul would pass this way. The birds couldn't have made off with it. So I knew at once who was at the bottom of it."

"Who?" asked Reb Levi Yitzchok.

"He," answered Berel the tailor, and pointed heavenward. "The Lord of the world. His doing it was, and no one else's. And of course I understood why. He, the great Lord, the mighty Master, did not want His slave, Berel the tailor, to take left-overs."

"Naturally," said Reb Levi Yitzchok in a gentle voice. "That's the law, as everyone knows. A tailor mustn't take the left-overs after a job. The law is very clear on that point."

"Law shmaw!" answered Berel hotly. "The Lord of the world knows as well as I do that custom is stronger than law. What's more," he added, "I didn't invent the custom of left-overs. It's older than any man can remember. And if the Lord of the world, that high and mighty Prince, doesn't want His humble servant, His slave, Berel, who's been serving Him all his life, to take tailor's left-overs, then it's His business to provide me with a livelihood. Isn't a prince responsible for his servant's keep? What's the idea? Neither my keep nor left-overs? No, sir. That I won't stand for.

"And therefore I decided to leave the service of the Almighty. And I've taken a vow on it. I'm through."

There was a growl from the congregation. Hands were lifted, bodies surged forward. Reb Levi Yitzchok cast one glance at the congregation. "Silence!" And turning to Berel he asked gently:

"And then what happened?"

"Why, nothing! Nothing at all. I came home that day, I refused to wash. My old woman started to ask the meaning of it. 'Out of the room!' I yelled. I went to bed—I refused to say the night prayers. My lips began to move of themselves; I bit them. In the morning, no prayer again, no washing of hands, no prayer-shawl, no phylacteries. 'Eats!' That's all I said to the old woman. She ran out of the house, to her father's, in the next village. So what? So I'll do without a wife. In fact, it was better that way. After all, I'm Berel the tailor, and she's nothing but a weak female. I don't want her mixed up in this business. And so I went on. Tabernacles came: no tabernacle for me, no palm branch, no citron. No holy days for me, no Sabbaths, no benedictions. Not even when I take a drop of whisky. At the time of the Rejoicing of the Law I put on sackcloth, like Mordecai in the Book of Esther. I'll show Him!

"The weeks passed, the months passed, and the Penitential Days came round, and there was a kind of tugging at my heart. The beadle makes the rounds before dawn, waking Jews to prayer; I want to go along—but I'm Berel the tailor. I'm a man of my word. And then the New Year —I don't budge. You can hear the blowing of the shofar all over town—I stuff up my ears with cotton. It wasn't easy, Rabbi; I felt myself being torn apart. . . . And I hated myself, I was sick of myself, unwashed, impure. There was a mirror on the wall; I turned it round, didn't want to see my ugly face. I heard the people going to the river to cast out their sins—I stayed put."

Berel the tailor was silent a moment and then cried out suddenly:

"But I'm right, Rabbi, I'm right. I won't take back a word."

Reb Levi Yitzchok meditated awhile, then asked: "Well, what is it you want, Berel? A livelihood?"

Berel was offended. "Livelihood nothing! He should have given me that before. Everyone's entitled to a livelihood. Even the bird in the air, and the worm in the earth. A livelihood is just a servant's keep. I, Berel the tailor, want more than that."

"Speak, Berel, what do you want?"

Berel paused. "Rabbi," he asked, "on the Day of Atonement those sins are forgiven which man has committed against his Maker; isn't that so?"

"Yes, Berel."

"But not those sins which man has committed against his fellow men?"

"No, Berel."

Berel the tailor drew himself up like a soldier on parade and declared: "I will not withdraw my vow, I will not re-enter His service, until He will declare that this year, for my sake, He will also forgive the sins of man against his fellow men. Am I right, Rabbi?"

"Absolutely," answered Reb Levi Yitzchok. "What's more, I advise you to stand firm on that point. You can't lose."

Then Reb Levi Yitzchok turned back to the Ark, looked up, listened awhile, and turned back to Berel with the report.

"Berel, you've won! Go home and get your prayer-robe and your prayer-shawl."

Many years later Peretz wrote a little pendant to this incident and called it: "A Man Has to *Davven*, Hasn't He?"

Davven is the Yiddish word for "pray." Its origin is obscure. Some connect it with "dawn" because the first thing a Jew does on waking is to wash his hands and utter a prayer. Others trace it to the Persian *divan*, "council." In any case, "pray" is the only possible English rendition, and it is misleading. When a Jew *davvens* he is undoubtedly saying his prayers; he is also communing; he is also performing a social function—even when he is alone. Anyone who has *davvened* with genuinely pious Jews knows, moreover, that *davvening* may be conducted attentively on two levels. On one, the words of the prayer guide the attention of the worshipper; he follows the meaning and puts his heart into it. On the other level, the mood of the prayer, or rather of the occasion, takes the lead. The individual words are then transcended, their meaning is of no importance, the utterance of the lips is as it were a genuflexion that accompanies the devotion of the soul.

Sometimes you will hear a worshipper gabble off the words: "BLESSEDaretheythatdwellinThyhousetheyshallpraiseTheeforeverselah!" He begins with a shout and trails off into a subdued drumfire of amazingly precise syllabification, right to the end of the psalm, coming up now and again with an occasional outburst of intelligibility, or pausing here and there for a roulade. You would swear that the man's mind is not on the words—and it is not. Then you would add that his prayer is perfunctory, and you would more often than not be quite wrong. His soul is in the posture of prayer; he may be in the mood of supplication, of adoration, or of humility; he is using the occasion of the common gesture for a private experience; the familiar syllabic exercise is a kind of hypnotic induction. *Davvening* is therefore the periodic contact with the religious emotion rather than the formal act of prayer.

And the religious emotion is a daily necessity to the pious Jew.

Berel the tailor reappears in the pendant I have mentioned. He now has a grown-up son who has taken his medical degree, and who returns to his native townlet, after a long absence, one Friday afternoon.

On the Sabbath morning Berel naturally proposes that his son accompany him to the synagogue, to *davven*.

"Father, I shan't go," answers the new doctor.

"What is it, son? Are you ashamed to be seen with me?"

"God forbid, Father! What an idea!"

"Is it because you're a doctor, and a doctor isn't supposed to pray to God or praise Him?"

"No, that isn't it, Father."

"What is it, then?"

"All right, I'll tell you."

The old man puts down his prayer-shawl and takes a seat. The young man begins to expound.

"Father, I want you to imagine that you're a rich man; so rich that a few rubles more or less don't mean anything to you."

The father sighs heavily. To see his son through college he had spent the last of his savings, sold the roof over his head, gone into lodgings.

"All right, I'll imagine."

"You're rich, and opposite you lives a poor widow, a poor, sick widow; maybe with a lot of children; and she needs help. What would you do?"

"Help her, of course."

"Would you wait for her to come and beg, would you wait for her to fall weeping at your feet?"

"What on earth for? As long as I know. . . ."

"Well, is God better or worse than you?"

"What kind of question is that?"

"Well!" crows the son triumphantly. "If God is better than you, and He knows of Himself what poor, sick, weak people need, do you think He's going to wait to be asked?"

"M-m-m, yes, but still—"

"You mean about praising Him?"

"If you like."

"Now, Father, how would you like it if someone were to stand up in front of you and start praising you to your face: a fine tailor, a wonderful tailor, an honest tailor. Oh, what a tailor! The true tailor! The only tailor!"

"It would make me sick, of course," said the old man impatiently.

"And why is that? Because you are not foolish, to take pleasure in foolish praise. And you're only a poor human being, who can be harmed by blame and helped by praise."

"Yes, but—"

"No buts, Father! No buts! God is wiser than we; do you think He needs our praise? Do you think He wants you to stand up three times daily and tell Him to His face: Oh, good tailor! Oh, wonderful tailor!"

"What are you talking about?"

"I mean: O good God, O wonderful God, Creator of heaven and earth. . . . Doesn't He know it better than you?"

The old man sank into meditation, then suddenly started up.

"You're right!" he exclaimed. "Absolutely right! But a Jew has to *davven*, hasn't he?"

||||||||||||||||||||||||||||||||||||||||||||||||||||||||||||||||||||||||||||||||||||||||||||||||||||||||

CHAPTER XV

Beyond Justice

❀

||||||||||||||||||||||||||||||||||||||||||||||||||||||||||||||||||||||||||||||||||||||||||||||||||||||||

Joy in God and loving-kindness to all human beings were for Chassidism only two aspects of the same thing. The opposite of these aspects would be fear of God and justice to all human beings. Where there is joy in God, fear of Him disappears, as we have seen; it becomes obsolete, it is remembered only as a primitive taboo or superstition. Where there is loving-kindness to all human beings, justice too becomes obsolete; it is remembered as the primitive set of rules designed for men without the inner guidance of love. Bacon (if I may be pardoned for introducing so incongruous a name into the discussion) says in one of his essays: "Revenge is a wild kind of justice." He implies, then, that justice is a tame kind of revenge. That is how Chassidism feels, and that is what Peretz brings out powerfully in his stories and anecdotes.

Sometimes the illustrations are on the factual level, sometimes on the miraculous. But always there is in Peretz's parables (they may so be called) a human poignancy that makes irrelevant the question of literalness. In the end we come to feel that goodness is the supreme miracle, and all other deviations from natural law, however spectacular, are by comparison trifling. But it all depends on the telling, which must startle us into a mood akin to the believer's.

There is, for instance, the little story about Reb Yechiel, which is not on the "miraculous" level, any more than the story of Him of Nemirov and the Litvak.

It is not clear from the story whether Reb Yechiel was a *Tzaddik* or a mere *tzaddik*. Without the capital the word means, literally, a righteous person. With it the word has a special Chassidic meaning. There is an analogous difference between Saint and saint. Whatever he was, Reb Yechiel, like many other *Tzaddikim* (or *tzaddikim*), was a specialist; that is to say, while he practiced all-round goodness, he had a peculiar gift for one branch of it—the art of sparing other people's feelings. Presumably the *Tzaddik* should be the *uomo universale* of goodness; but Chassidim were human and had their quirks. Reb Yechiel, then, being a genius at handling people in such wise as to overcome or circumvent their embarrassment or shame, did his best work in that field. We shall see in a moment how he dealt with a thief whom he caught in his house one evening.

Reb Yechiel is one of the few contemporaries whom Peretz introduces into his stories. Reb Yechiel's father, Reb Zischelle, lived in Zamoshch, Peretz's home town, and was "one of the great of his generation." His prototype was probably a certain Rabbi Samuel Wohl, whom Peretz remembered out of his childhood. Reb Yechiel must have inherited part of his gift from his father, of whom the following is related:

Leaving the house one day, he noticed that the door was practically off its hinges. At once he bethought himself that a passer-by might be tempted to break in and steal something. He was, then, tempting people to sin through his own carelessness. To extricate himself and others from the possible consequences, he looked up to heaven and said:

"Lord of the world, I call You to witness that I hereby relinquish the ownership of all goods in this house, of whatever nature they be, furnishings or cash, and whether I know of them or do not know of them. They are no longer mine. They are anybody's."

In thus turning the tables neatly on any putative thief, compelling him to be honest *malgré lui*, Reb Zischelle furnished Chassidic literature with an excellent example of the difference between loving-kindness and justice.

Reb Yechiel, his son, the specialist mentioned above, avoided all overt acts of charity. He would not serve on any collection committee and would not make a gift of money to any man. It was always a business transaction. "This is a loan," he would say to the receiver severely. "In God's good time you will pay me back, in a lump sum or in installments, as you think fit. And if I'm no longer here, you will give it to someone else."

Those who would not come to him for a "loan" he helped anonymously. When he knew of someone in need, he sent him the gift by mail and wrote the address with his left hand, since his natural handwriting was well known in the town. For many years it was believed that these anonymous gifts came from some thief who was doing penance and had no other way of making restitution. It was only after Reb Yechiel's death that the identity of the "thief" was discovered.

One evening Reb Yechiel came home and found a strange Jew in his house. At Reb Yechiel's entry the man started and turned white as a sheet. Then Reb Yechiel noticed that the man was hiding something under his coat, something he had obviously picked up there in the room. But the man was clearly not a professional thief. He had apparently come for a "loan," had found the house empty, and had, in the extremity of his distress, yielded to temptation.

Reb Yechiel went up to him with a friendly smile and said:

"Ah, I see you've come to borrow something on a pledge. Will you be kind enough to show me the pledge?"

The man stood as if paralyzed; only his teeth chattered wildly.

"Come, come," said Reb Yechiel quietly. "What is there to be embarrassed about? Fortune is a wheel—it turns; money is round, it rolls; today you have to borrow from me, tomorrow I'll be borrowing from you."

So talking, he approached the man, lifted up his coat, and took out his own two silver candlesticks. He put them thoughtfully on the table as if he were seeing them for the first time and were appraising their value.

The unhappy Jew wanted to flee from the house, but his feet seemed to be nailed to the floor.

"Well, Mister Jew," said Reb Yechiel, "what do you expect me to loan you on these?"

No answer.

"I see you're a very timid, shamefaced sort of person," went on Reb Yechiel. "I'll have to do your speaking for you. All you need do is nod for yes and shake your head for no. Let me see now; the Passover is approaching, and you probably haven't the money for matzos. Right?"

The man nodded.

"That was fairly easy," said Reb Yechiel. "One didn't need to be a prophet to find that out. It's written on your face. The next question is a bit harder. You have a daughter to marry off, what? Yes or no? Nod or shake your head."

At this point the man broke into tears.

"Now, now," said Reb Yechiel reprovingly. "What are you crying about? Haven't I just told you that the wheel is always turning?"

But the unhappy Jew could not contain himself. He went on sobbing. Reb Yechiel became quite stern with him.

"Look here, man. I am simply obeying the law. It is written, clearly: 'Thou shalt help thy neighbor.' That's the law, and I can't change it. But there's nothing in the law about my having to put up with your tears."

The man summoned his last energies and stopped weeping.

"I'll tell you what," said Reb Yechiel. "I'll simply lend you what I consider the value of the pledge. I doubt whether it can be resold for more than fifty rubles. I'll lend you thirty-five—all right, all right, I'll make it forty. Fifteen to see you through the Passover, fifteen toward your daughter's dowry, and ten more toward her wedding clothes. The rest God will provide. And when the time comes, you'll pay me back. Either in a lump sum or in installments; and if I'm not here, you'll give it to someone else."

Were they always quite sure of themselves, these great lovers of God and mankind? Did the intoxication hold, and did not suspicion cross their minds that life was made of grimmer stuff and that there were principles which overrode even compassion and loving-kindness?

Some glimmerings of doubt there were, just as there were frequent backslidings into sadness; the sadness and the doubt were in fact related. So it appears from a story about a billy-goat, told by the great Chassidic Rabbi Reb Nachman, or, as they called him affectionately, Reb Nachmanke.

As the sympathetic reader will see, Reb Nachmanke was himself the billy-goat of the story or parable. In his modesty he saw himself in the guise of that homey, unpretentious, and slightly comical animal. The obvious question raised by the story (and I would not mention it if there were not an unobvious point) is this: has the great saint a right to fritter away his mighty relationship with the Almighty in unimportant services to every Chaim, Shmerel, and Yankel? Has he not mightier tasks to concentrate on? The unobvious point, which Reb Nachmanke may have missed (but not, I am sure, Peretz), has to do with the unfortunate transformation of the *tzaddik* into the *Tzaddik*.

As Chassidism incorporated itself into a great loosely organized movement, the love that was poured out on the *tzaddik* (without a capital letter in the early days) washed away gradually the simplicity and tacitness of his role. He was transformed into the *Tzaddik*, the wonder-worker, the Saint, the vizier of the Almighty; and like many a vizier to an earthly potentate, he was credited with the real power, his Master being merely the complacent executor of *his* wishes. There came a time when many Chassidim believed that God did what the *Tzaddik* told him to do. This was of course the undoing of Chassidism; for, alas, the *Tzaddik* himself often behaved as though he believed his viziership to be the most important factor in human relations. The seed of this megalomania may be detected in the story that follows, Reb Nachmanke's story of the billy-goat.

He told it on a Sabbath evening, a few weeks after he

214

had been "revealed"—that is, made manifest to the world in his capacity as *Tzaddik.*

The "revealing" of a *Tzaddik* is—or was—usually accidental, and certainly unsought. Something about him must, of course, have been attracting attention or the process would never start. It goes something like this: for some reason or other a man or a woman in trouble will come to the *Tzaddik* (who is still an unknown *Tzaddik,* a *Tzaddik nistor*) and seek his advice; it may be concerning a match for a daughter, or a sickness, or merely a matter of livelihood. The *Tzaddik,* whose spirit has been sojourning in the upper spheres, is suddenly brought down to earth. He cannot refuse to receive the suppliant; and listening to the pitiful story, he is moved to say something: advice, admonition, comfort. The words prove to be prophetic. They are fulfilled. This happens once, twice, three times, then the truth swims out like oil on water. There is a Saint in our midst!

So it came about with Reb Nachmanke, for he was never the man to refuse anyone. A light went up in Israel, and all the windows shone.

The townlet rejoiced, of course; what a break! On the one hand there was misery aplenty; a *Tzaddik* would be extremely useful. On the other hand, it meant business. Jews would come from the four corners of the earth. And so little miracles multiplied, like mushrooms after a rain. The word went out among the near-by villages. Here's a Saint who refuses no one, and whatever he utters is law. Before the first week is ended, before the Sabbath has come, two walls in the *Tzaddik's* house must be broken through; a table is laid through the length of three rooms. There will be guests from the big city, guests from the villages. Wines and fruits will be needed—and the harvest, as it happens, has been a good one.

On that Sabbath evening, two or three weeks after the
revealing, the townlet was caught up in a wave of jubila-
tion. Such a singing of Sabbath-evening songs, such a
dancing about the laden table, had never been known
before. Only Reb Nachmanke sat apart. And when the
time came for him to say the valedictory prayer to the
departing Sabbath, a great sadness came over him, and
the winecup in his hand trembled so, that they feared he
would let it fall. After the valedictory prayer he sat down
again in a corner, murmured a last prayer to himself, then
suddenly rose and left the room.

The congregation made as if to follow him, but he
turned round and shook his head. They remained in the
room, but crowded to the window to follow him with their
eyes. They saw him cross the market-place with faltering
steps and disappear into the fields beyond.

And now a real heaviness of heart settled on the assembled. Some returned to the table, a few went home; those
who remained tried to strike up a melody—it did not
take. They sent for brandy—no one felt like drinking.

What was it? What did the Rabbi lack? What *could* a
man in his position lack?

"Well, as far as his livelihood is concerned—" began
someone, coarsely, and went no further, for the looks that
were turned on him froze the roots of his soul. And yet
the question remained: a man who had attained that degree of sanctity should radiate only happiness.

Reb Joshua the teacher, who had once lived in the
kingly presence (that is, he had known the Baal Shem in
person), exclaimed:

"Here is a man who can help thousands of Jews, and
yet he is sad. He can even cause a harsh decree issued from
above to be abrogated. Isn't that true?"

"Indeed it is," they chorused. For Reb Nachmanke had

already done much in these few weeks. And they began to
rehearse his miracles. I will not set them down here; they
are a drop in the ocean compared with his later wonders.
But one little story I will tell out of those early days, for it
shows his humility and his kindness.

There was an old woman in the townlet, a simple old
soul, the widow of some tailor. All she had in the world
was a nanny-goat, and this was what she lived off. The
nanny-goat was not worth a broken kopeck, but it was
enough for her. As the years passed, the old woman found
it harder and harder to milk the goat. Her hands became
very shaky, and so she would lose a few drops at every
milking—and there was not, God knows, too much milk
in the nanny-goat at best. Finally she dragged the animal
to Reb Nachmanke and lodged a complaint against it as
lacking in respect for an old woman and refusing to stand
still while being milked. Reb Nachmanke listened pa-
tiently and smiled; then he said: "Go home, woman. Help
will come for you." And help did come for her. Not that
her hands became any steadier—the poor creature was
every bit of eighty, or maybe nearer ninety; but a wonderful change came over the nanny-goat. It became as it were
another animal; it began to turn up of itself at milking
time; it would stand quietly with uplifted leg till the last
drop of milk had been squeezed out of it.

The assembly was so absorbed in the various stories of
Reb Nachmanke's wonders that they did not notice his
return. Suddenly they heard his voice at the window:
"Once again, Jews, a happy week to you all!"

There he was, his elbows on the sill, his head on his
arms. His eyes shone with a queer, gay light—gay, yet
somehow not happy.

"I am going to tell you a story," he said. "Listen and do
not think it strange."

They wanted to bring a chair out for him. No, he preferred to stand. So some of them came out, and some remained in the room, and standing thus in their midst, with the moon over him like a crown, he told them the story of the billy-goat and of the meaning of "revealing."

"Once," he began, and his voice was steeped in sorrow, "there was a billy-goat. A billy-goat like all other billy-goats. Or perhaps it was different, bigger. I don't know. No one ever measured it. For the billy-goat loved loneliness and never ventured among other living things. Perhaps this billy-goat was an eldest son—and perhaps not.

"Outside the village there was a ruin, which had been standing there as long as men remembered. It was said, and no doubt with truth, that it was the ruin of a holy place, a synagogue, or a Study House. Men had prayed here once, had studied the sacred books. When the building was destroyed, someone was martyred here, died for the Sanctification of the Name. Old stories, these were. Now grass grew in the ruin, a strange kind of grass that no one sowed and no one cut. In this ruin the billy-goat lived, and this was the grass he ate.

"The grass that grows in these ruins is, as I have said, no ordinary grass. It is a wonderful specific for horns. The horns of an animal cropping here grow to an unbelievable length. Such horns are likewise remarkable in another respect—they are alive. They can curl themselves up at will, and they can unfold and become revealed. And as long as they remain curled up, no one seeing them would suspect anything. But when they unfold they can reach to the uppermost heavens.

"This billy-goat of ours was a nazarite, a dedicated soul, attentive to his vows. No grass but such as grew in the ruin ever touched his lips. Nor would he eat at random even in the ruin. He had a great understanding for grass,

218

and he chose only the richest and best, both for taste and for smell. Here was a patch that grew in the heart of the sanctuary; there was a patch that grew in memory of particularly soulful prayer; elsewhere grass sprouted from soil that was soaked in the blood of a Jewish martyr. The billy-goat ate carefully, and the horns grew faster and faster.

"Being a nazarite and a hidden wonder, the billy-goat kept the horns curled up. Only in the night, when the townlet sleeps, save for those Jews who say their midnight prayers in the Houses of Study, in the night, when the heartache of the psalm 'By the waters of Babylon' is poured out between heaven and earth, an agony of longing would come over the billy-goat. Then he would stand up on his hind legs and straighten out his horns heavenward; and if there happened to be a new moon there, recently sanctified by Jewish prayer, he would hook the tips over the lower edge and say:

" 'What news, holy moon? Is not the hour of the Messiah come yet?'

"The moon would pass the question on to the stars, and they, in deep perturbation, would arrest their motion, and the moon's with it. Then the night would stand still, and the song of the night would break off. The attendants about the Throne of Glory, marking the sudden silence, would send down a messenger to find out the cause; and he would bring back word that moon and stars were motionless till they were told whether the hour of the Messiah had not yet come. But the only answer from the Throne of Glory was a melancholy sigh.

"Nevertheless, such questionings can have their effect."

Here Reb Nachmanke broke off. He covered his face with his hands, and the listeners saw clearly how head and hands trembled; and the moon, which hung over him like a crown, seemed to be trembling too. Then after a time Reb Nachmanke lifted up his head. His cheeks were pale, and his voice shook as he continued:

"Mark well that it was no small act of grace on the part of the billy-goat that he remained among us, here below, on earth. Another than he, possessed of horns that he could hook over the moon, would have swung himself up and entered paradise while yet living—what would he have cared about us? But this billy-goat had a compassionate soul; he thought of the congregation and could not bring himself to abandon it.

"For life is hard here below. Years of hunger come, and the congregation begins to break up. . . . The women sell their jewels, the men the gold and silver ornaments on their prayer-shawls. . . . The times grow harder, the little ones are taken out of school, there's no money to pay the Rebbi. . . . And still the misery grows, pestilence follows starvation—and now he *must* do something.

"Up in the heaven there is the Milky Way, as human beings call it. It is not a way at all, for no foot treads it and no wheels roll on it. It is a stretch of great fields sown with precious stones, with countless diamonds and pearls. These are diamonds and pearls for the crowns of the saints in paradise. No one knows or cares to know their number—they are like the sands on the seashore. They multiply from year to year, while the number of crowns needed for newcomers to paradise diminishes from year to year.

"Then at last the suffering on earth below becomes unbearable, and the secret owner of the hidden horns takes action. When it is midnight in the village, and voices in the Houses of Study are heard lamenting over the exile of Israel and the exile of the Divine Glory, the billy-goat rears up on his hind legs, straightens out his horns, and directs them toward the Milky Way. There he pulls out a precious stone and flings it all the way down into the market-place. The stone shatters into a thousand fragments, and Jews going home after their midnight lamentations see them sparkling on the ground—and so there is something to live on for a while.

"That is why the billy-goat cannot abandon the community."

Again Reb Nachmanke broke off, to resume sadly after a while:

"And his kindness of heart was the undoing of him. Because of his compassion and sweetness he was 'revealed.' I mean—his horns. And the beginning of it was so trifling —the snuff habit."

And now there was something utterly fantastic in Reb Nachmanke's tone; the listeners did not know whether it wept or laughed.

"The snuff habit," he repeated. "Jews took to snuff; it became a custom everywhere. They said it did them good: a sound sneeze cleared the eyes. And of course if people take snuff, they have to have snuffboxes. And snuffboxes are best made of goat's horn. So whenever a Jew finds a piece of goat's horn he makes himself a snuffbox. Sometimes he stops a goat, asks for a piece of horn, and gets butted for his pains. But one day a Jew happened to be passing the ruin and chanced on our billy-goat. He said:

" 'Billy-goat, first-born or not first-born, give me a piece of horn for a snuffbox.'

"In the kindness of his heart the billy-goat could not say no. He pushed out the horn, and the Jew cut off a piece and made himself a snuffbox. In the Study House he offers the other Jews a pinch of snuff, and they say: 'Where did you get such lovely horn?' He tells them—and in a few days every snuff-taker in the village has already sought out the billy-goat among the ruins. He never says

221

no to anyone. He bends down his head and lets them cut off a piece of horn. Before long the fame of his kindness has spread through the land. Jews come from every corner —and are provided with snuffboxes.

"And there is only one drawback to this kindness. Before long the billy-goat will not be able to reach the moon with his horns, to inquire after the Messiah. Neither will he be able to prize a jewel out of the Milky Way and cast it down to earth."

With that Reb Nachmanke stopped, turned from his listeners, and walked away. At the same moment a cloud covered the moon, and a mingling of sadness and fright fell on the assembly.

Nowhere did Peretz bring out more clearly the fundamental dispute between the old-style formalist scholar and the Chassidic Rabbi than in the story, or study, "Between Two Cliffs." The two "cliffs" or mountains were the famous Rabbi of Brisk, the Talmudist, and the equally famous Chassidic Reb Noah—or Noachke—of Biale. And the man that tells the story is the one who is trapped "between the two cliffs."

Very few Jews, Chassidic or otherwise (he begins), know that He of Biale was once a student in the Yeshivah of Him of Brisk; that after a number of years he broke away and disappeared took exile upon himself, became a beggar-wanderer, that is—and finally arrived in Biale, where his "revealing" took place.

Reb Noachke left his teacher for a number of reasons. At the Yeshivah there was of course much studying of the Torah, but Reb Noachke felt the method and approach were dry and lifeless. Not the substance itself: the laws of cleanliness in women, the dietary laws, the laws of property—they were all good. If there was a real case, a dispute between Reuben and Simon, a problem posed by a householder, a question of kosher and non-kosher, or whatever it might be, the law became alive and exerted its power over the world. But by itself, without application, pursued for its own sake, for its own substance, the law was dry, lifeless, and meaningless. Such was young Noachke's view. The study of mystical Kabbalah books was forbidden in this Yeshivah. He of Brisk was a *Misnaged,* an opponent of Chassidism, and a relentless one. He placed a curse and a ban upon anyone who read the Zohar or any other work of "concealed" wisdom. To show you how far he went: he once caught a student with a forbidden book; he had the man tied down and his beard shaved off by hired gentiles. What happened to the student after this humiliation can be better imagined than described; he fell into such melancholy, such self-loathing, that thereafter no Chassidic rabbi could do him any good. *That* was the Rabbi of Brisk. And yet—and yet how could one possibly tear oneself away from the illustrious Yeshivah of Brisk?

Young Noachke revolved the matter in his mind for a long time and reached a decision as the result of a dream.

He dreamed that He of Brisk came to him and said: "Come, Noah, I will show you the earthly paradise." He took his student by the hand and led him to a great palace. The palace was without windows and without entrances except for the door by which they entered. But it was light within, because the walls were made of a curious crystal which shone of itself; and they wandered through the palace for what seemed an endless time.

"Hold on to my gabardine," said He of Brisk; "the rooms here are without number, and if you let go of me you will be lost forever."

Noachke obeyed. They wandered on and on, and nowhere did they see a single stool, nor was there a sign of the master of the palace. "Here," said the Rabbi of Brisk, "no one ever sits down. One only wanders." The rooms became larger and larger, the light that came from the walls changed colors; some of the rooms were multi-colored. But never a sign of life.

Reb Noachke felt his legs giving under him. A cold sweat broke out over his body, and the cold penetrated his limbs. The eternal brightness of the walls was blinding him. And suddenly he was flooded by a great home-sickness for friends, for Jews, for Jewry at large.

"Be homesick for no one," said He of Brisk to Noachke. "This palace is only for you and me. Some day you too will be the Rabbi of Brisk."

These words only frightened young Noachke the more, and tottering to a wall, he put out his hand to support himself. But the wall burned him—not as fire burns, but as ice burns.

"Rabbi!" he cried. "The walls are of ice, not of crystal. Just ice!"

The Rabbi of Brisk did not answer.

Thereupon Reb Noachke cried out again: "Rabbi, take me out of here! I don't want to be alone with you. I want to be with all the other Jews."

No sooner had he uttered these words than the Rabbi of Brisk disappeared, and he was alone in the palace. Now he was utterly lost. An icy fear radiated on him from the walls; and the longing to see a fellow Jew and speak with him, let it be some cobbler, some tailor's apprentice, grew stronger and stronger. Reb Noachke burst into tears.

"Lord of the world," he wept, "take me out of this place. Better to be in hell with fellow Jews than here alone."

At once there appeared before him the figure of a simple Jew, wearing the red girdle of a wagoner and carrying a long whip. Without a word he took Reb Noachke by the sleeve, led him out of the palace, and disappeared. This was the dream that was sent him for a sign.

He awoke as the sky was growing gray with dawn, and understood that this was no ordinary dream. He dressed hastily, intending to go at once to the Study House, to have his dream interpreted by the scholars who passed their nights there. But hurrying through the market-place, he was pulled up by the sight of a great wagon, a vast, old-fashioned market-wagon, with horses harnessed to it. By the horses stood the driver, with the red girdle of his trade about his waist, and a long whip in his hand. Just such a Jew had led Reb Noachke out of the palace in his dream.

So this was the meaning of it!

He approached the driver and said: "Which way do you travel from here?"

"Not your way," answered the driver, boorishly.

"Please," insisted Noachke. "I might come with you."

The driver thought awhile, then said: "And what's the matter with your legs—a lad of your age? Go your own way."

"Where shall I go?"

"Just follow your nose," answered the driver, and turned away. "As if it's my business!"

Then at last Reb Noachke understood, and he went forth into his exile, into the period of homeless wandering.

Well, as I told you, the "revealing" of Reb Noachke took place a few years later in Biale. As to the manner of it I shall say nothing here, though the wonder of it would make your eyes start from your head. About a year after his revealing I too came to Biale, to be a Rebbi, or, as you would call it nowadays, a tutor, in the house of a Biale merchant, Reb Yechiel by name.

I was reluctant about accepting that post. Reb Yechiel, they told me, was a man of great wealth, an old-style grain-dealer bursting with money. His daughters used to get a thousand rubles each as dowry, and he married into none but the highest rabbinic families. At the last wedding he had become father-in-law to the daughter of Him of Brisk!

I don't think further explanation is needed. If the Rabbi of Brisk was an enemy of Chassidism, the families he married his children into could hardly be friends of it; and I, as you have probably guessed, am a passionate follower of the Chassidic Rabbi of Biale. How could I possibly become tutor in one of those families?

And yet—Biale! The sacred city of my Rabbi! To be near him day and night! I could not resist that. I thought the matter over, hesitated briefly—and accepted.

Reb Yechiel turned out to be a very simple, decent sort of man; I'll take my oath on it that his heart was really with us—I mean, with the followers of the Chassidic rabbis. He was not much of a scholar; if he understood one word in ten when He of Brisk held forth, he was doing well. He did not forbid my visits to Him of Biale, but would have nothing to do with him himself. When I introduced the subject of my Rabbi, he pretended to yawn, though I could see he pricked his ears up. His son, the son-in-law of Him of Brisk, would frown, and look at me with a mixture of anger and derision. He did not argue with me, however; he was not much of a talker anyhow.

Not long after my arrival in Biale, it was announced that Reb Yechiel's daughter-in-law, the daughter of Him of Brisk, was about to be confined. Nothing extraordinary or terrible about that, you would say; it happens every day. Ah, but this was a special case. It was known that since He of Brisk had caused a student to have his beard shaved off for reading a book of Kabbalah, he had lost his standing on the list of the righteous. Within five or six years two of his sons had died, and none of his daughters had borne male children. More than that, all three of them delivered their young with the most frightful sufferings; one never knew—God save us!—whether they would come through alive. It was clear to everyone that this was the punishment decreed against Him of Brisk; clear to everyone, that is, except him. He, for all the keenness of his vision, could not see it; or would not. He still continued to persecute the Chassidim with denunciations and excommunications, as was not uncommon in those days.

I was sorry for poor Gitelle (that was the young woman's name), first in a general way; but more particularly because she was such a saintly creature—I've never known a saintlier one. No penniless bride of Biale ever made her wedding without Gitelle's help. An angel, I tell you. And *she* had to suffer because of her father's obstinate anger. So when I saw the mother-in-law—Reb Yechiel's wife— making the preparations for the childbirth, I began to move heaven and earth to have them send to Reb Noachke. Let them send only a note, without the usual redemption fee: did my Rabbi need or want redemption fees? Everyone knew that he despised them.

The first one I approached was the husband himself, Reb Yechiel's son. I knew that there was a great love between him and his wife—his soul was bound up in hers. He tried not to show it too much, of course; but the sweetness of their home life was like a perfume in every corner of the house. What a reception I got from him! The idea of turning to a Chassidic Rabbi! At the mention of the name he spat out and walked away, leaving me standing there open-mouthed.

I went next to Reb Yechiel himself. His answer was: "But it's the daughter of the Rabbi of Brisk! I wouldn't do such a thing to him even if her life were at stake. Good heavens!"

In my desperation I tried Reb Yechiel's wife, a good, honest, simple soul. She answered with these words: "Let my husband only say so, and I'll send your Rabbi my holiday headcloth—it cost a fortune—and my earrings. Otherwise I won't send anything, not even an eggshell."

"But just a note," I pleaded. "No redemption fee, only a note. What harm can it do?"

"Without my husband's knowledge I can't do a thing," she said, like the honest Jewish wife she was, and she turned away from me to hide her tears. Her heart, her mother's heart, was filled with foreboding.

When I heard the first scream from the young woman, I ran to the Rabbi myself.

"Shmaya," he said to me. "What do you want me to do? I will pray."

"Rabbi," I begged, "give me something for her: a note, an amulet, a coin you have blessed—anything at all."

"That," he said, "might only make matters worse, God forbid. Where there is no faith, such things are harmful, and she has no faith in them."

What was I to do? We were at the beginning of the Festival of Tabernacles. I could not return to the house where the young woman was agonizing. I decided to stay with my Rabbi. I needed no invitation—I was a familiar there. I would remain with him, I would catch his eye whenever I could, I would plead with him, perhaps he would take pity. . . .

The reports from Reb Yechiel's were not reassuring. The birth-pangs had lasted three days, and the end was not in sight. Everything possible had been done: prayers in the synagogue, appeals before the Scrolls of the Law, supplications in the cemetery, candles by the hundred in the synagogues and Study Houses. And charity, of course, without stint or calculation. Every clothes closet stood open in the house; on the table in the living-room lay a huge heap of coins. The poor entered, took what they wanted, unwatched, unchecked. And all the time the pain in my heart grew.

"Rabbi," I said, "is it not written: 'Charity saves from death'?"

The Rabbi answered, quite beside the mark, it seemed to me: "Perhaps He of Brisk will come!"

That very instant Reb Yechiel entered the room. He addressed no word to the Rabbi; it was as if he did not see him; to me he said:

"Shmaya!" And he caught me by the lapel. "Shmaya! A cart stands ready outside. Get into it and go bring the Rabbi of Brisk. Let him see for himself, and let him tell us what to do!" And the face of the man was—how shall I put it? I've seen faces with more life on them in coffins.

I set out at once, thinking: "If my Rabbi already knows that He of Brisk will come, great things may happen. We may have peace! Not between Him of Brisk and Him of Biale; it wasn't necessary; they had never fought each other. But peace in general, between the two parties in Israel. For surely if the Rabbi of Brisk will come, he will see for himself. The man has eyes, hasn't he?"

But it looked as if it was not Heaven's will to make things too easy for us. Hardly had we left Biale when a tremendous cloud began to roll across the sky. A cloud? It was more like a river of pitch. And with the cloud came a frightful wind, howling like a thousand demons. The driver pointed to the sky with his whip and crossed himself. We were in for a rough trip. And indeed the wind redoubled its fury, and driving against the cloud split it into two gigantic fragments, which it proceeded to pile one on top of the other, like a river piling the ice floes on one another. I took it rather lightly at first; I already knew what it meant to be soaked to the skin. Nor was I afraid of thunder. To begin with, it never thunders after the Feast of Tabernacles. And even if it did, we of Biale knew that after our Rabbi had blown the shophar for the High Holy Days, the thunder of heaven was powerless for a year. Which was all well and good; but when that rain suddenly slapped me in the face once, twice, and three times, the blood in me curdled down to the bottom of my boots. It was as plain as the nose on my face that the heavens were set against my journey.

The poor driver, too, was imploring me: "Let's turn back!"

But I knew it was a matter of life and death. Sitting there in the wagon, I could hear the moaning of the woman in labor; I could see the young man striding up and down the room, wringing his hands, cracking his finger-joints. There rose up before me Reb Yechiel's deep-sunken, blazing eyes in the more-dead-than-alive face. "Go on!" he begged me, "Go on!" And we went on.

The water came down in torrents from the clouds above; it squirted up in fountains from under the wheels. The road disappeared under the water: no roads, no fields —a lake. We were more like a raft than a wagon. And we lost our way, of course. But I didn't turn back.

We brought the Rabbi of Brisk to Biale. But truth is truth, and I have to set it down that the moment He of Brisk mounted the wagon, everything quieted down. The clouds divided, the sun came through, and we went back in peace over the drying roads.

And when we got to the house—you should have seen

the women, and the way they greeted the Rabbi. They almost fell at his feet. Nothing could be heard from the next room, where the suffering young woman lay; either because of the lamentations of the other women, or because—God forbid—she hadn't even the strength to moan. Reb Yechiel didn't even see us. He was standing at the window with his burning forehead pressed against the pane. The son-in-law, too, didn't turn round to greet Him of Brisk. He, too, was very far gone; he stood with his face to the wall, and you could see his body trembling through all its length. Such a feeling of pity overcame me that I thought I would faint away. A chill went through my limbs, my body, my soul.

But the Rabbi of Brisk—I don't know if you've ever seen him—there was a man for you. A pillar of iron! He towered above others "from the shoulders up," like King Saul of old. A regal presence, I tell you; terrifying. A gigantic white beard. One point of it—I remember as if it were yesterday—had slipped under his girdle; the other lay quivering above it. Massive white eyebrows overshadowing half his face; and when he lifted them—great God! —those eyes! They flashed like blades. The women fell back as before a thunderbolt. And he, with a voice like a lion, exclaimed: "Out of the way, women!"

Then, more softly: "Where is my daughter?"

They showed him into the other room, and I remained frozen to the spot. That presence! That look! That voice! How could two such men as He of Brisk and He of Biale inhabit one world? The eyes of the Chassidic Rabbi of Biale shine with such a mild and kindly light that the heart expands with joy; his glance is like a shower of gold; and the sweet, loving voice—so caressing, so comforting—it melts your heart and draws it out of you. Never a touch of fear; only the longing of your soul to become one with his soul. You can feel it fluttering inside you, like a moth that is drawn to the flame. And the Rabbi of Brisk—nothing but majesty and terror: a Master of the days of old!

I was thinking: "What can such a man do for a sick woman? He will frighten the last bit of life out of her." And I ran to my Rabbi.

He met me with a smile.

"Have you seen the majesty of the Torah?" he asked. "Pure kingliness, is it not?"

I was comforted. If the Rabbi could smile, all was well.

And indeed all came out well. Within a short time the young woman was delivered of her child, and by the Day of the Rejoicing of the Law the Rabbi of Brisk was holding forth to an assembly gathered around the table. For myself I would have preferred to be at another table, that of my own Rabbi; but I was afraid to leave, all the more as I happened to round out the number of ten for the prayers.

What shall I tell you of the Rabbi of Brisk and his mastery of the Torah? If the Torah is an ocean, He of Brisk was its leviathan. In one sweep he flashed from end to end of the ocean, cutting through a dozen tractates on the way. With a single gesture he gathered in the world of the Talmud and its commentators. The waters seethe, fountains rise, a foam of quotations breaks into the air. It made one dizzy trying to follow him. But the heart knoweth its own bitterness. There was no joy for me that day of the Rejoicing of the Law. I remembered Reb Noachke's dream, and my blood froze. The sun sent its level rays through the window; on the table the wine sparkled; the wrinkled foreheads of the listeners were bedewed with drops of sweat—and I was chilled through and through.

Over there at the table of my own Rabbi another kind of Torah was being uttered. . . . Over there everything was bright and warm; every word was steeped in earnestness and love; angels hovered in the room; you could catch the flutter of their great white wings. . . . My heart was filled with longing, but to leave was out of the question.

Suddenly the Rabbi of Brisk broke off his discourse and asked:

"Who's the Chassidic Rabbi in this town?"

"Some fellow by the name of Noah," was the answer.

The words cut me like a knife! Toadies! Lickspittles!

"A wonder-worker?" went on the Rabbi of Brisk.

"Not very much. At any rate, we hear little. The women talk about him, to be sure—but who listens to them?"

"So? He takes money without working wonders?"

They told him truthfully that this particular Chassidic Rabbi took little money, and most of what he took he gave away.

The Rabbi of Brisk meditated.

"A scholar?"

"A great one, they say."

"And where does he hail from, this Noah?"

No one could answer, so all eyes were turned on me.

"Wasn't he once in Brisk, this Noah?" asked the Rabbi.

"Was my Rabbi once in Brisk?" I stammered. "Yes, I think he was."

"Ah!" exclaimed the Rabbi. "A follower of his!" And it seemed to me that he started, as if he had seen a spider.

He turned to the assembly. "I once had a student by the name of Noah," he said. "He had quite a good head on his shoulders, but he hankered after those others. I spoke to him about it once, and twice, and I was going to give him a third warning, but he disappeared. I wonder if this isn't the man."

234

"Who knows?"

And the Rabbi of Brisk began to describe him: a gaunt little man, black-bearded, with black, curling earlocks, an abstracted air, a gentle voice, and so on.

"That's probably the man," they commented. "It sounds very much like him."

After the meal and the grace something utterly incredible happened. The Rabbi of Brisk got up from his chair, approached me, took me aside, and said in a low voice: "Take me to *your* Rabbi, *my* pupil. But listen: no one is to know about it."

I obeyed, as you may well imagine. And on the way I asked him, terrified: "Rabbi of Brisk, what is your intention?"

He answered quite simply: "During the grace it occurred to me that I had judged him in his absence. I want to see him for myself." Then he added: "Perhaps, with God's help, I will rescue an old pupil of mine from their hands. Do you know, you young heathen"—a touch of playful mockery crept into his voice—"if your Rabbi is indeed the Noah who studied with me, his name may yet be great in Israel; he may be Rabbi of Brisk some day."

And now I was quite certain that it was the same Noah, and my heart jumped into my throat.

So these two mighty cliffs came face to face, and I was caught between them. It was a miracle that I wasn't flattened out.

He of Biale—his memory be our blessing—followed a custom of his own on the Day of the Rejoicing of the Law. He would send his Chassidim out of the Study House and tell them to go strolling in the open air, and he himself would sit on the veranda and take pleasure in the sight.

Biale is no longer what it was. In those days it was little
more than a village—clusters of tiny, low houses, with the
synagogue and the Rabbi's Study House standing out in
their midst. The veranda was on the second story, and
below it the village and its surroundings lay as in the palm
of your hand, enclosed between the hills on the east and
the river on the west. The Rabbi sits up there and looks
down. If a group of Chassidim passes without singing, he
throws them the opening notes of a melody, which they
take up and carry away with them. So group after group
goes by and, singing, spreads out into the fields, filled with
true happiness, as is proper on the Day of the Rejoicing
of the Law; and the Rabbi would remain up there and
never stir from his place.

The Rabbi must have recognized our footsteps, for on
this occasion he rose and came forward in salutation.

"*Sholom aleichem,* greeting, Rabbi," he said modestly,
in his low, sweet voice.

"*Aleichem sholom,* Noah," answered He of Brisk.

The Rabbi of Brisk sat down, and He of Biale stood
before him.

"Tell me, Noah," said He of Brisk, lifting his eyebrows,
"what made you run away from my Yeshivah? What did
you lack there?"

"Air, Rabbi," said He of Biale gently. "I lacked air. I
couldn't catch my breath."

"Come, come, Noah; how can that be?"

"I mean my soul lacked air," said He of Biale in the
same voice. "It was being stifled."

"Why, Noah?"

"Your Torah, Rabbi, is only law and judgment, without compassion. It is a Torah without a touch of tenderness. And therefore it is without joy; the breath of life is
not in it. Only iron and bronze, iron laws and tablets of

bronze: a lofty and majestic Torah, for scholars and for choice spirits."

He of Brisk was silent, and my Rabbi continued: "But tell me, Rabbi, what Torah have you for the common people—for the wood-gatherer, the butcher, the laborer, the ordinary, everyday Jew? And particularly for a sinful Jew. What have you, Rabbi, for those who are not scholars?"

He of Brisk still remained silent, as if he did not know what was being said to him. And He of Biale went on again, in his sweet, low voice:

"Forgive me, Rabbi, but I must be truthful with you. Your Torah was hard, hard and arid, because it had only the body and not the soul of the Torah."

"The soul?" said He of Brisk, and rubbed his forehead.

"Indeed, Rabbi. Your Torah, I said, was only for scholars, for the elect, for a few chosen spirits, and not for the masses of Israel. But the Torah was given to all Israel, and the Divine Glory must rest on all Israel, for the Torah is the soul of Israel."

"And your Torah, Noah?"

"Do you want to see it, Rabbi?"

"See it? See the Torah?"

"Come, Rabbi, I will show it to you. I will show you the glory of it, the joy that streams out from it for all Israel."

The Rabbi of Brisk remained seated.

"Come, I beg you, Rabbi. It is not far."

And he led the Rabbi of Brisk out on the veranda. I followed silently. Nevertheless my Rabbi heard me, and he turned and said: "You may come too, Shmaya. Today you will see, and the Rabbi of Brisk, too, will see, what the Day of the Rejoicing of the Law is—a true rejoicing in the Torah."

That which I saw differed in no way from what I had seen on previous occasions; but the manner of my seeing it was different. It was as if scales had fallen from my eyes.

I saw the wide, enormous heavens, infinite in extent, and blue, radiant blue, so that the eye was filled with delight. A host of little silver clouds floated up there, and if one looked closely one could really see that they quivered with happiness, as if they were dancing in the Rejoicing of the Law. Below, within the circle of the hills and the river, the townlet lay embedded in green, a dark and living green; one would have said that a living spirit breathed among the grasses. The spirit broke out here, there, elsewhere, like an odorous flame, which danced between the bushes, kissing and caressing them. . . .

On the meadows, among the flames and grasses, little groups of Chassidim walked to and fro. Their satin gabardines—and even those of plain cotton—glittered like mirrors: all of them, even those that were ragged. And the flames that danced among the grasses touched the holiday attire of the Chassidim and played with it; it was as if every Chassid was surrounded with exultant, joyous fire. And the Chassidim turned their longing eyes to the veranda, and the light in their eyes was drawn from the eyes of their Rabbi. And as the light grew, their songs became louder, gayer, and even more sacred.

Every group sang its own melody, and the melodies mingled in the air and came to us in a single harmony. And not only they sang; the heavens sang too, the upper spheres sang, and the earth under their feet sang; the soul of the world sang—everything sang.

Lord of the world! The sweetness of it melted my heart!

And yet the moment I had hoped for did not come.

"It is time for evening prayer!" exclaimed He of Brisk sharply. In that instant everything vanished.

The scales covered my eyes again. I looked and saw an ordinary sky, and under it ordinary fields. On the fields wandered beggarly Chassidim in tattered gabardines. The flames were extinguished.

I turned to my Rabbi. His face, too, was extinguished.

No, they did not come to an understanding. He of Brisk remained an opponent of Chassidism. But the visit was not without effect. From that time on he no longer persecuted the Chassidim.

CHAPTER XVII

"Transmigrations of a Melody"

❁

Says an eager little Chassid in the pages of Peretz:

What's in a letter? It depends on how you read it. What's in a melody? It depends on how you sing it.

Here, for instance, is a melody steeped in love. But what kind of love do you mean? There's love of the Eternal One, and love of our fellow creatures, and love of our fellow Jews. But there's also self-love and, God help us, the love of another man's wife.

And here's a melody that's all lamentation. But a melody may weep for the triumph of the serpent and the exile from paradise, or for the destruction of the Temple, or for our glory which lies in the dust. And it may weep for the lovely and beloved one who's fled.

And here's a third melody, full of vain-longing. But is it the vain-longing of the soul that hungers to return to its divine source, or is it the vain-longing of the old dog who remembers the lusty days of his youth?

The notes themselves can no more make a melody than a heap of stones can of themselves make a house. These are but the body of the melody; the melody must have a soul.

I, gentlemen, believe that that which gives joy to life must itself be possessed of life. A melody lives, and a melody can also die, and be forgotten, just as a man may go down to the grave and be forgotten.

Once that melody was young and fresh, bursting with life. The years passed, the strength went out of it, and then it breathed its last. It is no more.

But a melody may also experience a resurrection!

Suddenly someone remembers an old melody; it rises in him as if from nowhere and breaks out from his lips. Involuntarily he puts a new feeling into it—that is, a new soul; it is almost as if a new melody had been born.

This is what I call the transmigration of a melody. And about this I have a story to tell.

A dozen miles or so beyond Berdichev, just where the forest ends, there's a townlet by the name of Machnovke, and in Machnovke there used to be a decent little orchestra. The conductor, Reb Chaiml, was a first-class musician, a pupil of Podhutzer's, of Berdichev. Reb Chaiml was no creator of melodies, he was not what they call a composer; but he excelled in execution and interpretation, in the giving of heart to a melody.

He wasn't much to look at—a little dried-up man but when he began to play he turned into another person. His eyelids, which were forever drooping, lifted slowly, and from the quiet eyes there spread over the pale face a look of deep compassion. You could see plainly that the man was somewhere else; the hands played here, but the soul had taken flight and wandered about in the universe of song. Sometimes he so far forgot himself that he actually began to sing, too; and he had a clear, ringing voice, like a clarinet.

If Reb Chaiml hadn't been a pious simple Jew—I almost said a simpleton—he wouldn't have starved with his wife and eight children in Machnovke. He'd have been playing or singing in a theater; and maybe he'd have been choir-leader in some great synagogue in Paris or Berlin. Only that sort of thing seldom happens to people who come from Berdichev. Chaiml stayed home in Machnovke and ran up bills in every grocery in town on the strength of the next high-class wedding. Sooner or later one would have to turn up.

And on this occasion that I'm telling of what turned up was the very best in town: its richest home, that of Berel Katzner's widow.

Berel Katzner (his ghost may come and choke me for this) was a big usurer and a bigger miser. He begrudged himself every mouthful of food: he used to pick up the leavings from his children's meals. A man with a heart of granite.

Just before his death, when he was practically at the last gasp, he called in his eldest son, asked for the account-book, and with his own finger, which was already turning a bluish-brownish color, went over the list of defaulters. "And don't you dare to extend their notes," he said. "I forbid it, by the authority of a father!"

Then he called over his wife and told her to put away the copper pots hanging on the wall. "If anything happens to me," he said, "nothing will be safe around here." And with that he gave up the ghost. He left half a million rubles.

Well, as I said, it was the widow who married off the daughter; and she was in a hurry because she was thinking of a match for herself. It was as if a stone had been lifted from her heart; she'd got a new lease on life. And since our Reb Chaiml also had a daughter to marry off, you may imagine that he waited for this wedding as if it would bring the Messiah.

Then what do you think happened? The widow took it into her head that no musician would do but Podhutzer himself, from Berdichev. And the reason? The new in-laws were from Kiev, big city people with an ear for music; so she wanted, at the ceremony of the covering of the bride, a new melody for the *El Moleh Rachamim,* which would be sung in memory of the father; none of the old hackneyed stuff. What did a few rubles more matter? She'd show those visitors from Kiev!

When Chaiml got the news he nearly died; and the town took it nearly as badly as he. Chaiml was beloved of everyone; and even if he hadn't been, what was the idea? Was there no pity for a pauper? So delegations went to the widow to work out a compromise. It was finally agreed that Chaiml and his orchestra should be hired; but before the wedding he was to slip into Berdichev and bring over a new *El Moleh Rachamim* from Podhutzer. The widow was to pay his expenses.

Chaiml took the few rubles, gave more than half to his wife, hired a cart, and set off for Berdichev. And here begins the story of the melody.

Pauper's luck! Just as Chaiml drew in at one end of Berdichev, Podhutzer left at the other. He had been invited to Tolny, to the Sabbath valedictory. Our Reb Dovidl of Tolny, you must know, thought the world of Podhutzer. "His melodies," he would say, "are filled with the secrets of the Torah. It's only a pity that he can't decipher them."

Chaiml wandered about the streets utterly beside himself. What was to be done? To go back without an *El*

Moleh Rachamim was out of the question—there would be the devil to pay. To follow Podhutzer to Tolny, or wait for his return, was equally impossible. He simply hadn't the money. The widow had given him little, and he'd left his wife a lot. Chaiml was utterly distracted.

As he wandered thus about Berdichev, he came upon this scene: right in the middle of a fine week-day a young woman parades the street holding in her hand a great big silver tray. She's dressed in the loveliest holiday attire, or, as they say in those parts, to the nines; and on her head she wears a queer bonnet, with long, bright, multicolored ribbons. She's followed by a little group of musicians, and she goes from house to house, from shop to shop, and in front of every door she does a little dance. The music attracts crowds of people, the doors and windows are jammed. The music plays, the young woman dances, the colored ribbons flutter in the air, the tray flashes in the sun. The crowd shouts: *"Mazel tov!"* and coins are thrown toward the tray; the young woman dances forward to catch them. The coins ringing on the tray seem to be keeping time to the music.

What is it? Nothing extraordinary, really. Berdichev, the great Jewish city, has Jewish customs of its own. This is how they collect a dowry for a poor bride.

Chaiml was acquainted with the custom. He knew that the women thought up the dances, while Podhutzer composed new melodies for them; this was the good deed Podhutzer specialized in. They'd come to him and tell him about the bride, about her family, her prospective marriage, her poverty. Podhutzer would listen silently, closing his eyes and putting his hand before his face. When they had ended, there would be quiet for a while; then Podhutzer would begin to hum a melody.

All this was familiar to Chaiml. Why, then, did he stand

there, rooted to the spot, open-mouthed and all ears? Never in all his born days had he heard so gay and fetching a melody. It wept and laughed, it exulted and lamented, all in one: heartache and happiness, inextricably intermingled, flowed from it. Just the melody for an orphan's wedding!

He started suddenly, as if he had been stung. He had it!

On the way back the driver took on several extra passengers. Chaiml had no objection. As it happened, they had some feeling for music. They told afterwards that as soon as the cart entered the forest, Chaiml began to sing.

He sang Podhutzer's new melody; but as he sang it, it became something altogether different. The *Mazel tov* of the bridal collection was reincarnated in a genuine *El Moleh Rachamim;* and against the murmurous background of the rustling trees the sweet and gentle melody floated up as if sustained by the subdued tones of a choir. Softly and tenderly it lamented, pleading for compassion before the Throne of Grace, as a sick man pleads for his life. Then, from the soft and tender, the melody passed over to the urgent, to a staccato sighing and importunation. It pleaded now, not for life, but for remission of sins. Was this the Day of Atonement, or was it a deathbed confessional?

The melody soared again and became even more fragmented; it was choked by tears, torn by anguish. Then, after a few deep sighs, a sharp cry, and again a sharp cry, which broke off completely. Silence. Someone had just died.

But no, it was not the end. The melody woke again, and became a series of blazing, passionate outcries, directed toward the heavens, an outburst of mourning, as at a funeral; and in the midst of it all, a thin, childish voice emerged, tremulous, terrified, damp with tears—a young voice intoning the Kaddish.

Images and ideas without number, echoes of visions and memories, passed through the mind, and were succeeded by a slow, gentle strain: consolation and encouragement; infinite goodness and devotion, faith as deep as the sea: all will yet be well, life will be sweet once more. The longing for life returns, and with it the will to live, the will to hope.

The listeners in the traveling cart were dumbstruck.

"What is it?" they asked at last.

"An *El Moleh Rachamim,*" answered Chaiml. "For Katzner's orphan."

"Too good for them!" they said. "It's a shame to waste such a melody. But the whole world will take it up—and those guests from Kiev will simply pass out."

The visitors from Kiev didn't pass out. The truth is that the Katzner wedding wasn't the good old-fashioned affair it should have been. The *El Moleh Rachamim* was out of place. The visitors from Kiev preferred dances with lady partners; "custom," "tradition," "morality"—who had a mind for these things? Besides, in whose memory was the *El Moleh Rachamim* sung? That old miser's?

Had the old miser been alive, the bride's dowry wouldn't have been half of what it was. Nor would she have had a trousseau. It would have been an altogether different wedding. If he had risen from the grave and seen the white satin dress, with its lace trimmings, and the veil; if he had seen the costly wines, the fish and meat dishes under which the tables groaned, he would have died again forthwith, and this time in real torment.

And anyway, who needed the whole ceremony, the

veiling of the bride, the singing of the *El Moleh Racha-mim*—stupid old customs!

"Faster!" shouted the Kiev visitors.

Poor Chaiml! He had given the orchestra the signal for silence; with beating heart he had drawn the bow across the violin strings; the simple, ordinary folk at the wedding had already begun to blink away their tears; and suddenly someone—a Kiev visitor—cried out:

"What is this? A wedding or a funeral?"

When Chaiml ignored him and went on playing, the fellow from Kiev began to whistle. And, as it happened, he whistled extremely well. He had caught on to the tune, and he whistled it correctly enough, but faster and faster, more and more brutally, vulgarly, shamelessly. And yet still the same melody.

The orchestra was silent. Nothing was heard but the battle between the decent violin and the dissolute whistling. And the whistling won. It caught up with the bow and left it behind. And now the bow no longer wept; after one groan of pain it began to laugh. Chaiml had stopped for a moment and jumped over to a higher string. With blazing eyes and tightened lips he speeded up the melody and set out after the whistling, determined to overtake it. No, this was no longer playing. Wild, broken cries issued from the violin, circling as in a whirlwind. Everything seemed to dance now, the room, the orchestra, the guests, the bride—and at last Chaiml himself with his violin.

Now the melody was neither a gay piece nor an *El Moleh Rachamim*. It was a dancing madness, an epileptic seizure, God help us. And it went on until the string snapped.

"Bravo, Chaiml, bravo!" shouted the Kiev visitors.

Perhaps you think their applause was some sort of recognition of the old miser for whom the *El Moleh Rachamim* was played. Not a bit of it!

A few years later the melody turned up in a theater—brought there by one of the Kiev guests at the wedding.

I don't know what you think about the theater. The old-time *Maskilim,* the first modernizers, used to believe that the theater was worth half a dozen morality books. You, I suppose, look on the theater as something slightly less kosher than pork. We, on the other hand, simply say that it all depends on what's being played.

The thing happened in Warsaw.

The theater was packed, you couldn't have squeezed a pin in. The orchestra struck up. And what did it play? It didn't play; it merely produced a kind of pandemonium, a babel of notes. Chaiml's *El Moleh Rachamim*—but in place of the original Wallachian theme, an unrecognizable tumult, a screeching and banging and rattling. No majesty to it, no thunder and houses falling: just plain hullabaloo. You'd think you heard the demons skating on the ice of the northern seas, or a thousand evil creatures had escaped from hell.

Suddenly the bass viol breaks through. He seems to be angry. Now we have something, it appears. No, we haven't. It's all false. The anger is put on. Then a queer little flute comes dancing up and flashes zigzag through the orchestra like an outbreak of lightning, laughing meanwhile like a clown: Ha! ha! ha! and hee! hee! hee! The clarinet takes off in pursuit. He's beside himself with excitement: to hell with everybody.

And now three or four violins come swimming out, playing with a strange, wild sweetness, as sweet as lust itself, as sweet as the demon temptress when honey drops from her lips. The playing steals into their hearts, as smooth as oil, as intoxicating as old wine. A flame wraps the audience round; eyes glitter, lips are parted.

At last the curtain rises, and "he" and "she" appear— the "king's son" and the "queen's daughter"—and they sing. The melody has words, and the words come out of their mouths like flaming, flying serpents. The fires of hell are reflected from their faces as they dance toward each other. . . . The kissing and caressing, the singing and capering, go faster and faster, get wilder and wilder. The whole theater is caught up in the blaze: the galleries with their men and women, the perspiring faces, the burning eyes. The whole theater sings. An ocean of lust lifts it and carries it away.

This is what became of Podhutzer's charity bridal song, via Chaiml's *El Moleh Rachamim,* with the help of the fellow from Kiev.

But there are depths below depths.

The Jewish theater closed its doors; the "kings' sons" became cobblers and tailors again; the "queens' daughters" returned to their chimney-corners. And some of the theater melodies were reincarnated in hurdy-gurdies.

Our melody is scarcely recognizable.

Somewhere in the courtyard of an apartment house a shabby rug is spread on the ground. The acrobats are here, two men in tights and a thin wretched-looking little girl whom they have kidnapped. One of the men balances a ladder on his teeth. The little girl scampers like a squirrel up to the top rung, jumps down, and lands neatly on the shoulder of the other man. Then, with a somersault, she comes to the ground and stands with a beggar's hand stretched out to the spectators.

This too is a theater, but for the lower orders, for serving men and servant girls. It plays under the open sky, so it can afford to be cheap. Tickets are not needed, a kopeck dropped into the hat is enough. And the thin little girl does it all so cleverly.

Big drops of sweat run down her painted young face, her sunken eyes are filled with sadness; but this the onlookers do not see. Her breathing is labored—the onlookers do not hear it. They see only the acrobatic tricks and hear only the lovely music of the hurdy-gurdy.

The soul in the body of the wretched stolen child, and the melody in the hoarse tinny hurdy-gurdy weep together; together they plead for rescue and restitution.

Rescue and restitution awaited Podhutzer's bridal melody.

Wandering from courtyard to courtyard, from town to town, the men dragged the unhappy girl along with them until she fell sick. This happened in Radziwill, near the frontier. They left her lying under a fence and stole across the frontier. Hunt the wild wind in the fields! Half-naked, with blue bruises all over her, she lay there in a fever till people found her and carried her compassionately to the poorhouse. When she recovered from the attack of typhoid she was totally blind.

She left the poorhouse and became a beggar. Blind, she crept through the streets from door to door, singing. She hardly spoke. She could not beg with words. She stood with hand outstretched and waited. Then she would begin to sing, and it was the melody that the hurdy-gurdy had played.

What does the melody say now? It says: "Pity an unhappy child. Wicked men stole me from a good father, a loving mother, a warm home. From these I was torn away, to be used up and cast aside. Pity an unhappy child."

It said: "It is cold, and I am in tatters. I am hungry. I have nowhere to lay my head. And I am blind, blind, blind."

Thus the melody pleaded, and this was its first step in purification and ascent—it provided occasion for charity.

In Radziwill there lived a *lamdan*, a scholarly Jew. He was no opponent of Chassidism, certainly not one of its persecutors; but he had not attached himself to any Chassidic rabbi, had not become a follower. He hadn't the time for it! He was too busy with his Talmudic studies. The thought of an interruption filled him with dread. Out of this same fear he did not study in the synagogue, but at home. All day long he studied, while his wife attended to the shop, and the children were at Hebrew school.

Sometimes the idea did in fact cross his mind: "Oughtn't I to choose a rabbi, become a follower, and make visits from time to time, as the custom is?" This was the good spirit in him. The wicked spirit countered by disguising itself as the good spirit and arguing back: "Yes indeed, one ought to make these trips to a rabbi. But this isn't the time. Get through, first, with this Tractate of the Talmud, and then with that one." And so the months went by, and the years.

But it was the will of Heaven that this scholarly Jew should become a follower of our Reb Dovidl of Tolny. And this is what came to pass:

One day he sat, as usual, bent over a folio of the Talmud when he heard a singing at the door. Thereupon he became angry with himself. "A man absorbed in the Talmud should be unaware of things in the street, or at the door. One must be lost in the Torah." But what was the good of saying that?—he could still hear the singing. He stopped his ears up with his fingers. The song came through. He became angrier still, shoved the point of his beard into his mouth, chewed on it, and concentrated with all his power on his studies.

It was no use; the singing persisted. It even gathered strength. Suddenly he became aware that it was a feminine voice—a girl was singing! That was too much. He cried out loudly: "Wanton! Begone from my door!" The singing ceased. But, horror of horrors, the melody sang itself in his ears, in his soul. He exerted himself to grasp the problem on the page before him. In vain. The soul of the man was filled with the melody.

He rose from the table, closed the folio, and began the afternoon prayer. But he could no more *davven* than he could study. The melody was like a silver bell inside him. And so it was all that day, and the next day, and the following days. It became unbearable. A killing gloom threatened to settle on him. He tried fasting, to no avail. He could not get rid of the melody. It haunted him in the days, it woke him in the nights.

And this was a man who had never led a congregation in prayer, had never sung a canticle. On Sabbath afternoons he would simply read off the singing prayers, and instead of singing he would give another hour to the Talmud.

It dawned on him at last that this was no simple and straightforward matter.

"Devil's work!" flashed through his mind, and his spirits fell still further. Now was the time, obviously, to set out on a visit to a Chassidic rabbi. "Certainly," said the evil spirit to him. "But to which rabbi? Who is the true saint of this generation? Who can really help you?"

And while the scholar pondered the matter, heaven prepared another sign for him. Reb Dovidl of Tolny had to take flight, and he passed through Radziwill.

I suppose you know something about the denunciation of Reb Dovidl to the Russian authorities. My own firm opinion is that the thing came on him as a punishment. It was wrong to steal Reb Dovidl away from the community of Vasilkov and bring him to Tolny. First, what a humiliation for Vasilkov! Second, the community was utterly ruined. The hostels and inns all closed down, no one earned a kopeck, starvation or beggary was all that was left to the Jews of Vasilkov. And now some informer in Tolny denounced Reb Dovidl and the same fate threatened Tolny.

Reb Dovidl, as you remember, had a golden armchair, and on it were engraved the words: "Long live David, King of Israel." That was enough for the informers, and for the government. The words were interpreted politically. *We* know of course that the words referred to the realm of Jewish learning. But how could you explain it to a Russian general?

Anyway, Reb Dovidl had to flee, and, passing through Radziwill, spent the Sabbath there; and our Jew, the *lamdan*, went, in a happy hour, to attend the Sabbath-afternoon meal. The evil spirit, however, put up a last fight. For when the *lamdan* entered the crowded room, he saw, at the head of the great table, a diminutive little figure, a dwarf almost, crowned with an immense silver-fur headgear; and the room was silent—no Torah was being said, no wisdom was being expounded. So that our visitor's heart sank, and he said to himself: "Is this all?"

Then Reb Dovidl perceived him, and greeted him with: "Sit, *lamdan*." It was enough. That single glance from Reb Dovidl penetrated his soul. You've heard, I take it, about Reb Dovidl's eyes: from them shone princeliness, sanctity, and power.

The table was crowded; but when Reb Dovidl said: "Sit," they made room for him.

Then Reb Dovidl said: "The *lamdan* will be honored with a melody," meaning that the visitor was to sing for them; whereupon the visitor almost fainted. He and a melody! But his neighbor slapped him on the back. "If Reb Dovidl says 'Sing,' you sing!" So there was nothing for it but to sing.

All confused, and in a quavery voice, he began; and what was he to sing if not the orphan's melody? Indeed, he knew no other. He trembled and stammered—and sang. And now the melody rose to another stage; it had a touch of Torah, of Sabbath sanctity, and of a scholar's penitence. Singing, the *lamdan* got the spirit of the melody; his voice took on assurance, the singing became fuller and freer.

As the *lamdan* proceeded, Reb Dovidl began to hum with him, as his custom was. The assembly followed suit. As they warmed up, the *lamdan* warmed up with them, and soon he was completely caught up in it. Amazement took hold of him: he was singing! He was really singing!

The melody flowed on, it spread, it streamed forth like a river of light, like a river of healing warmth. The room became too small for it; it burst through the windows and flowed into the street: a river of holiness, of flaming holiness; and the crowd which was gathered about the house cried out in wonder:

"The orphan's melody! The orphan's melody!"

Thus salvation came to the melody—and to the scholar.

Before he left, Reb Dovidl called the scholar to one side and said to him:

254

"*Lamdan,* you affronted and humiliated a daughter in Israel. The root and sources of her song were beyond you. You called her 'wanton.' "

"Rabbi," implored the scholar, "what penance can I do?"

"No penance is needed," answered the Rabbi. "There's something better than that—there's a good deed to perform."

"What good deed, Rabbi?"

"Find a husband for the girl. The marrying off of an orphan is among the highest deeds of merit."

There's a little epilogue to the story.

Some years later, when the girl had been married for quite a time to a widower, a learned scribe, they finally discovered who she was and where she came from. She was the granddaughter of old Katzner, the miser of Machnovke, and her father was the man from Kiev. One evening her parents had gone out to the theater, leaving her, their only child, alone. It was then that she had been kidnapped. By now the mother had been dead for many years, and her father had long since emigrated to America.

CHAPTER XVIII

"The Kiss of Moses"

❊

For the last of the retold Chassidic stories of Peretz I have chosen one that he calls *"Mekubalim"*—that is, "The Kabbalists"—which I have renamed for the English reader "The Kiss of Moses." It is an episode rather than a story; and perhaps an atmospheric piece rather than an episode. It does not stand by itself; its meaning—like the meaning of all moods—must be gathered by implication from the background. And here the background is manifold, a composite of many backgrounds.

There is the background of decline—sunset over Chassidism and over Polish Jewry. There is a strange contrast between the willful optimism of Peretz the public leader, with regard to the future of Polish Jewry, and the mournfulness—I will not use the abrupt word "pessimism"—of Peretz the poet and prince. The contrast is just as strange, and just as pathetic in retrospect, between the high hopes of Polish Jewry at the end of the first World War and the objective reality of its condition. I do not refer here to the unforeseeable catastrophe of the complete mass slaughter twenty years later, but to the substantive facts of the time, the undeniable facts, which were largely ignored. The pogroms that accompanied the liberation of Poland deflected the attention from the deeper and darker processes of destruction in Jewish life. Pogroms were a familiar, recurrent, but evanescent phenomenon. Reiterating this hopefully, the Jews of Poland encouraged themselves to forget that for a long time their historic economic foundations had been crumbling away. Long before the outbreak of the first World War Peretz had made a statistical sociological study of the Jewish villages and found them in hopeless decline. But he, too, encouraged himself to believe, at least in his publicistic capacity, that the process could be arrested and turned back. In his capacity as guardian of Jewish values he knew better, even if only instinctively. Again and again he sounds the purely nostalgic note, and nowhere more clearly than in "The Kiss of Moses."

If one must die, one does well to make death meaningful. This is the theme that is implied against another element in the background of the story. Death by physical starvation is hideous—in one sense the most ignominious form of death, betraying the most elemental failure. Death by fasting is at the other end of the scale, if the fasting is deliberate and part of a purificatory or expiatory rite; and the death of Polish Jewry, the death of the student—these are interchangeable symbols in this story.

And a third background is the Chassidic-kabbalistic, in which death is seen as reabsorption of the soul into its mighty fount. The return to the fount is open to all, but the manner of the return is also significant. Moses set the first Jewish example of translation without the ordinary humiliations of death. Enoch, whose disappearance from life is recorded simply as "and he was not, for God took him," lived before Abraham and therefore before Judaism. Moses confronted the Angel of Death with non-recognition; he did not desire to live forever, he simply would not recognize the universal sovereignty of the executioner. God, in turn, recognized the protest and, stooping to earth, drew out the soul of Moses with a kiss. To die *b'nshikah,* with the kiss of Moses, is, then, the symbol of the transfigured death.

Thus when Reb Yankel of the one-time glorious Talmudical College of Lashvitz was left, in the decline of the village, with only one pupil, Lamech; when the poverty of the villagers became such that it could no longer supply "days" to students (to "eat days" was to be assigned to certain houses for meals on certain days of the week); when depopulation, hunger, and worry had sapped the spiritual as well as the economic resources of the dwindling community, and the little that was sent to sustain the life of Reb Yankel and the student Lamech was sent ungraciously; when things had reached this pass, master and pupil turned for solace to Kabbalah and mysticism.

The master in tatters, the pupil in rags; the old, lean man with his long, unkempt beard and sunken eyes, the lean young man with the tremulous Adam's apple and burning black eyes; both without shirts under their coarse outer garments, both in clumsy boots too large for them: this was all that was left of the illustrious Yeshivah of Lashvitz. Reb Yankel would not leave—he was too old to begin life again; he would die here. And his beloved pupil remained with him to do him his last earthly service, close his eyes and put the potsherds on them.

They had become familiar with hunger, and with its consequences. Those who eat little do not sleep well; and those who stay awake nights for lack of food feel a longing for mystical experiences, for Kabbalah. "Let's turn it to account," said Reb Yankel. Let the lack of food become fasts, let the nights become vigils; in the fasts and vigils they would make acquaintance with the demons and angels and other mysteries of the world of Kabbalah.

Day long and night long, then, they sat over the Book of Splendor and other mystical works. They sat at the long table about which so many pupils had once been ranged, they two, alone. And one afternoon, when the villagers had already eaten the midday meal, but Rabbi and pupil were still waiting for breakfast, one afternoon Reb Yankel was explaining to Lamech the kabbalistic significance of melody.

"There are many levels of melody and of knowledge," he said. "One man will know only a fragment of a mystic melody, another man as much as a half, a third, or—and this is rare—an entire melody. My Rabbi, of blessed memory, possessed an entire melody together with a supplementary harmony. And I—" the voice sank sadly—"I know just about this much." And he measured off a fraction of his forefinger with his thumb.

"There are melodies," he went on, "that must have words. Such melodies belong to the lower levels. On a higher level a melody sings itself without words—pure melody. But even such a melody, to be sung, must have a throat, and delicate though that instrument is, it is nevertheless material, and therefore gross. Let us even concede that the voice is halfway between spirit and matter—the melody that needs a voice is still tainted with the earthy. It has not attained to pure spirit. And therefore the true melody is one that does not need even a voice. It utters itself within, in the heart, in the organs. That is the secret meaning of King David's words: 'All my bones shall praise the Lord.' The marrow of the bones becomes vocal, and then the melody is the highest praise of the Eternal. Nor is this a melody that a human brain has thought up. No, it is part of the melody with which God created the world, the melody of the soul which He poured into her. It is also the melody of the congregation of the blessed hosts;

and it is the melody of my teacher, of blessed memory."

The lesson was interrupted by the entry of a big, slovenly youth with a rope about his middle—a pack-carrier. He came into the Study House and deposited on the table, near Reb Yankel, a bowl of grits and a piece of bread, saying coarsely: "Reb Tevel sends this food to the head of the Yeshivah." He turned and went, calling over his shoulder: "I'll come back for the bowl."

Pulled out of his lofty mood by the rude interruption, Reb Yankel rose to wash his hands before eating. As he walked back and forth, his clumsy boots dragging and slapping on the floor, he still talked, but some of the enthusiasm had departed from his voice.

"As for me, I cannot even grasp the nature of that melody, or guess to which level it belongs, by which gate it enters. But I can tell you"—here he smiled sadly—"what exercises of self-discipline and self-mortification and self-purification lead to that melody. And these I will teach you this afternoon."

The eyes of the pupil started from their sockets, and with wide-open mouth he swallowed every word uttered by the Rabbi. But now the latter broke off. Having washed his hands and uttered the prayer, Reb Yankel seated himself before the bowl. As the warm steam rose about his bony face, he took the spoon in his right hand, and with his left caressed the bowl, warming himself. Lamech watched, and when the first mouthful was lifted to the trembling lips, he felt a contraction of the heart. He covered his face with his hands and shrank in on himself.

A few moments later another youth entered the Study House with a bowl of grits and a piece of bread:

"Reb Joseph sends this food to the student."

Lamech did not take his hands away from his face. Reb Yankel put down his spoon, rose, and went over to his pupil. For a moment he looked at him with proud love in his eyes; then he wrapped his hand in the skirt of his gabardine and touched Lamech's shoulder.

"They've brought you food," he said affectionately.

Lamech took his hands from his face; his face was paler than before, his eyes glittered more wildly.

"I know, Rabbi. But I will not eat today."

"The fourth day in succession?" asked Reb Yankel. "And without me?" There was a touch of reproach in his voice.

"It is another kind of fast," answered the pupil. "It is an expiatory fast."

"What are you saying? Expiatory?"

"Yes, Rabbi. I must expiate something. Just a little while ago I sinned in thought. At the moment you began to eat I transgressed against the commandment: 'Thou shalt not covet.' "

That same night, at a late hour, the pupil woke his Rabbi. They had fallen asleep stretched out on two wooden benches, opposite each other.

"Rabbi, Rabbi," he called weakly.

The old man started up, frightened by the voice. "What is it?" he asked.

"I have just been on the topmost level."

"How do you know?"

"The singing was inside me."

Reb Yankel sat up, half asleep.

"How was it? Tell me, how was it?"

"Rabbi, I hardly know myself." The pupil's voice became weaker. "I couldn't sleep, so I thought as closely as I could on your discourse of yesterday; and my soul insisted

261

ın reaching that melody of the spirit. . . . And because I couldn't reach it I began to weep with disappointment. And the weeping spread through me, so that all my limbs wept before the Almighty. But all the time I kept repeating the disciplines and purifications you had taught me; not with my lips, but within me. And a strange, wonderful thing happened. A light burst on me. I kept my eyes closed, but I was all light within."

"Yes!" The head of the Yeshivah bent over toward his pupil.

"The light spread in me, and I felt so good, so bodiless. It seemed to me that I had lost all bodily weight, and that I could fly."

"Yes, yes!"

"And out of that lightness there came joy and gaiety. I was filled with laughter. My face did not move, my lips were motionless, and I was laughing. Wonderful, pleasant, hearty laughter."

"Yes, yes, yes! Out of pure joy!"

"Then a humming and murmuring began inside me. . . ."

Old Reb Yankel leapt from his bench and sat down eagerly by his pupil's side.

"And then? And then?"

"Then I heard that singing inside me."

"Tell me what you felt! Quick! What?"

"I felt that all my senses had been sealed off from the outside world, and there was a singing inside me. The real kind of singing that you spoke of, a singing without words."

"But the melody! What was the melody?"

"No, Rabbi, I can't. I thought I knew the melody, but I don't now. Then the singing changed. It became—it became—"

"Became what?"

"A playing on instruments instead of a singing. As though there were a violin inside me, and Jonah the fiddler were seated near me, as in the old days, when there used to be assemblies at your table and there was singing of holy melodies after the grace. No, it was better; it was a playing much more of the spirit; a playing that had no real sound, but which I heard within me."

"Ah!" cried the Rabbi. "Happy, happy, happy youth!"

"And now it is gone," said the pupil mournfully. "My senses are open again on the world. And I am so tired, so tired. . . .

"Rabbi," he cried suddenly, and put a hand to his heart. "Say the confessional with me! They've come for me! They need a singer up in the heavenly choir! They need a singer with white wings. Rabbi! 'Hear, O Israel—Hear' . . ."

There was not a man in the village of Lashvitz who did not envy Lamech his death. But the old head of the Yeshivah was dissatisfied.

"Only a couple of fasts more," he lamented, "and he would have died with the kiss of Moses."

CHAPTER XIX

"Translators Are Traitors"

❀

T HE closing chapters of this book are in the nature of a tacit apology and an attempt at an explanation. It is hoped, however, that they will serve more than the translator's purpose of confession of his inadequacy, that they will, for him who has read thus far and reads farther, throw back on the preceding pages a touch of illumination.

At the outset of this book, speaking of "understanding the Jewish world," I said that goodwill is not enough. There is also the need for a sustained intellectual effort. Is that effort worth while? To this the answer is always individual. But for those who say "Yes," the warning is here issued that only those will think they can get the soul of a Jewish writer in a hurry who also believe they can get the essence of Shakespeare in two shakes of a Lamb's Tale. It is impossible to penetrate to the Yiddish world by mere translation; there must be, on the part of the reader, a willingness to devote some attention to the peculiar, revealing character of Yiddish, to whatever extent this character can be conveyed in English. We will begin by admitting and discussing the limitations; we shall then see what can be done about them.

It is useless to try to explain why the rules of good Eng-

lish forbid you to say: "He made himself a non-perishable
name by inventing an imperishable food." You let it go
with the remark that that happens to be the genius of the
English language—and then add hastily that "genius" as
here used does not mean extraordinary gift of native
power, but pervading spirit. Every language has its genius, which is non-transferable; and on one level Yiddish
differs from English or French or Italian just as these differ from one another.

It differs in the same way from the German, even though
it has taken from a German dialect about eighty-five per
cent of its raw material. In one very important sense the
primitive roots of a language are like foods absorbed by
different persons: the end results are incommensurable.
Ivan eats a potato and it becomes Ivan, Hans eats the same
potato and it becomes Hans. From this point of view it is
wholly wrong to identify Yiddish with German, and especially silly to call it, as some do, a corrupted German. (It
is of course equally absurd to suggest, as others are
tempted to, that German is a corrupt Yiddish.) When the
Jews of the Rhine valley had, after some centuries, di-
gested the German roots, these were no longer recognizable as far as the spirit is concerned.

True, the Yiddish words *tish* (table), *mensh* (person),
kop (head), *ferd* (horse), are, as raw material, pretty much
the same as in German, and a pidgin German-Yiddish
conversation can be carried on by their means. But the
moment spirit enters, the communication is broken. A
couple of instances will suffice:

The simple Yiddish phrase *dem Rebbens shnur* (the
Rabbi's daughter-in-law) is in one sense easily understood
by a German, only he would say *die Schnur des Rabbiners,* although *Schnur* is now archaic and *Schwiegertoch-
ter* is the modern equivalent. Actually *dem Rebbens*

shnur and *die Schnur des Rabbiners* are worlds apart, for reasons which, even if we could elucidate them, would not help us at all to make the two worlds one.

Dem Rebbens shnur! It is a phrase loaded with many values, each of which is brought out by its appropriate intonation. Say it one way and it is quiet and dignified, evocative of Friday-evening candles and the Sabbath loaf. Say it somewhat differently—pulling in your chin a little —and it becomes an epitome of small-town snobbery: the young woman walking down the street, *her* chin pulled in a little, and the whisper passing from door to door: "*Dem Rebbens shnur!*" A third manner, and the physical image vanishes; it becomes an abstraction, a function in a lofty tradition, an institution for which there is no substitute. But *die Schnur des Rabbiners,* like *the Rabbi's daughter-in-law,* is merely a young woman who married the son of a rabbi—a statistical fragment.

There is a curious and charming portmanteau word in Yiddish, *Staitch!* which can best be described (if described at all) as an expletive of expostulation. If one Jew has told another a tall story that can be neither accepted nor denied, it is not impolite to answer with the exclamation: "*Staitch!*" In this sense it may be tormented into English as: "Bless my soul! You don't tell me!" Or if someone has committed a misdemeanor (as distinguished from a serious crime), he may be reproved with a somewhat distressful: "*Staitch!*" which amounts more or less to: "But, my dear fellow, one can't do that sort of thing!" Or if someone makes an unreasonable demand, you counter with an appeal to the sense of proportion: "*Staitch!*" —which now becomes an ironical but not unfriendly: "How d'you get that way?" And still again, recalling to an ingrate the benefits he once received, "*Staitch!*" approximates to: "Man alive! In the face of all I've done for you?" And in a similar spirit, though on other grounds, it may be adressed to the Almighty Himself, meaning then: "Father in heaven! After all our faithfulness!"

It all depends on the intonation which may be:

1. courteously skeptical (the tall story),
2. fraternally admonitory (the misdemeanor),
3. amicably derisive (the excessive demand),
4. speechlessly distressful (the ingrate), or
5. intimately but unresentfully accustatory (the Almighty).

And I do not speak of the possible permutations and combinations of these numbers, which, in the mouth of an unusually expressive person, may achieve incredibly edifying results.

Now the word *Staitch!* has been traced back to the German phrase *wie heisst's auf Deutsch?*—"What do you call that in German?" It may originally have been an innocent question or a provocative challenge. I have heard Americans, confronted with some baffling or offensive statement, cry back: "Say, what's that in American?" Or, as Maria says to the clown in *Twelfth Night,* "Make that good." *Wie heisst's auf Deutsch* was gradually consulted from four syllables into one, and the shorter it grew in pronunciation, the wider it grew in implication. What connection is there now between the Germanic raw material and the Yiddish finished product? Who can translate the latter back into the former? As well try to unscramble an omelet and hatch a chicken from it. It is of course interesting and instructive to trace the transmutation; but the information this provides brings the outsider no nearer to the insider's "*Staitch!*" And in the same way, if someone were to trace the steps by which *imperishable* and *non-perishable* acquired their specific tonalities in

267

English, he would not thereby learn the usage of the words; that comes from practice plus instinct, rather than from logic.

Personal names are fascinating instances of spiritual molds. Why is it that the English name *Tom* has become synonymous with manliness and honesty?—in combination, naturally, with honest and manly surnames. Fielding's Tom Jones and Hughes's Tom Brown are two of the most famous exemplars of English solidity of character. To be sure, they corresponded to widely divergent ideals; Tom Brown would have shrunk from Tom Jones as a gross and sensual early Georgian, and Tom Jones would have grinned at Tom Brown as a mid-Victorian milksop. But each was to his age the embodiment of grand old English grit and mettle. I feel that it is useless to seek the why of this distinction; at best we may get part of the where and when. Still, why is it that *Caleb,* on the other hand, is naturally a villain, a tricky lawyer, a heartless collector of mortgages? One is tempted to look back at the Hebrew original: *Kelev,* a dog. But Caleb was not a name of evil association among the Hebrews. On the contrary, a well-known Caleb—namely, ben Yefunneh—shares with Joshua ben Nun the distinction of having brought back from Palestine the first favorable minority report. Of the twelve spies sent in by Moses, only these two were undaunted by the dangers of the conquest. We see, then, that names, passing from one language or people to another, may undergo transvaluations just like other words. And what can translators do about it?

The extent to which Yiddish has remolded the raw material it has taken over may be studied in proper names. *Shprintze* is an especially lovable girl's name in Yiddish. It has gaiety and goodness. One thinks of Shprintze as young and bright-eyed; one sees her running, basket on

arm, to the village market, her shining, pointed nose innocent of powder, her lips parted in a happy smile. She is
poor but jolly, betrothed, or recently married, to a sturdy
workman, who is admittedly not much of a scholar, but
respectful of learning, observant of the tradition, and prepared, of course, to give his children the finest education
obtainable. That is Shprintze. The name is derived from
the Spanish *Esperanza,* and was brought (it is surmised)
by Spanish Jews at the time of the expulsion into the valley of the Rhine, where Yiddish was already in an advanced stage of crystallization.

Now, I do not know what suggestions the name Esperanza carries with it for most Spaniards. The word means
"hope," but that may go for nothing. A girl called Hope
in English unfortunately suggests one from whom there
is little to be hoped, just as *Friedrich,* in German, suggests
anything rather than its literal meaning, "rich in peace."
For me (and since I do not know Spanish my feeling about
the name has nothing to do with its Spanish overtones)
Esperanza suggests alternately the cloister and the guitar;
on the one hand a nun's name, but also, on the other, the
name of the young woman whose eyes, "more darkly
bright than love's own star," were hidden by the lattice
from those of the serenader below. Well, whoever Esperanza was, she has become Shprintze, altogether unrecognizable; and never again will Shprintze be Esperanza.

In a like way the Yiddish girl's name *Yente*—it is really
not a girl's name, somehow one thinks of it always as be-
longing to a grown woman—goes back to the Italian *Gentilia.* Yente has become for the Yiddish world synonymous
with noisiness and vulgarity, with some implications of
rough good-heartedness: it is the equivalent of "washer-
woman." It would be absurd, in translating a Yiddish
story into Italian, to make Yente Gentilia again; but nei-

269

ther does the Italian get a hint of the author's intention if the name is left as it is.

Possibly the extremest instance of such a transformation is found in the Yiddish name *Feivish,* which began as Phœbus Apollo. Now Feivish—especially when coupled with Yukel—is perhaps the most comical-trivial man's name in the Yiddish-speaking world. Zangwill found an equal for it in Soshe Shmendrik, which is, however, synthetic. Not only is Feivish utterly remote from any physical suggestion of Phœbus Apollo ("He was a man born with thy face and throat, lyric Apollo," sings Browning in "The Dead Grammarian"); no writer would dream of assigning to a Feivish the smallest task calling for dignity, common sense, learning, or even clear enunciation.

I have referred to the immense range of intonation that endows the word *Staitch!* with countless variations of meaning. Spoken Yiddish differs, again, from spoken English, in relation to their written models, in a manner which I obviously cannot hope to convey here; but the spoken language has naturally reacted back on the written; and in Yiddish the context of a phrase or word carries a larger hint of intonation than in English.

All this is intended to illustrate that Yiddish has its separate genius, and more particularly to make clear that the etymological origins of Yiddish words are no longer a clue to their living identity. The result is—as I mentioned in *The World of Sholom Aleichem*—that it is just as hard to translate classical Yiddish into German as into English or French. I have always been skeptical of the language-scholars who try to clarify the meaning of living words by reference to their roots in a dead language: skeptical, that is, on this one point; their material has great value and interest in other regards. Actually it is harder to translate classic Yiddish (I shall explain farther on what "classic"

Yiddish is) into German than into French or English or Italian, precisely because of the physical affinity of German and Yiddish. There is an additional obstacle. When a ghetto Jew wanted to sound cultured in the modern sense, superior to his surroundings, and tony generally, he Germanified his Yiddish; that is, he tried to reassemble the omelet. Thus a serious translation of Yiddish into German savors of the outlandish and affected, at least to the Yiddish ear, so that the translator is thrown off balance. Besides which German, either in its involved and stately mood or in homely mood, is not so apt as Anglo-Saxon English to convey whatever can be conveyed of Yiddish to a non-Jew.

Of the languages I know, Yiddish is by far the best for reading aloud—as the reader must surmise from what I have already said about it. But the reading aloud of even a good English translation from the Yiddish is extremely dangerous. I once witnessed an English performance of Ansky's *Dybbuk;* the acting was good, and the translation —as I thought back on it—not at all bad. But the actors had an Oxford-cum-Harvard accent, and their cultured epiglottal voices, issuing from the bearded faces of gabardined Chassidim, turned the tragedy into a grisly comedy.

Now, when Jews speak of the "impossibility" of translating Yiddish into English, they have in mind just those differences of spirit and idiom which are the ordinary barriers between all languages. They will ask, for instance: "How on earth can you say in English: *'Hayre off tzu hacken a tchainik'?" Hacken a tchainik* (literally, to chop or wallop a teakettle) is to talk nonsense long and earnestly on a given subject. *Hayre off* is "stop," or "give over." To make it harder they will cite: *"Er hot gehackt a tchainik off vos die velt shteht"* (he walloped a teakettle on what the world stands on), meaning "incessantly," "interminably," or, in idiom, "to beat the band." But when such instances are given—and it should be noted that we have to do here with words of non-Hebrew origin—they are really beside the point as far as the particularity of Yiddish is concerned. *These* difficulties do not make of Yiddish a uniquely untranslatable language; they merely show that Yiddish is neither more nor less translatable than other languages and has nothing special to complain of. There is another level on which Yiddish is in fact unique, and I shall come to that in the next chapter.

Meanwhile I am willing to concede that perhaps Yiddish is in fact somewhat more difficult of translation than other languages even on the ordinary level. In *The World of Sholom Aleichem* I called Yiddish a "knowing language," because of the special intramural hints, allusions, and interjections in which it abounds; it is also that because of intonation and gesticulation. I have not yet come across a theory which explains why some languages—Chinese, for instance—give the same syllable-words entirely unrelated meanings on different pitches. I am tempted to suggest that the early crystallizers of Yiddish, speaking a dialect that was then much nearer to the originating language, and therefore intelligible to the hostile strangers around them, began to develop a technique of gesture and intonation which enabled them to converse on two levels simultaneously, one for themselves, one for the outsiders. There is a popular Yiddish story about a Jew who is being tried for the theft of a chicken: asked by the judge—via an interpreter—whether he pleads guilty or not guilty, he answers in quiet despair: "*I* stole the chicken!" The interpreter, obviously not a Jew, translates: "Guilty," whereas a Jew would have known from the intonation that "*I* stole the chicken," thus uttered, means the exact opposite, and in its extremest form.

Later, when Yiddish was spoken (in Poland, Russia, Rumania) among surrounding peoples that could not have understood it, the presence of a gentile may have impelled the Jew to develop the gesture as an auxiliary of speech, and occasionally as a substitute for it. But gesticulation is common, though in varying degrees. The French gesticulate much more freely than the English, the Americans, or the Germans. But I do not find in French gesticulation the peculiar congruence with meaning which I find in Yiddish. The Frenchman seems to gesticulate because he is energetic, the Jew because he is subtle; the Frenchman emphasizes his meaning by a tone, the Jew changes it.

There are of course Yiddish phrases and idioms that are the crystallization of purely Jewish experience or social form. *Dem Rebbens shnur* is what it is in Yiddish because of the accumulation of associations round a specifically Jewish institution. A phrase like *areinfallen vie a Yoven in Sukkah* (to blunder like an ignorant boor into a festival tabernacle) condenses a world of circumstance. The *Sukkah* is the ritual tabernacle that Jews put up during the festival of Sukkoth. To adorn the *Sukkah* beautifully, to take one's meals in it ceremoniously, to sit there whenever possible, is a commandment and a delight; there is about the *Sukkah* a peculiarly intimate and tender complex of memories and emotions. The image of an insensitive stranger blundering into a *Sukkah* as if it were an ordinary hut or lean-to is therefore vivid and painful. *Yoven*, a Greek (figuratively, any boorish fellow) may be an echo of Maccabean times. "Bull in a china shop" is the best I can do with the phrase in English.

There are phrases and turns of speech which are quite hopeless from the translator's point of view. A certain type of Jew is described as *a shadchan a badchan a ganev a lamdan a Yid*. Literally, a *shadchan* is a marriage-broker,

a *badchan* a wedding jester, a *ganev* a thief (but the word
is used jestingly, too), a *lamdan* a scholar, a *Yid* a Jew. But
these professions or attributes are each embedded, for the
Yiddish-speaking Jew, in entire sub-worlds of association,
and a man who is all those things put together is a one-
man civilization. The best I can produce here, for rhyth-
mic effect and friendliness of tone, is: "a rascally son-of-
a-gun of a scholarly matchmaking Jew." Not very helpful.

Sometimes there is an incredibly felicitous approxima-
tion. *Gott die neshomeh shuldig* (literally, owing God his
soul; i.e., blameless as a babe unborn) is hit off perfectly
in English by "butter wouldn't melt in his mouth." The
phrases cover each other perfectly, nothing missing, nothing left over. And it is amusing—as well as rather touch-
ing—to observe how two such disparate peoples as the
Jews and the English, and two such disparate languages,
have found the identical attitude of good-humored derision toward impudent rascality parading as injured inno-
cence.

Alas for the good souls who dream of a universal literal
language, Ito or Esperanto or Basic English, even as an
auxiliary. Man is born to idiom as the sparks fly upward.
The difference between literal language and idiom is the
difference between barracks and a home. From the intimi-
dating efficiency of the first we turn to the coziness and
privacy—and dangers—of the second. And if we live in
barracks for more than a week or two, we create little corners in it, corners for ourselves and our clique, to which
outsiders are aliens: little intimacies, attachments, and
idiosyncrasies spring up about the shape of the wall and
the places of the cots. What a hullabaloo there will be in
the Esperanto world when—as they must sooner or later
—idioms spring up unbidden. Or have some appeared already? (I severed my connection with the language after a

high-minded and barren affair with it many years ago.) No doubt more idioms will be needed in Esperanto to express the consternation of the Esperantists at the first deviations from literalness.

I come back to my Yiddish and its idioms, and repeat: in respect of the points I have discussed so far, Yiddish is a language like others, with certain inalienable values and an inalienable spirit; these are not my reason for stating that classic Yiddish cannot be translated. Extraordinary things have been done in the way of translation. The Bible in English at once springs to the mind, and after it Shakespeare in German. Almost as great as these, for ingenuity and insight, is Scott Moncrieff's translation of Proust. And as an instance of what can be done by way of murdering someone in a foreign language, we have only to look at the English translations of *Faust*. There is a special delight in reading the Bible with the Hebrew and English side by side, or Shakespeare with the English and German: there are neatnesses and profundities of transmission which bring a sudden smile of joy to the lips. I say "joy"—for it is that kind of happiness which attends the breaking down of seemingly insuperable barriers between one people and another, one language and another. And yet: one becomes alive to the paradox that very often the better the translation, the more it wrongs the original. The less it reads like a translation (and is not that the conscientious translator's aim?), the more uneasy the original creator, wherever he may be, must be feeling at the transformation. "Very wonderful," he murmurs wryly, "but is that really me?"

But even this pleasant discomfort will forever be denied the three classic Yiddish writers (among others): Yal Peretz, Sholom Aleichem, and Mendele Mocher Sforim. And why this must be so, why the utmost genius cannot

conceivably find a way of doing them justice in translation, will be talked over in the next chapter.

NOTE ON PRONUNCIATION. I have been at a loss as to how
to deal with the transliterations. There are certain scientific rules familiar to scholars, and to few others. I thought
it would be a nuisance to introduce them here. I decided
to trust to my ear, and to use the ordinary English repro-
duction of the sound of Litvak Yiddish. (Except for the
ch, which must be pronounced as in German. Where I
need a *ch* as pronounced in English, I write *tch.*) That,
however, is only half the problem. There are at least two
ways of pronouncing Hebrew: the modern Palestinian,
also called the Sephardic, which is a revival of the surmised ancient Palestinian pronunciation; and the Ashkenazic (itself subdivided into groups) used by Yiddish-
speaking Jewry. Jews who speak both Yiddish and Hebrew have a strange way of using both pronunciations!
When they are speaking Hebrew *only* they will most
probably use only the modern (revived ancient) Palestinian or Sephardic pronunciation. When they are speaking Yiddish and use some of the Hebrew words current in
Yiddish, they will pronounce these as they have always
been pronounced in the Yiddish-speaking world, before
the revival of Hebrew.

For instance: *chatunáh* is wedding or marriage, Sephardic pronunciation; the Ashkenazic pronunciation is *chásseneh.* The most unbending purist among modern Hebra-
ists would not (assuming he spoke Yiddish at all) say in
Yiddish: *"Er hat chatunáh gehat,"* for "he got married."
He would say: *"Er hat chásseneh gehat."*

The difference between the Sephardic and Ashkenazic
can sometimes be very wide. In one form of the Ashkenazic, "closed doors" is approximately: *dlóóssess sgééress.* In

the Sephardic it is *dlatót sgoorót*. In the Ashkenazic the first syllables are accented; in the Sephardic the second.

Of the various Yiddish pronunciations, Galician, Rumanian, Litvak, Polish, I will only say that they make little difference to the content. There is much less of a gap, in idiom, between Galician Yiddish and Litvak Yiddish than between Ayrshire English and Somerset English. Nevertheless that little difference is important because to the Yiddish reader it is the clue to differences of types: the logical Litvak, the excitable Galician, the nervous Pole, the earthy Rumanian. It is obviously useless to try to indicate such differences in a translation. That, again, is a difficulty not peculiar to Yiddish. All attempts to translate the dialect of one language into an equivalent in another language must fail. I once saw some songs of Robert Burns translated into local dialect in a Bordeaux newspaper, and it threw me into a state of melancholy for weeks.

CHAPTER XX

A Language with a Policy

❀

A LANGUAGE cannot be born of a program, witness the failures of those estimable projects Ito and Esperanto, already cited; it cannot even be remade by a policy, witness the failure of the German nationalists to substitute in popular usage *Fernsprecher* for *Telefon* and *Funkspruch* for *Radiogram*. The peculiarity of Yiddish is that, possessing as a language both a policy and a program, it is nevertheless natural and authentic.

Between ten and twelve per cent of classical written and spoken Yiddish consists of Hebrew words. These, however, are not, like many of the German root words, transformed in spelling and meaning. They remain pure Hebrew, written as Hebrew is written. They are almost never mutilated into the phonetic Yiddish spelling. (Of the rare exceptions I can think only of *bahavent,* adept, and—occasionally—*ballebatim,* householders.) Sometimes they are given Germanic prefixes and suffixes; in that case the Hebrew word is retained intact, and in writing is separated from the prefix and the suffix by an apostrophe.

Thus: *harog* is Hebrew for "to kill." It is written *hrg*— Hebrew has no written vowels. When the word is used in written Yiddish it is also spelled *hrg,* although Yiddish has vowels—it uses some of the Hebrew letters for that purpose. In Yiddish, *killed* is written *ge'hrg'et* and pronounced *geharget*. One does not tamper with the spelling of the Hebrew root.

The same rule applies to *ge'chlm't* (pronounced *gecholemt*), dreamed; *ge'yrsh'nt* (pronounced *geyarshent*), inherited; *ge'gnv't* (pronounced *geganvet*), stolen; *ge'ml't* (pronounced *gemallet*), circumcised, etc. And of course Hebrew words that stand alone, without prefix or suffix, are spelt in the original. Thus, *smchh* (pronounced *simchah*), rejoicing; *yllh* (pronounced *yellolloh*), lamentation; *kbtzn* pronounced *kabtzan*), pauper; *sf* (pronounced *sof*), end, etc. (Cf. *gekidnapped, gecatched,* etc.)

Now, the oddity is that in Yiddish most of these Hebrew root words have their Germanic root doubles, and the two words are used side by side! It is sound folk Yiddish to say *"a simchah a freid"* (German *Freud*), for "a rejoicing"; *"a yellolloh a gevein"* (German *weinen*), for "a lamentation"; *"a kabtzan an orreman"* (German *armer Mann*), for "a pauper"; *"a sof an ek"* (German *Ecke*), for "an end."

One would almost think that it is an echo of the poetic dittology so familiar in the Bible: *"Hear,* O heavens, and *give ear,* O earth . . . I have *nourished* and *brought up* sons. . . , Ah, *sinful nation,* a *people laden with iniquity.* . . ."* But it is not that at all. For in the Hebrew the repetition has variation, and the rhythm has an ascending effect; it is a reinforcement. In the Yiddish the effect is quite different, and will be explained below.

A parallel to this type of repetition is to be found in archaic English. Louis H. Gray, in his fascinating *Foundations of Language,* quotes from the Book of Common Prayer: "to acknowledge and *confess,*" "to *assemble* and meet together," "to *pray* and beseech." The italicized words are of Romance origin, their parallels of Anglo-

Saxon. And again: *"mortify* and kill," *"perceive* and know," *"power* and might." Professor Gray then points out that in the Roman missal, from which the above prayers are taken, there is only one Latin word where the English translation has two: *mortifica* becomes *"mortify* and kill," *videant* becomes *"perceive* and know," *virtutem* becomes *"power* and might." The reason for this practice, as we know, lies in the history of the English language, in the need that once existed to make public utterances intelligible equally to speakers of Anglo-Saxon and of Norman French—namely, during the period of the fusion of the two languages.

We are tempted to assume that the Jews of the Rhine valley adopted a similar device. The mass of the people spoke a Germanic dialect, the learned spoke Hebrew; the repetitions were a sort of bridge; in time the two languages would fuse into one, each losing its separate identity. But the explanation will not do. It was never in the mind of Yiddish-speaking Jews (let alone Hebrew-speaking) that Hebrew should be lost. The pattern of their lives was directed at the perpetuation of the national-religious identity, with Palestine as the land of the return, and Hebrew as the language of the redemption. All the prayers, with a few very minor exceptions, were said in pure Hebrew even by those who understood them imperfectly, or not at all. Both the ritual and the prayers are unintelligible unless they are seen from the point of view of national-cultural conservation. Classic Yiddish writing derives its stylistic strength and charm from the deliberate emphasis on Hebrew phraseology. Yiddish had a policy which gave it its folk-character—and that was: to keep Hebrew alive.

Quite a number of simple Hebrew words so established themselves in Yiddish that the German repetitive explanatory word was hardly needed, or not needed at all. So one says *ganev* (thief), never *Dieb; Lamdan* (scholar), seldom *Gelehrter*—and then only for non-Jewish learning; *matbeya* (coin), never *Münze; meshugas* (lunacy), never *Wahnsinn; mumcheh* (specialist), seldom *Spezialist.*

There are some minor oddities in the language which only point up the thesis I am presenting. Jews became so accustomed to the repetitive technique that in a few cases they applied it without the purpose I am suggesting— namely, the conservation of Hebrew. They say *"an umglick a malayre,"* "a misfortune," *the umglick* being German, the *malayre* French *(malheur)*. *(Malheur* and *égal* came into the Yiddish of Russian Jewry with the Napoleonic invasion of Russia in 1812.) They also say: *"a shoiteh a tipish"* (a fool), though both words are Hebrew. But these are rare instances. There has also crept into Yiddish a queer and charming form of repetitiveness direct from the Hebrew. *"Ki goonav goonavti m'eretz ha-Ivrim,"* laments Joseph in Egypt. *"Goonav goonavti"* are the same verb; literally: *"to be stolen I was stolen* from the land of the Hebrews." The regular translation is: "For indeed I was stolen." In Yiddish we say: *"Essen fleg er essen in der heim, nor shlofen fleg er shlofen by der mummen";* literally, "To eat, he used to eat at home, but to sleep, he used to sleep at his aunt's." I have even met, in Peretz and elsewhere, this phrase: *"Isn is er a nar";* literally, "to be, he is a fool"; meaning: "As for what he is, he is a fool."

It would not help us much to discuss the extent to which the national policy of Yiddish—that is, the conservation of Hebrew—was conscious among some groups. We merely see the effect: one cannot speak good Yiddish without using a great many Hebrew words; and writing a good Yiddish, we preserve the original spelling of the He-

brew words, isolating them by punctuation from the con-
tamination of Germanic affixes. Only the most ignorant
Jews would spell the Hebrew words in phonetic, Germanized style: *neshomeh* for *nshmh, chasseneh* for *chtnh, kal-
leh* (bride) for *klh,* and so on. What is more significant is
that precisely this type of Germanized spelling was
adopted by modern Jews opposed to Zionism and the
Hebrew-nationalist spirit. With them, certainly, the
change was purposive and was directed at the elimination
of the separate Hebrew element. They wanted the Hebrew and the Germanic to fuse as the Anglo-Saxon and
the Norman French fused into modern English.

I have referred several times to "classic" Yiddish writing and to its leading practitioners, Peretz, Sholom Aleichem, and Mendele Mocher Sforim. In their most typical
work they have loaded their Yiddish so heavily with Hebrew—over and above the common usage as already described—that it is impossible to read them intelligently
without a good knowledge of Hebrew; and the beauty of
their style springs, strangely enough, from the naturalness
of this bias. Still more strangely, they do not simply put in
Hebrew quotations, phrases, verses from prayer and Holy
Writ: in most instances they translate them at once into
German-origin Yiddish. And yet it does not sound like a
translation, but rather like a repetition. The effect is not
one of pedantry and affectation, as if an English writer
were to strew his pages with Latin tags. On the contrary,
the style thereby becomes more homey and authentic. It
has echoes of childhood and the cheder, of winter conver-
sations about the stove in the Study House, of the nostalgia for learning which was a perpetual mood with the
Jewish masses, echoes of spiritual salvation, of the synagogue, the cemetery, and the festivals.

This programmatic and purposive character of good

Yiddish, aiming at the teaching of Hebrew, cannot of course be rendered in translation. For if a Jew says: *"a sof an eck,"* you can only translate it as "an end"; and if he says: *"sein bas yechidah, sein eintzige tochter,"* he has merely said "his only daughter," once in Hebrew-origin Yiddish and once in German-origin Yiddish. It does not sound at all repetitious in the Yiddish; it is on the contrary charming and natural; it has a "dying fall," and a little touch of melancholy, or perhaps of mere reflectiveness. But in English I can neither say "his only daughter, his only daughter," nor can I insist on "his *bas yechidah,* his only daughter," since my reader does not want to learn Hebrew, and even if he did he would have to go about it without mutilating the English narrative.

Beauty, we are told, must be functional if it is not to be meretricious, trivial, or decadent. One of the functions of Yiddish, therefore one of its sources of beauty, is—or was —precisely this teaching of Hebrew. It does not matter if the Yiddish reader happens to know Hebrew perfectly. We are told, regarding the Passover ceremony of the seder, that no matter how wise and learned we may be, it is meritorious to dwell once again on the completely known story of the exodus from Egypt; so, knowing Hebrew thoroughly, it is still proper for us to use the repetitive Germanic and Hebrew words side by side. It is a ritual, sanctified by usage; it expresses, implicitly, the ancient hope that Hebrew will one day be restored, with the Jewish homeland; it is a reminder that the secular must always be at the service of the sacred. We speak Yiddish not only to convey our transient thoughts, but to keep in touch with the eternal language. So Yiddish is a double instrument; and when we translate it into English we remove one element of beauty by defunctionalizing one half of the instrument.

Here, at last, is the core of the difficulty, about which there is a group of peripheral difficulties. I mention one other. The fusion of the secular and sacred in Yiddish makes possible a charming transition from the jocular to the solemn and back again. Well-worn quotations from sacred texts mingle easily with colloquialisms, and dignified passages jostle popular interjections without taking or giving offense. There is about it all a suggestion of an Oriental bazaar.

In the first Peretz story given in this book, "Devotion unto Death," there is, in the Yiddish, a passage that I have omitted from the translation. It tells of the coming of Reb Chiya, as a young man, to his father-in-law in Safed. The Prince of the Babylonian Academy recommended him as a son-in-law to the merchant-scholar and Rabbi; and the entire passage offers an illustration of my point. The Hebrew words that I reproduce below are there, in the original Yiddish text. They are not current words in ordinary Yiddish, yet a moderately well-educated Jew is supposed to know their meaning and should not need a translation. Nevertheless they are followed by translations into simple Yiddish (just as they are followed, below, by my English translation). But after the solemn and scholarly Hebrew, the simple Yiddish adds a touch of homely humor, as if the author were digging his reader in the ribs, implying without so many words: "I know you know what the Hebrew phrases mean, so I'll give their translation a slightly comical twist." And, thinks the author to himself, slyly: "If you don't know any Hebrew, no harm done."

Here is the little passage:

"And the Prince of the Babylonian Academy wrote to the Rabbi of Safed, concerning the young man Chiya, neither more nor less than the following: *ateret roshi v'ateret ha-yeshivah,* which is to say, the crown of the Prince's head, and the crown of the Academy itself; and, what was more, *shalshelet hayuchsin,* of the loftiest descent—that is, the *crème de la crème,* the pick of the basket." (I am afraid this is not much fun in English.)

In one of the strongest Yom Kippur prayers there is a phrase, *moshul kecheres ha-nishbor*: "the likeness is that of a broken potsherd," alluding to the worthlessness of the life of man. Yiddish has taken over the phrase and has put it to colloquial, ironical use. If someone utters an incongruity, or commits a grotesque non-sequitur, it is *moshul kecheres ha-nishbor*. And in another prayer the life of man in the hand of God is likened to "clay in the hands of the potter, which at his will he draws out or cuts short," a moving if not particularly original simile. The Hebrew phrase *"birtzoso marchiv u-birtzoso mekatzer,"* "at his will he draws it out, and at his will he cuts it short," is applied in Yiddish to all sorts of situations, from someone making a speech to someone taking a nap. And it is a remarkable circumstance that the colloquialization of these solemn phrases has not robbed them of their force in their original context. A Jew at his Yom Kippur prayers, encountering these phrases again, sees them re-endowed with their first pathos; he is not in the mood to remember their workaday usage. They are now clothed, like himself, in dignity.

Perhaps I can come nearer to the tone of that kind of Yiddish narrative by inventing rather than translating a passage. I offer the following:

"And behold, Yechiel cast his eyes upon Sarah, and the maiden found favor in his eyes, so that his soul was bound unto her soul, even as the soul of David was bound unto the soul of Jonathan, by which I simply mean to say that he fell head over heels in love with her. And she said unto him: 'It is written, thou shalt speak unto the maiden's father,' at which words the soul of Yechiel ran out of him like water; that is to say, he nearly dropped dead from fright."

This sort of thing, done at any length in English, becomes tedious, for it is not native to the language. Neither, for that matter, can it be long sustained in Hebrew. It is a very odd circumstance to be confronted with—that classical Yiddish cannot be translated into Hebrew! For there is no need to teach Hebrew to the Hebrew reader; repeating the phrase would be as pointless in Hebrew as in English. In fact, the whole folkloristic machinery that was erected to keep Hebrew and Palestine alive in the mind of the Jews becomes obsolete in the Jewish homeland. It has fulfilled itself. And it may be said of this machinery, while it is being dismantled, that it succeeded in a task that baffled other peoples—the Irish, for instance, who never set up a similar machinery for the conservation of Gaelic and now find themselves unable to revive it.

It served its purpose well, but gave up its task most reluctantly, even in Palestine. It had, so to speak, become enamored of its job. There were Jews in Palestine, in the early days of the Zionist movement, who wanted Yiddish to become the language of the reborn Jewish National Home. The means had become so precious and interesting that they were now an end in themselves. But then Zangwill tells us of the old Jew who settled in Palestine, and every day at the Wailing Wall repeated the prayer: "Next year in Jerusalem."

CHAPTER XXI

The Episodic and the Permanent

❁

THIS, then, is or was the classical Yiddish, a language with a nationalist-Hebrew-Palestinian technique; a language largely untranslatable because it was created—in part—to serve only one people for a purpose that interests no other people; a language which became beautiful in the service of that purpose with a beauty known only to itself.

What, then, do we obtain when we translate classical Yiddish into the English? The reader must judge for himself, from the foregoing pages. What we do not obtain, however, is the stylistic grace. It disappears in translation, and it has disappeared from neo-Yiddish as distinguished from classical Yiddish.

Neo-Yiddish is the westernized and internationalized Yiddish, which is stripping itself of the Hebrew-nationalist function. It is a Yiddish that can be translated as easily as—or with not more difficulty than—any other language. While it does not Germanize the spelling of the Hebrew words, it reduces Hebrew to a minimum, avoids the introduction of Hebrew phrases from the prayer-book, the Bible, and the Mishnah, and drops the musical and instructive repetitiveness I have described. It is not redolent of the synagogue, the *cheder* and the festivals; it is a language without nostalgia.

The neo-Yiddish style is capable of powerful effects. It is the style of Sholem Asch's later works, and of much of I. J. Singer. And it must strike us at once as something very relevant that Asch's later works, and part of Singer's, have found wide audiences in English and other languages, while Asch's earlier works, closer to the classical Yiddish, have found a much smaller audience. This is not due to the superiority of, let us say, *The Nazarene* over *Salvation;* and not even to the more universal theme of the former. The fact is, simply, that *The Nazarene* is translatable and *Salvation* is not. The very titles furnish a clue. The first book is called, in Yiddish, *Der Man fun Natzeret*—literally, *The Man of Nazareth.* This phrase is international in its freedom from particular associations. But the second book is called, in Yiddish, *Der T'hillim Yid,* literally, *The Psalm Jew,* which conveys nothing in English. *Salvation* is an evasive and quite misleading title; but after long effort I have come to the conclusion that I at least cannot find an English title that will retain anything of the simple and heart-warming grace of the Yiddish original. A *T'hillim Yid*—quite apart from Sholem Asch's story—is an unlettered Jew who cannot worship God with the wisdom and learning of scholars (cf. the story in this book: "A Chapter of the Psalms"); he is the pure, untutored soul whose devotions consist in repetitions of the Psalms; he is the obscure, devout little man, full of loving-kindness, for whom the Baal Shem, the founder of Chassidism, took special thought. All this is in the phrase *Der T'hillim Yid,* which is classical, not modernized and denaturized Yiddish.

Peretz, it must be said, was a master of the neo-Yiddish as well as of the classical Yiddish style. We see that in

288

"Stories" (p. 133). The technique of "Stories" is wholly different from that of Peretz's most characteristic works. In the former he is the modern sophisticated intellectual, the ingenious weaver of plot, the self-conscious artist who is perfectly at home among the techniques of trained and refined craftsmen. In the latter, while not less—in fact infinitely more—the artist, he pours himself out with at least a seeming spontaneity, and a thousand echoes of the folk-nostalgia sound in the pages. In the former you sense the contemporary who has studied all the literary theories and is *au courant* with the latest movements; in the latter you see only the native teller of tales, in the style, and for the comfort, of the un-Europeanized, Palestino-centric, Bible- and Talmud- and Chassidism-conscious folk. But the clearest indication of the point with which I am now concerned is found in a simple statistical fact. In the original of the first page of "Devotion unto Death" there occur thirty Hebrew words and phrases in the Yiddish; on the first page of the neo-Yiddish story there occurs only one, and that is the title itself: *Maisses.*

I return to the question: what do we obtain in translating classical Yiddish into English? We obtain the permanent Jewish, non-Yiddish value. This needs some explaining.

Jewish life has always been conscious of the permanent and the episodic in history. Permanent was the faith, which comprised the developed ethics and the religious sense, the Messianic hope and the Palestine promise. Episodic were the separate historical incidents or experiences: the Babylonian, the Spanish, the east-European. The Yiddish-speaking episode in Jewish history, comprising an entire civilizational creation, was only one of many. Its basic values were not different from those of the other episodes. The wide folk-interest in moral problems, the worship of learning, the lively immediateness of remote figures like the Patriarchs, Moses, Elijah, King David, the peculiar intimacy with God, are the permanent features of the large Jewish record. But each separate chapter had some special cultural technique for the nurture and increase of these values. These permanent values make up the translatable element; it is the episodic that is untranslatable.

And yet the episodic is so intimately the garb of the permanent. It is quite fantastic to note how the Yiddish-speaking civilization took elements from the surrounding world and turned them to its peculiar use. The Yiddish language itself is the most striking instance, but it is certainly not the only one. There are folk-religious customs that the naïve east-European Jew regarded as having the same sanctity as the law from Sinai, which nevertheless were of local gentile origin. The *kaftan* and *shtreimel* (gabardine and flat, circular fur headgear) of the Polish Jewish pietist were the national dress of the Poles before the coming of the Jews. The Jews adopted them, the Poles dropped them. Among the Jews that long *kaftan,* that round *shtreimel,* became sacrosanct symbols of Jewishness. If a wayward son threw off the *kaftan* and put on a short coat, his father was as like as not to count him as dead and mourn for him in the prescribed ritual of death.

There was the wearing of the *sheitel,* or wig, obligatory for married women. Every pious Jewish bride had to crop her head before marriage, and the tragic theme has been woven into a thousand Jewish stories. But there is absolutely no mention of such a law in Talmudic literature; nor is the practice known to non-European Jews. Dubnow (I believe) traces it to the practice of cutting off the hair of a bride—and not only of a Jewish bride—so that she might sell it to the wigmaker, and with the money buy herself out from the *jus primæ noctis* of the medieval lord. The Jews retained the symbolic gesture long after the necessity had disappeared, and they made it so Jewish that the refusal of a pious Jewish daughter to sacrifice her hair before marriage was considered the equivalent of apostasy.

The *gefilte* fish of the Friday-evening meal is of Christian (and pre-Christian) origin; the *Chassidic* melodies are Ukrainian and Moldavian; and just as these have become completely and tacitly Jewish in the Yiddish-speaking civilization, so certain east-European places like Vilna, Medzibozh, Volozhin, Belz, Zhitomir have become sanctified in Jewish memory. You say "Vilna" to a non-Jew, and his response is: "The capital of Lithuania." Say it to an east-European Jew, his response is—or would have been a little while ago: "The Jerusalem of Lithuania." Volozhin is for everyone else an obscure village in Russia; for the Jew it was a glorious center of scholarship, a name precious to him and to the Almighty, whose sacred word was studied in its famous Talmudic Academy.

All this is the episodic, which cannot be recaptured. In its day it created its proper illusion of permanence, so that even some Jews were misled; they thought it would endure until the coming of the Messiah. Certainly Peretz, though not a Messianist, believed that it would endure along with the rest of the world. He was, as we have seen, confident of a time, close at hand, when anti-Semitism would disappear; he kept on hoping that the Jews by changing their way of life would win the good opinion of the world. And carried along in these illusions, he could never have guessed what in him was episodic and what permanent. He did not know that his essential concern

291

was with the moral being of the Jew, according to the tradition, which he wanted purified whatever the world would think of the Jews. He could not know that if he was to survive beyond Yiddish it would have to be as the traditional Jewish folk moralist.

Biographical Note

❊

ISAAC LOEB (Yitzchak Leibush, or "Yal," from the initials) Peretz was born on May 18, 1852, in Zamosch, Russian Poland, of a scholarly and orthodox Jewish family, probably—as the name indicates—of Spanish origin. His father, though extremely pious, was a modernist and permitted his son to learn Polish and Russian while pursuing his regular Jewish studies; he did not, however, go so far as to send him to a non-Jewish school.

Young Peretz was known as an *ilui,* a child genius. He began to write at the age of fourteen, but for many years was uncertain of his medium, wavering between Polish, Hebrew, and Yiddish and experimenting in verse, prose, narrative, and drama. Most of his early productions are lost.

He married at nineteen, was divorced at twenty-three, and remarried at twenty-five. After an unsuccessful venture in the beer-brewing business he prepared himself for the law, and practiced successfully in Zamoshch from 1877 to 1887. At one time he employed as many as seven or eight assistants. In 1887 his license was revoked as the result of his denunciation to the Czarist police for radicalism.

He moved to Warsaw and supported himself for a time by giving private lessons. In 1890 he obtained a position in the office of the Jewish Community (*kehillah*), and he retained this until his death in 1915, his salary rising from an initial forty to two hundred rubles a month. At no time did he make any money to speak of from his writings.

He did not begin to write consistently and seriously until he was in his middle thirties and did not become widely known to the Jewish reading public until 1894, when he began to issue his *Yomtov Bletter (Festival Journals).* These were published irregularly for Jewish holidays, and contained stories, poems, essays, dramas, editorials, and so on, by himself and others. A great deal of his work appeared in this form. Very often he was editor and publisher as well as chief contributor. (Cf. enterprises like *The Tatler* in eighteenth-century England.) By this time Yiddish had become his exclusive medium.

His professional and literary duties took up only part of his energy. He was active as an educator and conducted popular classes in the social and natural sciences, with Yiddish as the language of instruction. He also exerted himself to improve the Yiddish theater, for which he wrote many plays. His dramatics work, however, like his poetry, does not rank with his folk and Chassidic tales.

By the beginning of the twentieth century he was one of the leading figures in the Jewish world, known equally for his literary work and for his championship of Yiddish, of Jewish nationalism, and of the working-class movement.

The outbreak of the first World War was a great blow to his hopes for the Jewish people and for mankind generally. Used up by his efforts for Jewish refugees, he died on April 3, 1915.

Peretz had two children, both by his first wife. One died in infancy; the other, Lucien, survived him, but disassociated himself from the Jewish people.

MERIDIAN BOOKS

12 East 22 Street, New York 10, New York

JEWISH PUBLICATION SOCIETY SERIES

MERIDIAN BOOKS

12 East 22 Street, New York 10, New York

M44 GOTHIC ARCHITECTURE AND SCHOLASTICISM *by Erwin Panofsky*
M45 FREUD AND THE 20TH CENTURY *edited by Benjamin Nelson*
M46 POLITICS AND THE NOVEL *by Irving Howe*
M47 A SHORTER HISTORY OF SCIENCE *by William Cecil Dampier*
M48 A GUIDE TO CONTEMPORARY FRENCH LITERATURE *by Wallace Fowlie*
M49 THE RENAISSANCE OF THE 12TH CENTURY *by C. H. Haskins*
M50 NEW POETS OF ENGLAND AND AMERICA *selected by Hall, Pack, and Simpson*
M51 ST. AUGUSTINE: HIS AGE, LIFE, AND THOUGHT
M52 CIVILIZATION ON TRIAL *and* THE WORLD AND THE WEST *by Arnold Toynbee*
M53 RELIGION AND CULTURE *by Christopher Dawson*
M54 PROUST: A BIOGRAPHY *by André Maurois*
M55 ST. THOMAS AQUINAS *by Jacques Maritain*
M56 MEMOIRS OF A REVOLUTIONIST *by Dwight Macdonald*
M57 DEBATES WITH HISTORIANS *by Pieter Geyl*
M58 POLITICS: WHO GETS WHAT, WHEN, HOW *by Harold Lasswell*
M59 GODS AND HEROES OF THE GREEKS *by H. J. Rose*
M60 RELIGION IN AMERICA *edited by John Cogley*
M61 MEN AND IDEAS *by Johan Huizinga*
M62 WITCHCRAFT *by Charles Williams*
M63 SCENES FROM THE DRAMA OF EUROPEAN LITERATURE *by Erich Auerbach*
M64 THE HUMAN MEANING OF THE SOCIAL SCIENCES *edited by Daniel Lerner*
M65 ARISTOTLE *by W. D. Ross*
M66 THE DISINHERITED MIND *by Erich Heller*
M67 THE BOOK OF JAZZ *by Leonard Feather*
M68 THE WORLD OF ODYSSEUS *by M. I. Finley*
M69 THE SCROLLS FROM THE DEAD SEA *by Edmund Wilson*
M70 GREY EMINENCE *by Aldous Huxley*
M71 THE LOGIC OF THE SCIENCES AND THE HUMANITIES *by F. S. C. Northrop*
M72 HISTORY 1
M73 ON MODERN POETS *by Yvor Winters*
M74 THE MAIN STREAM OF MUSIC AND OTHER ESSAYS *by Donald Francis Tovey*
M75 JONATHAN EDWARDS *by Perry Miller*
M76 THE CONFEDERACY *edited by Albert D. Kirwan*
M77 TALENTS AND GENIUSES *by Gilbert Highet*
M78 APES, ANGELS, AND VICTORIANS *by William Irvine*
M79 PAINTING AND REALITY *by Etienne Gilson*
M80 MOZART'S LIBRETTOS *translated by Robert Pack and Marjorie Lelash*
M81 PHILOSOPHY IN THE MIDDLE AGES *by Paul Vignaux*
M82 THE RECOLLECTIONS OF ALEXIS DE TOCQUEVILLE *edited by J. P. Mayer*

Titles listed here are not necessarily available in the British Empire